THE DAY TRADER

THE DAY TRADER

From the Pit

To the PC

LEWIS J. BORSELLINO
WITH
Patricia Commins

John Wiley & Sons, Inc.
New York • Chichester • Weinheim • Brisbane • Singapore • Toronto

Copyright © 1999 by Lewis J. Borsellino. All rights reserved.

Published by John Wiley & Sons, Inc.

Published simultaneously in Canada.

The opinions expressed in this book are solely those of the author based on his own experience and in relating those experiences, certain names have been changed to respect individual privacy. This book is sold with the understanding that the publisher is not engaged in rendering professional services and neither the author nor publisher intend this book as substitute for professional services. The book does not constitute nor should it be construed as an offer or solicitation of an offer to buy or sell investments. Any investment decision by readers should be undertaken following appropriate independent advice.

Library of Congress Cataloging-in-Publication Data:
Borsellino, Lewis J., 1957–
    The day trader : from the pit to the PC / Lewis J. Borsellino with
Patricia Commins.
        p.   cm.
    ISBN 0-471-33265-8 (cloth : alk. paper)
    1. Floor traders (Finance)   2. Index and Option Market (Chicago
Mercantile Exchange)   I. Commins, Patricia, 1959– .   II. Title.
HG4621.B67   1999
332.64'4'0977311—dc21   99-10019

Printed in the United States of America

10 9 8 7 6 5 4 3 2 1

In Memory of My Father
Tony Borsellino
1930–1979

CONTENTS

There are very few arenas for the warriors among us these days. There are few opportunities to do battle in business in which you are on your own, armed with only your intellect and your nerve. Trading is one of those rare arenas. Yes, there are computer programs to analyze the market, technical charts that plot the support and resistance, and wireless phones that connect the computer screen at the trading floor. But, in the end, an independent trader takes on the market alone, whether on the trading floor or at the computer screen.

I went to the futures market at the age of 22, and I have remained there for nearly half of my life. I began as a runner on the floor of the Chicago Mercantile Exchange, making roughly minimum wage. I was a clerk, a broker, and then an independent trader. Today, I am a fund manager.

I am fortunate to have been a trader during some of the most exciting, and sometimes controversial, times in the pit. I was there when the Merc launched the Standard & Poor's 500 Stock Index contract, which soon outshone anything else traded on that floor. As the S&P contract grew in volume, I matured as a trader and became a bigger player. I looked around one day and realized I was the biggest player in the S&P pit.

But, the business of trading is changing. Technology, as in much of the business world, is making its inroads into trading. The debate rages as to whether the PC will ever replace the pit. Once again, my professional life mirrors that pit. I am trading both on the floor and at the computer. In both venues, however, I am still a trader. I will always be a trader.

When I was first approached to write this book, I laughed and said my life was only half over. I was also partly serious. I am in transition from the pit to the PC, from independent trader to fund manager. I still have a lot more stories to collect by living them. But, I have many lessons to share about trading and about life—about managing risk, being disciplined, handling losses, and, when times are good, letting the profits run. These are key lessons for any trader, from a member on the floor of the exchange to a trader at the screen of an electronic system.

This story is also a personal one. I cannot explain about my career without sharing details of my life. The sum total of my experiences affected me not only as a man, but as a trader. By understanding myself, both my strengths and my weaknesses, I became a better trader. In fact, knowing yourself—how you react to winning and losing, how well you handle success and failure—is just as important as studying the technical price charts. It's not the market that will ever break you, it's *you* who can break you. Too much risk. Too much leverage. Not enough discipline. A lack of focus. I know. I've committed those sins of trading, just as every trader who is honest with himself has. But, that's how you learn what *not* to do. You process your mistakes, accept responsibility, and come back to trade another day.

ACKNOWLEDGMENTS

The story of *The Day Trader* **does not belong to me, alone. In many ways, it is** the story of my family. In a special way, I wish to thank them for their support, love, and encouragement throughout this process, especially my wife, Julie, my mother, Florence "Tootsie" Borsellino, and my brother, Joey, who is also an outstanding S&P trader in his own right, and his wife, Theresa. This story is also a legacy to the next generation: my children, Lewis, Anthony, Briana, and Joey, who carry the Borsellino name; my stepchildren, Nicole, Jamie, and Nick; and my brother's children, Anthony, Joey, Johnny, and Marla. I am also blessed with a tightly knit family that includes my aunts and uncles—Norfe and Dolly, Louisa and Gus, Josie and Mimi, Caroline, Tina and Tony, Antoinette ("Cookie") and Vince, Sammy and Donna, and Frank and Theresa, as well as "extended" family, and my many dear friends.

I acknowledge my friends who have been with me over the years, including my mentor, Maury Kravitz, Jack Sandner, Joni Weber, who has worked for me some 15 years, and the "Boat People." I thank my colleagues at Borsellino Capital Management, including my partner, Edward R. Velazquez, II, Joe DeLaurentis,

Brad Sullivan, Luke Matthews, Joe Kale, Anthony Ruggerio, Laith Kubla, Louie Lazzara, and my cousins, Marianne Palumbo and Antoinette "Toni" Marino, who also work with me. I wish to thank Jim Sebanc for his contribution of historic market data and the legend of Galileo, the trader, and also Mario Alberico for his insights into electronic trading.

I extend a special thanks to the staff at John Wiley & Sons, especially my editor, Pamela van Giessen, for her help, humor, and extraordinary patience, and to my agent, Ariela Wilcox, who first suggested this book.

Finally, *The Day Trader* salutes the Night Writer, who burned the midnight oil to get the job done.

To contact Lewis Borsellino, please see his Web site at www .borsellino.com.

THE DAY TRADER

CHAPTER 1

High Times

I was nowhere near the trading pit on Black Monday. I was out of Chicago, out
of the country and, at that moment, out of touch with the market. It was late in the afternoon on October 19, 1987, when I
stepped into the Piaget store in Zurich, Switzerland, to buy a
watch. The salesman behind the counter was a middle-aged
Swiss man, as conservatively dressed as any banker I had seen
on the Bahnhofstrasse in Zurich's financial district. He laid four
watches on a black velvet cushion and waited while I looked
them over. I glanced up from the watches at an electronic sign
outside a bank. I don't read German, but could still figure out
what the sign said. The Dow Jones Industrial Average was off
500 points.

"That must be broken," I said to the salesman, gesturing
toward the sign on the bank. I picked up one of the watches for
a closer look.

"No, sir," the salesman said quietly in his clipped Swiss
accent. "The U.S. stock market crashed today."

All the color drained out of my face. I threw the watch at the
salesman and ran for the door. "Sir, don't you want the watch?"
he asked, confused by my behavior.

"Forget the watch," I yelled back. "I've got to get back to Chicago."

Back at my hotel, the message light on my telephone flashed ominously. There were messages from my wife and my brother, repeating what the clerk in the watch store had told me. The stock market had crashed.

My first trip to Europe was cut short. There were seven of us—all businessmen, and I was the youngest at 30—on a 10-day excursion to Europe for rest and a little relaxation. We had left the previous Friday afternoon bound for Italy then Switzerland. I was short 25 Standard & Poor's 500 Stock Index futures (S&P) contracts when I got on a plane from Chicago to New York on Friday afternoon, but had left an order to fill them at the close. By the time I arrived in New York for my trans-Atlantic flight, I had made $250,000 on that trade. I was already up $2 million for the year. It was going to be a great trip.

After a weekend in Italy, we arrived in Zurich. I was staying in the Beau Rivage Hotel, the best of the five-star hotels in Zurich. My mind was admittedly on leisure and not on business when I walked into that watch store. When I left moments later, all I could think about was getting back into the trading pit as fast as I could. On Tuesday morning, I caught a flight to London where I hoped to get the Concorde to New York. To my amazement, the flight was full and I had to go standby—to the tune of $5,000 for a one-way ticket. But even that sky-high price was worth the investment to get me back to the trading pits where, in the wake of the biggest single-day decline in the stock market, opportunity awaited me.

I was so antsy on that three-hour flight to New York that I couldn't even enjoy the fact that I was on the Concorde for the first time. My focus was getting back to that trading pit where, I imagined, the S&Ps would probably rebound after Monday's sharp drop. But there was another pressing issue on my mind— something that only I could handle. I had 1,000 eurodollar call options, giving me the right to be long eurodollars at 94.00, which I had bought for $25,000 about two and a half months before. My reasons for buying the options were twofold: I wanted to become more familiar with options, which were fairly new to me. And, in this instance, the 94 calls would be very valuable should there be a cut in short-term interest rates.

As a futures trader, specializing in the Standard & Poor's 500 Stock Index contract at the Chicago Mercantile Exchange, I wanted to learn more about options. The interesting thing about options is that they give the holder the right—but not the obligation—to take a position in the futures market in return from a premium. Options carry a particular exercise, or strike, price. The closer the strike price is to the market, the more valuable the option (and the higher the premium). The farther away the strike price is from the market, the less valuable the option.

There are several diverse and complex strategies to trade futures and options together, and I had begun to dabble in them. The first time was in cattle options. I had the idea that cattle prices were going up, based in part on what I heard from a friend in the wholesale meat business. I decided to buy calls— 2,000 of them—for about $25,000, gaining the right to be long cattle futures at 65.00 cents. Just as I had hoped, the market rose steadily until cattle prices were just 0.20 cent away from my strike price. If only I knew then what I know now. I would have sold futures when the market was at 64.80. If I pursued that strategy then, if prices rose, I'd be long cattle at 65 by exercising the call options. If prices fell, I'd be short from 64.80. My only risk was that 20-point differential between the call options and the futures price. That amounted to about a $61,000 invest-ment—the cost of the options and my exposure on the futures trade—which would have been more than offset by the money I could have made on the trade.

Instead, I held onto my options, thinking that my 65 strike price was going to be hit. Then, the U.S. Department of Agri-culture came out with a report that indicated a larger supply of cattle than previously estimated. Cattle price went limit down for five days, and my options expired worthless. If only I had sold the futures contracts at 64.80—my estimated profit on that trade would have been a cool $750,000.

The second time I tried an options play was six weeks before

I left for Europe. Eurodollars were at 92.00 when I bought those 1,000 calls to be long at 94. But it looked like the scenario I had hoped for—a cut in short-term interest rates—was not going to materialize. When I left Chicago, eurodollars were down to 91.50. Interest rates would have to be reduced by two and a half basis points for my strike price to be hit. That seemed to be a pretty far-fetched proposition. My options were in the cabinet, meaning that although they had not yet expired, they were virtually worthless.

Then the stock market crashed, and Alan Greenspan, in an effort to calm the panic in the market, announced the Fed would loosen rates. On Tuesday morning, my eurodollar options went from just paper to solid gold. I could have parlayed them into about a $1 million profit, but I didn't know that at a cruising altitude of 50,000 feet.

There were no phones on the Concorde, and by the time I reached New York, the eurodollar market had not yet opened. I had to wait until I was on the plane from New York to Chicago to place a call to my floor broker. But, for some reason, the phone on that plane was not able to read my credit card when I ran it through the swiper. I was panicked now. Nobody knew about those options, and I was stuck in a plane with a phone that didn't work. I approached the flight attendant with a $100 bill and a question: "Do you have a VISA or an American Express card?"

She looked at me a little puzzled.

"I'm a commodities trader. The market is really crazy. I have to place a call and take care of something. But the phone won't read my credit card. I'll be on the phone two minutes. I'll give you $100 if you let me use your credit card."

The flight attendant took pity on me, and she wouldn't take the $100. "It's a five-dollar telephone charge," she said. "Give me five dollars and you can use my credit card."

When I finally reached the trading desk on the floor of the Merc, I learned eurodollar futures had opened at 94.50, but then retreated from the highs. My options were still worth something—but nowhere near what they could have been worth. I sold them for a $250,000 profit, which was still a 10-fold profit on a $25,000 investment.

Looking back, however, I would have done things very differently had I been on the floor that day. I could have sold my 94 options and made $500,000, or I could have sold 1,000 eurodollar futures to be short at 94.50 and stayed long options at 94 for a guaranteed 50-tick profit. Three days later, eurodollars were back down to 92, and I would have been short from 94.50. All in all, I figure I lost out on at least a potential $1,250,000 profit. Granted, I did make $250,000 on the options that I had thought were worthless. But, like much of what happened to me during the Crash of 1987, I made some big money—but also left a lot on the table.

When I reached the trading floor at the Chicago Mercantile Exchange at one o'clock Tuesday afternoon, it looked like a battlefield after heavy casualties. Some local traders had busted out, never to return. Others were yanked out by their clearing firms because they didn't have enough money in their trading accounts to cover potential six-figure losses. Other traders were just scared and stayed away until the smoke cleared. The traders who remained looked shell-shocked.

"You should have been here, Lewis," one trader said. "You would have made $5 million on Monday."

Another trader stopped me on the way to the S&P pit. "I swear to God you would have made $5 million," he said. "It was unbelievable."

Five million—every time somebody saw me, I heard that number. I would have made $5 million on Monday. It was not what I wanted to hear.

I made $500,000 on Tuesday as the market roared back about 350 points. Wednesday was another crazy, volatile day in the pit, and I netted another $500,000. Volatile days present huge opportunities for a day trader like myself. The more the market moves intraday—rising and falling, testing support levels, and breaking through resistance points—the greater the potential for profit. But a volatile market is a little like going white-water rafting. When you're in control, it's a great ride, but if you lose your focus and your discipline, things can get dicey very quickly. Luckily for me, I have this ability that the crazier the market becomes, the more focused I am. This ability has served me well in times of crisis, both personal and professional. When the world around me goes nuts, I become more sane. The wilder the market gets, the more disciplined I become.

Then came Thursday morning. The trading pit has a mood that reflects the thoughts, fears, hopes, and biases of the people in it. When negative news has hit the market, the pit feels like a top-heavy boat that's about to capsize. You know it's going down. On days when the market is bullish, you can feel the optimism that we're going to test the old highs, build enough momentum and break through them. Reading this mood comes with experience, from being in the pit day in and day out since I first arrived on the trading floor as a runner in 1981. I developed an instinct that grew out of listening to my gut as much as my brain. I've been wrong and I've second-guessed myself and been burned as a result. But, like a lot of veteran traders, I've learned to rely on an ability that is like a sixth sense when it comes to reading the market.

On the Thursday after the crash, there was definitely something in the air. As I walked into the S&P pit a few minutes before the opening bell, I noticed the brokers who filled customer orders seemed nervous and edgy. I had been an order-filler, myself, for four years before I began trading solely for my own account. I remembered well the nervous anticipation of having a big order to fill at the opening. That's what I saw across the pit that morning. I could see it in the way their eyes darted around them and the uneasy fidgeting of their body language. They were sellers, I decided at that moment. After a day of historic loss on Monday, followed by two days of high volatility on Tuesday and Wednesday, the sellers were coming back into the market.

Just before the market opens, the brokers are allowed to announce their bids and offers, which sets the tone for the opening trades. That morning, a broker announced he was offering to sell S&Ps 400 points lower. Then another broker, this one from Shearson, stepped up. He offered to sell 1,000 points lower. In those days, the S&P pit had no trading limits. Today, there are limits to control how far—and how fast—S&Ps can fall. These protective limits act like a brake to slow a sharp decline. But in those days, the market rose and fell at the whim of the bids and offers.

If the Shearson broker was willing to offer 600 points below the first broker, I wondered just how low this market would go. "I'm 2,000 lower!" I roared into the pit.

The Shearson broker didn't hesitate. "I'm 3,000 lower!" he bellowed back.

Holy shit! I thought. This market was down 3,000 points and we hadn't even started trading yet. To put this in perspective, in those days a 400- or 500-point rise or fall was a significant move.

"4,000 lower!" I yelled.

"5,000 lower," the Shearson broker countered.

With that, S&Ps opened about 5,600 points lower. It was a freefall, but we had to be near the bottom, my gut told me. "Buy 'em!" I started to say to the Shearson broker across the pit, until the trader behind me grabbed my arm.

"Lewis! I'll sell you 150!"

"Buy 'em!" I yelled back.

I scribbled the trade on my card and looked up.

A second later, another broker caught my eye. "I'm selling 300," he told me.

"Can't do it," I signaled back. I had just bought 150 contracts, and didn't think I could stomach taking the risk of another 300 in a market that could just as easily crash or rebound.

Two seconds later, a trader across the pit grabbed my attention. Using a combination of hand signals and lipreading, he asked me, "What are you doing?"

"I'm a seller," I replied.

"I'm a buyer," he signaled back.

I offered those 150 contracts—which I had bought less than a half-minute before—for 2,000 points higher than my purchase price. I made $1.3 million on that single trade. But I also knew that, if I had bought the other 300 contracts, my profit would have been a cool $5 million. But I couldn't look back. I had reached my internal risk limit. I made a few smaller trades, netting another $40,000 or $50,000. Then I had enough. I handed my last trading card to my clerk, walked out of the pit, went into the bathroom, and threw up.

I splashed my face with cold water and stared at my reflection in the mirror. Red veins striped my blue eyes and my skin looked gray. I ran my hands through my blond hair, cut short as in the days when I played college football. My mind reeled at the enormity of what I had pulled off, which my ego was just beginning to grasp. I was 30 years old, and I had made over a million dollars in less than a minute. But, I tasted the bile in the back of my throat and knew what my gut was telling me—it could have just as easily gone the other way and I'd be in the bathroom puking my guts out for another reason. If the market had turned against me, I would have been wiped out.

Trading provides the highest highs and the lowest lows of any profession, and I have had my share of both. For 18 years, I've stood in the S&P pit at the Merc, through the Reagan years, the Persian Gulf War, the Russian coup, the longest bull run in the market's history, and the Asian financial crisis. One way or the other, I'll be trading S&Ps for a long time to come—on the floor or electronically, from Chicago or from anywhere else. It doesn't matter. I'll be there in the market during whatever comes next. I've averaged well over seven figures a year—just trading my own money. I take risks that are not for the insecure or the faint-hearted, and reap the rewards that come from patience, discipline, and a competitor's drive.

My success has brought me my share of the good times. And, I've endured my share of the bad. But just as when you're on a roll at the craps table, you have to enjoy the winning streak for as long as it lasts. There are other rules that I live by, a kind of personal code I've hammered out—or that's been hammered into me—over the years. Never lose your focus, your discipline, or your control, and never forget who you are.

I've come a long way from Taylor Street on Chicago's Near West Side, where Italian was spoken as often as English and street-smart kids played tag on the sidewalk and down the alleys. I've gone far from the old neighborhood, where nearly everybody had some kind of racket on the side and, when it came to gambling or running the numbers, everybody knew somebody who was in on the game. I've curbed much of my quick temper, which never let me walk away from a fight, replacing it with the cooler head of a strategist. I've come a long way, but I haven't forgotten where I was born in April 1957. Nor have I lost the heart and nerve of a fighter with a toughness, mental and physical, that has made me successful. Those attributes have given me the strength to endure everything from FBI investigations to a bitter divorce and not lose my focus. I've become what I am, both in spite of my background and because of it.

Now, as I write at age 41, I have lasted 18 years in a profession in which the majority cash out, burn out, or crap out after only a few years. I no longer stand bell-to-bell as in the old days. I leave those grueling long days to younger traders, some a little more than half my age. I am leaving the pit, not just because I lack the stamina to be a player, but because the game is changing. I have entered a new arena as a fund manager, which calls upon both my ability as a trader and my focus and discipline.

Over the years I have persevered during the bad and profited in the good. For nearly two decades, my turf has been about a one-foot square spot on the second step of the trading pit. My brother, Joey, whom I consider to be the biggest S&P trader these days, stands to my left. Looking out into that pit, where hundreds of traders, brokers, and clerks swarm like bees in a hive, I see new faces. They trade for a while, and then they are gone. On the entire trading floor there are only a handful of guys who have traded as a long as I have. We greet each other with a nod or a wave like veterans of some foreign war.

I have seen it all—from the end of dual trading, which once allowed brokers to trade for themselves and fill orders for customers, to the advent of electronic trading, which threatens to make floor traders into an endangered species. I remember well a long sting operation at the Chicago Merc and its sister exchange, the Chicago Board of Trade, when the FBI tried to catch traders in the act of allegedly making illegal trades. A few minor infractions were handed out, but the majority of traders were found to be clean. And we've bumped into some of the biggest and supposedly best in the financial world.

Take the day George Soros filed what was tantamount to a class-action suit against the S&P pit following the Crash of 1987. It only took a day for the rumor to leak out regarding who was behind all that heavy selling on the Thursday after the crash. The Shearson brokers were filling a sell order for speculator and fund manager George Soros. But the Soros order, we learned, was for 2,500 contracts. The desk manager had somehow entered the order twice. Shearson inadvertently sold 5,000 contracts instead of just 2,500. The rumored loss on that sale was said to be around $60 million.

It was in early 1988 when attorneys representing Soros deposed me. I was called into a conference room at a posh law firm in which a group of dark-suited attorneys waited for me.

"You have the right to have an attorney present," one of Soros's lawyers counseled me.

"I don't need an attorney. Just ask me what you want to know."

They asked me everything from where I stood in the S&P pit to how long I had been a floor broker before I was a trader. Then they got down to business. They wanted to know if the Shearson brokers had somehow disclosed the order to me before the market opened.

"No," I replied firmly.

"Why were you selling the market down?"

"Because it was apparent to me that there were a lot more sellers than buyers in the market," I replied.

Under open outcry, trades are transacted based on the best bids and the best offer. On that Thursday morning, I had every right to make an offer as long as I was willing to take on a buyer at that price. "Each time I offered," I continued, "the brokers dropped their offers even lower."

"Isn't that disclosing a customer order?" the attorneys pressed.

"No, it isn't. Listen, I paid $150,000 for my seat on the exchange so I could know first-hand where the market was and to see who was doing what. Anyone is more than welcome to do exactly what I have done—buy a seat and watch the market."

The attorneys paused. I watched the reel-to-reel tape recorder make one revolution. "What was your intention?" they asked me.

"I was ready to buy from Shearson. But I didn't. I bought 150 contracts from another trader." By the attorneys' faces, I'd guess that statement was a piece of news to them. Someone hadn't done their homework.

The deposition was soon over, and the suit against the floor brokers and traders was eventually dropped. In the end, the dispute remained between Soros and Shearson. Theories have circulated for years about what supposedly caused the Crash. Some blame computerized sell programs that sparked the wholesale dumping of stock positions. Others have pointed an accusatory finger at the S&P pit itself, claiming that weakness in futures caused the sell-off in stocks. Whatever the reason, in the aftermath of the Crash, margin calls on stock portfolios were astronomical. Brokerage houses had to cough up billions of dollars to keep trading, and the Fed came to Wall Street's rescue.

But while Wall Street was on shaky ground, the Chicago Mercantile Exchange stood tall. Specialists at the New York Stock Exchange kept some stocks closed for two and three days after the Crash, saying they had to wait until they had buy orders. The S&P pit was closed only for a few hours on the Tuesday after the Crash. Anyone who was short the S&P contract was facing a 40-point discount to the cash market. To offset that risk, traders turned to the Major Market Index based on 20 of the largest stocks in the Dow Jones Industrial Average. This *maxi* contract, which traded at the Chicago Board of Trade at the time, was not perfectly correlated to the S&P, but it was close enough. When S&Ps were closed, the maxi was at an 80-point discount to the cash market. By the time S&Ps reopened, the maxi was at an 80-point premium, which fueled a rally in S&Ps. Sifting through the events surrounding the Crash and the days that followed, I believe the maxi and the rebound in S&Ps helped stem the tide of losses in stocks, and kept a severe crash from becoming even more catastrophic. This also turned the sentiment of the market, and program trading turned from massive selling to buying.

In time, the Soros incident faded from the pit talk, although we still—even today—occasionally razz the guy who was the Shearson desk manager that day. ("Wanna sell 5,000?" we'll tease him.) As for me, I keep on trading as aggressively as I always have. Trading is my life. It is my business. It is what I do to distinguish myself.

CNBC once described me as being among the biggest and best traders in the S&P pit. I acknowledge the compliment. I know that I am among the best when it comes to reading support and resistance in the market, interpreting floor-order flow, and anticipating how the market will react to the next twitch or itch of the Federal Reserve Board. But that is only part of my story. What has made me successful as a trader is where I have come from, the past that I've not only risen above but come to terms with. I am my own man, but I am also Tony Borsellino's son. In that, I am the product of his hopes and dreams for me.

My father's life, on the surface, was very different from mine. He operated in a different world, one he should have avoided. But he made choices based on the options that were available to him. What he did was for us, his family, to give us a better life than he had. If I heard him say it once, I heard him say it a million times: *"I do what I do so you won't have to."* It echoes in my memory.

My story, you see, is my father's legacy. I can't look at my life without explaining my father's. I see the success that my brother, Joey, and I have enjoyed, and I know we have Dad to thank—but not in the way that people might think. The rumor I've heard is that Dad supposedly left Joey and me a bundle of cash, which we used as seed money to trade at the Merc. That, the story goes, is why Joey and I have both been so successful. The truth is, when Dad died, there was no money.

Sometimes I joke with the guys in the pit. I say, "What did your Dad leave you—$15 or $20 million? My Dad left Joey and me a ski mask and a gun and a note that said, 'Go make a living. Take care of your mother.' That's what we got."

My background is not a secret among my fellow traders, although no one ever asks me about it. In fact, I suspect that most of them are afraid to even bring up the subject for fear of offending me and facing my temper. As a result, the other traders have sometimes treated me differently, as if they were not entirely comfortable around me. To counter that, I sometimes joke about our childhood. I'll tell the "ski mask" story, which puts some people at ease and shakes others up a little bit.

But the truth is, Dad didn't really leave us a ski mask and a gun, either. He would have beaten the crap out of us if we ever thought of following in his footsteps when it came to the way he made his living. My father was a truck driver, legitimately, for 17 years. If something "fell off the truck," he made a little money on the side. Then came the temptation, the chance for a big score. There was no turning back.

The inheritance my father left Joey and me was worth more millions and will last longer than a trust fund. He left us integrity, self-reliance, intelligence, strength, toughness, and the ability to stand on our own. He made us men, even when we were little boys. And he loved us. Unconditionally. Unquestionably. Undeniably. His love for us and his belief that we could do whatever we set our minds to became the foundation for our success.

I was playing cards with Michael Jordan one day. A line like that usually gets somebody's attention. But it's true. We were relaxing in the clubhouse at a private country club after a golf tournament that included the top executives of some of

Chicago's leading corporations, a few sports celebrities, and independent businessmen like me. We sat around the table, smoking cigars and having drinks. Somebody pulled out a deck of cards, and we played a few friendly hands of gin. I realized that evening that, if it weren't for the money, Michael Jordan would never have been part of that card game and neither would I. We come from different worlds than the men we were associating with that evening. They are great guys, to be sure, but I know who I am and where I come from. And no matter what club I am admitted to, no matter who I know or how much money I make, I'll never blend in completely with that crowd. By choice, I am and will always be a man apart.

Being blond, blue-eyed, and college-educated, I could have slipped into another name or identity the way I change into a golf shirt or a business suit, but that would have been only on the surface. I could never negate the impact of my upbringing on my character, and I certainly know I would never try. I am an Italian-American, and I am proud of my heritage and my ethnicity. My grandfather, Luigi Borsellino, emigrated from Sicily and scratched out a living, first as a bootlegger during Prohibition. Then, he and his two brothers started the first spaghetti factory in Chicago and also ran an olive oil–importing business.

My paternal grandparents had four children. The oldest son, Norfe, was born in Italy, where he spent the first nine years of his life with his mother after his father had emigrated to the United States. Arriving here at last, Norfe had no memories of his father, only the stories that his mother told him. That first meeting was soured by a trick played on Norfe, which became a family joke for the next 70 years. Someone called Norfe aside and told him in Italian that his father, who was not much more than five feet tall, had a new English nickname that he loved to be called. So Norfe smiled at his father for the first time since he was a baby and said loudly the English phrase he had learned just a minute before: "Hiya, Shorty!" He never understood why his father slapped him the minute he saw him.

After Norfe came Louisa, my father, Tony, and Josephine, whom everyone calls "Josie." My mother, Florence, or "Tootsie" as she is called, was also of Italian descent with a large family: Sammy, Caroline, Frank, Antoinette (whom everyone calls "Cookie"), and Tina. On paternal and maternal sides, ours was and still is a tightly knit group of aunts, uncles, and cousins. We have been there for each other during the hard times, which makes the occasions we have to celebrate all the sweeter. That to me is the essence of growing up Italian-American. I was raised to believe there is no sacrifice that you wouldn't make for your parents, your children, or your siblings. I remember the story of when my parents were newlyweds and living in an apartment one floor above my father's parents. Dad was so worried that his mother, who had a heart murmur, might suffer a heart attack while walking up the stairs that he carried her up three flights every day.

In an Italian family, we are all responsible for each other. That means if somebody has a problem, we *all* have a problem. The phones start ringing from one house to another until the problem is hashed out and a solution is found. When I was a kid, that solution was usually my father. He was the original "Solutions Provider," as the software people call their troubleshooters today. Even though he was not the oldest of the family, he was the one everyone turned to for help and advice. I'd be a billionaire today if I had a dollar for every time I heard my father say, "Don't worry about it. I'll take care of it."

My father was tough, with an iron will and nerves of steel, but he could also be gentle and compassionate, generous and fun-loving. He was loved by those who knew him well. I was reminded of that last April, when my wife, Julie, and I and the seven children we have between us were in Las Vegas to celebrate my 41st birthday. Two limousines were parked at the curb as we left Caesar's Palace for a night on the town. The driver of one approached me.

"Are you Mr. Borsellino?" he asked.

"Yes, that's me," I replied, figuring that the driver just wanted to be sure he was picking up the right party.

"Are you Tony's son?" he asked, his voice softening.

I was shocked at the mention of my father's name after all these years. "Yes, I am. I'm Lewis Borsellino."

The driver shook his head, smiling in disbelief. "My God. Tony's son. You look just like him. He was the best guy in the world."

You know the old saying, "Honor among thieves." It applied literally to my father. He broke laws by stealing from a company, diverting a load into his own hands. But he would never rob or steal from a person. I'm not splitting hairs nor am I defending what my father did. It was illegal and it was wrong. I don't like what he did and I don't approve of it. My father could have made a living with a legitimate business, relying on his brains and his balls to put a deal together. I'm angry that he didn't do that. I'm angry that he never saw my success and my brother's success. I'm angry that he never saw his grandchildren. And I'm angry that my mother has been a widow for nearly 20 years, since she was 43.

But he was my father and I love him. Regardless of the choices he made, he was a man who loved his family, who moved us out of the old neighborhood and into the suburbs to give us a better chance. It was a lifestyle change he couldn't afford, though, and he paid the price for getting involved with the wrong element. I'll never forget that. What he wanted was for us to have a better shake in life than he had.

"I do what I do so you won't have to."

My father never minced words, whether he was giving out advice or telling me straight out about himself and his life. He used his life as a lesson to my brother and me. He knew fear. He knew risk. And he was comfortable with both of them. With honesty and candor, Dad told Joey and me the truth about life as he saw it. I remember when I was 18 and prowling the clubs with my friends. My father would smile and say, "You like going out cabareting, huh? You like the good life? You better get a good education and get a job." Or else he'd take me to a club and point out the guys at the bar. "You see that guy? He's a judge. The other one is a lawyer. He's a doctor. The other guy owns his own business . . . You want to be like them? Get an education."

In so many ways, my father made me the person I am today. Whatever success I have enjoyed as a trader, I have to thank him and the lessons he taught me about survival, discipline, and endurance. From the beginning, my father wanted my brother, Joey, and me to be our own men, to be independent and self-reliant. To this day, I can still hear my father saying to me, "Don't follow the crowd. Be a leader."

I inherited from my father an intense passion for what I love and believe in, especially my family and those who are close to me. That passion is both my biggest asset and my nemesis. The times I have lost control or gotten myself in trouble were because of that passion; however, I can never tame or lose it. It is the core of who I am, my edge and my advantage.

My father taught me other lessons about life, particularly the celebration of it. When life was good, my father lived it up. When we were boys, Joey and I knew it was summer when we got buzz cuts and Mom packed us up to spend the summer at a house we rented in Lake Geneva, Wisconsin, which is to Chicago what the Hamptons are to New York. In 1964, my father bought a boat for $12,500 in cash. He drove a brand new Oldsmobile and Mom had a new Thunderbird. I remember that he always paid cash for everything and he always had a wad on him.

Little wonder then that, when I made it big as a trader, one of the first things I did was to buy a house in Lake Geneva. It was for my family and me to enjoy. But in my heart, it was also for Dad who used to joke, "Some day I'm going to buy a house on the lake and sit on the deck. When people come strolling by, I'm gonna yell, 'Hey, get off my property.' "

But there is more to being a trader than making money. Surely, I have enjoyed the monetary rewards of my profession, just as I have lived it up during the high times. But handling success can be as difficult as dealing with failure. In fact, I believe the worst thing that can happen to a young trader is a string of wins the first week. It's so easy to believe that you are just *that* much smarter than the rest when you perceive every trade you made goes your way. When the market goes against you, and you're squeezed in a long position in a fast-falling market, or scrambling to cover a short position in a rally, you believe you are cursed.

The key is to never believe you can master the market. Oh, there have been times when I've called it so sweetly on the money that I've enjoyed a six-figure day without breaking a sweat. But there are others when I've violated my own rules, believing I *knew* when and where the market was headed instead of letting the market reveal its own timing. I've had my head handed to me on those days.

The market, as they say, rules. Every effort must be made— whether trades are made via an open outcry or an electronic exchange—to preserve the integrity of the market. Equal access must be guaranteed to all players, whether broker or independent "local trader," because in the end, it's the market that must be served by the players and not the other way around.

That's why I consider the Crash of 1987 to be one of the worst things that could have happened to our market. Sure, I was as wrapped up in the instant-gratification euphoria as everyone else. There were a lot of us who made a ton of money, just as there were those who were caught on the wrong side of the market and wiped out. But I would have preferred making $1 million a year for 30 years, rather than to make $4 million in 1 year and destroy the market and its integrity.

There were those who went around gloating after the Crash. To me, they were like the proverbial fools who killed the goose that laid the golden eggs in hopes of getting all the treasure at once. But, as the story goes, the goose only laid the golden eggs one at a time, and the fools with the butcher knife had a big mess on their hands. Moral of the story: patience and prudence, even in things financial, are their own reward. Perhaps that is the ultimate lesson of the high times. Live it up while you can. Enjoy the good fortune that life brings you, but understand that times will change. Just like the market, life has its up and down cycles. The high times never last forever.

The Trading Life

The day I went to the Merc for the first time, I knew I had found my calling—
I heard the noise, I saw the chaos, I felt the energy and the
excitement—and I loved it. People yelled and screamed at each
other, waving their hands and throwing trading cards in the air.
There was money in the air.

I was 22 years old when I visited the floor of the Merc for the
first time in January 1980. I was in the midst of a painful transition and unsure of what to do with the rest of my life. Then I
came to the Merc and I knew I had found my place.

Today, computers are making inroads into trading. Open
outcry is being challenged by the advent of electronic exchanges.
I've made my move already, setting up an off-the-floor trading
operation with a room full of computers and the ability to trade
for myself and investors. If the institutions have their way, the
trading floor will probably disappear and open outcry will be
silenced. But trading will continue. Banks will still hedge their
interest rate exposure, institutions will still use S&P futures to
offset their stock portfolios, and the locals who survive will still
scalp profits between the ticks. When the Merc is a museum
someday, I'll still be trading. I'll be sitting in front of a bank of

computers in my office two blocks from the Merc or relaxing with a laptop and a cell phone at my summer home on the shores of Lake Geneva.

It's hard to explain to people outside a small circle what I do for a living. Someone on a golf course hears that I'm a trader and wants to know what I think about Intel or IBM or some other stock. I explain that I don't trade individual stocks. My specialty is S&P futures, a contract based on the overall value of the S&P 500. The guy's eyes usually glaze over, and then he asks if I got killed when the market went down the week before or did I clean up when it rallied.

It doesn't matter what direction the market takes, I explain. A trader can make money when the market rises or when it falls. We trade from the long and short side. If I haven't completely bored him by this time, I'll go on to explain: It's like placing a bet with a buddy on the Super Bowl. Maybe you think Dallas is going to win so that's the way you bet. But you could just as easily bet against Dallas and go with the Broncos. Same thing with S&Ps: If you think the market is going up, you go long by buying contracts; if you think the market is going down, you go short by selling at the current price.

Some people use gambling as an analogy for trading. Granted, both are risky propositions, and in both arenas there are the high rollers and those who clutch their money to their chests, doling out one quarter at a time. But, when you roll the dice in Vegas, you're just as likely to come up with a five as a seven. Professional gamblers use strategies to improve their chances, but the odds still rule. In trading, you're speculating on what you believe will happen in the market, based on your analysis of the fundamentals and technical aspects. You know what influences the market, whether it's a piece of good news about the Asia crisis or a warning from Alan Greenspan that the economy is too hot. Still, even the best trader can get chopped up in a market that turns suddenly for no apparent reason. He's long in a market that drops suddenly, and he can't sell his contracts until the price is far lower than where he bought. I've been there more times than I care to think about or admit—every trader has. Focus and discipline, however, bring you back into the game. You make back what you lost—and more.

I start my day in my office, two blocks from the Merc, where a half-dozen traders and I meet before the opening to discuss where we think the market is going. We pour over technical price charts that look, to the untrained eye, like the ramblings of a mad mathematician or mystic chartist.

What the charts reveal are the price patterns, or levels in the market that pose support and resistance. Knowing where these key price levels lie, traders can execute a strategy for the day. Say, for example, S&Ps are trading around 1050. But looking back at the prices of the previous trading days, you can clearly see that 1065 was the point at which the market had difficulty going higher. It tested that level a few times but, failing to stay above it for any length of time, prices declined. As the market moves above 1050, the next target to watch will be 1065. If it loses momentum there again, the market will be decidedly bearish. But if S&Ps break through that level, the tone becomes bullish.

These technical price points act like magnets attracting trading activity. This is largely because traders and market technicians are all looking at the same price points. Although technical analysis does vary, certain key levels—such as previous highs and lows, or transition points where the market changed direction—will be common to most systems. So when the market nears these prices, you know all eyes will be on what happens next.

We examine the charts and discuss the numbers each morning, acquainting ourselves with the key price points to watch. "1065. That's the do-or-die level," one of the traders pipes up.

I nod in agreement, sitting behind a wide dark-wood desk on which three baseballs, autographed by Joe DiMaggio, Ted Williams, and Mickey Mantle, are displayed under glass. "If the market's above 1065, it's a buy signal," I concur. "Below that, we're going down."

I glance at my computer screen that's still etched with yesterday's market activity, and tune in for a second to CNBC headlines. Then, it's time to trade. The traders file out of my office and into the room next door where a wall of computer screens display price quotes and indicator lines. Phones are picked up and orders placed. The market will be open soon and the bets are on.

I stand alone in my office for a moment, surrounded by photos and tokens of the passions of my life. First and foremost is my family. On my walls are photographs of my wife, Julie, and the seven children we have between us. I have also inherited my father's love of sports and his competitor's heart. Photos of my golf partners and me at various tournaments are clustered on one wall. Walter Payton's signed jersey is framed under glass. A Notre Dame helmet signed by every Heisman trophy winner at that university sits on a lucite table in front of my desk.

I slip on my white trading jacket bearing my trading badge that reads LBJ. Although my initials are LJB, I turned them around to make a more memorable acronym. (Remember Lyndon Johnson and "all the way with LBJ?") Our trading badges are our signatures, the more inventive the better. My brother, Joey, went with "OEJ." Others use choice buzzwords like POW and WOW. My dear friend and mentor, Maury Kravitz, once suffered from a medical condition that caused him to fall asleep suddenly. Because of it, he choose ZZZZ as his trading badge. Whatever the label, the goal is to grab and hold somebody's attention across the pit, so they'll remember you on this trade—and the next.

I leave the office, knowing that in an hour or two I'll be back. I leave the grueling long days to the younger traders, some a little more than half my age, who coattail my trades. They buy when I buy, sell when I sell. I still maintain a presence in the pit because trading activity there is too important to ignore. As long as there is a pit, my firm and I will be represented there. But the future is out of the pit and upstairs at the PC.

Walking into the Merc, I exchange a wave with another trader. Outside the pit, there is room for camaraderie or even friendship. In the pit, it's another story. Whether the market ticks slowly or swings wildly, it is nothing less than war. I'm only as good as my last trade, whether I'm up $100,000 or down $50,000 on any given day.

Just before the market opens, I claim my turf. I stand on the second step from the top, nearly opposite the podium where the Merc keeps track of prices and trades. My brother, Joey, is already there, standing to my left. In the minute before the buzzer blasts and trading begins, I think back to the first time I came to the Merc in 1980.

I had graduated from college nearly a year before and was making a living driving my father's truck. It was not the plan I had for my life, but then again nothing had turned out the way I had hoped. After hours, I played handball with a man some 15 years my senior named Lou Matta, a man from the old neighborhood who had done well as a trader at the Chicago Mercantile Exchange. I had been reading in *The Wall Street Journal* about the price of gold, which was soaring in those days, and I was interested in trading gold futures off the floor for my own account.

When I mentioned this to Lou, he suggested I visit him at the Merc. "Come down to the floor some day," he said to me, "and see what trading is all about."

The day I went to the Merc, Lou Matta offered me a job on the spot. I don't know if it was the noise or the adrenaline rush, but I knew, intuitively, that I could thrive in this environment. I became a runner, which is the only way to learn the ropes at the Merc. It doesn't matter if you are the smartest guy in the world—a nuclear scientist with a Nobel Prize—when it comes to working at the Merc, you have to start at the bottom as a runner. For minimum wage, you take orders that come in from customers and bring them from the desk to the brokers who stand in the various pits—cattle, pork bellies, currencies, eurodollars, and so forth.

After a few days as a runner, I saw a man who had figured large early in my life, and who would remain one of the most influential people in my career and a dear friend to this day: Maury Kravitz. Maury hadn't seen much of me since I was nine years old and my mother was working as his legal secretary. His back was to me when I spotted him on the floor of the Merc. "Hello, Maury," I said. "Do you remember me?"

Maury peered at me over the top of the reading glasses he wore. "Hello, Lewis," he said warmly. Then he spotted the badge and my Merc jacket. "What are you doing here?"

"I'm a runner for Lou Matta."

"Why didn't you come to me for a job?" Maury asked, sounding genuinely hurt.

I hadn't wanted to ask any favors of Maury or anybody else. I had come to expect nothing more from people than a pat on the back and the hollow ring of the old "good luck to you" speech. But Maury was different. He truly cared about people, and when he offered me a break, he meant it. "Come see me in two weeks," he said. "I'll make you my clerk."

When I told Lou Matta what Maury had offered me, he smiled. "Lewis, if Maury Kravitz offered you an opportunity like that, you have to take it." Lou and I shook hands when we parted ways professionally, but he remains a good friend to this day. Then I went to the gold pit to become a clerk for Maury Kravitz, a legend among traders.

Maury has made a name for himself by his intelligence, his business acumen, and his wholehearted pursuit of life. During his career, both as an attorney and later as a trader, he was associated with both Leo Melamed and Jack Sandner. In fact, Maury and Leo had been law partners long before they formed a trading company, Dellsher, named for their two daughters. Jack Sandner was a young attorney who came to work for Maury. My mother, who was Maury's secretary for years, used to type legal briefs for Jack when he was just starting out in law practice.

In my early days at the Merc, there was a cordial business relationship between Maury, Jack, and Leo. Years later, a bitter feud over control of the exchange would embroil Leo and Jack. The Merc membership would be effectively split in two factions. From the beginning, I was associated with Maury, who was closely aligned with Jack. By default, I was part of Jack's camp. Leo and I, as the years progressed, would fight some bitter battles.

By the time I started out at the Merc, Maury and Leo had split up their businesses. Maury retained the law firm while Leo kept ownership of Dellsher. Jack was president of RB&H Financial Services, a clearing firm that had established a stronghold in cattle brokerage and handled a sizeable amount of the trades conducted at the Exchange. Through my association with Maury, I gained immediate entree into the inner circle.

In the early days, Maury was the king of the gold pit. In the early 1970s, even before the United States was off the gold standard, Maury had the foresight to approach several major brokerage houses about handling their business should a gold contract be launched some day. Maury persisted through the years until the brokerage houses, to appease him or just shut him up, agreed to give him their gold business. Then Maury's pipe dream became a reality. When the Merc launched its gold futures contract, Maury had virtually all the business from the large and small brokerage houses. He became so dominant, the Merc later made him split up his customer deck among other players.

When I went to work for Maury, he was still a major trader in gold, and I assisted him in handling the "deck." The deck is a stack of customer orders, with buys at one end and sells at the other—and all arranged around the current market price. As clerk, I handled the deck, arranging the trades for the brokers who executed the customer orders in the pit. In those days, trading was a different game than it is now. As the market moved, I reshuffled the buys and the sells, keeping track of the customer orders for the brokers in the pit. The job of the clerk was to keep the deck in line with the time and price of the market so that brokers could execute the trades the best way possible. In the process, I showed Maury that I had the instincts and the feel for the market to become a trader.

I was working for Maury only a few months when he invited my mother and me to his daughter Sheryl's bat mitzvah at his home in Skokie. Maury called my mother aside at the party following the ceremony and told her something that she repeated to me in the car on the way home.

"Maury told me not to worry about you, that you're going to be a millionaire," my mother said proudly.

"Yeah? Well, I wish it would happen soon because we could use the money," I said, not sure whether to believe what Maury had said.

My mother laughed. "Be patient," she said. "It will all happen when the time is right. Maury's a good man. He's been like a brother to me. He'll always treat you well."

Maury Kravitz was, and still is, a man motivated by friendship and loyalty. That can be said about very few people, especially in the markets, where money is the motivating factor. For most people in this business, money is their god; it is what they worship and live for. Ultimately, it becomes their Achilles' heel. At the extreme, some people will do anything for money, including putting themselves at risk of a major trading violation out of fear of losing a few thousand.

I've made my share of money, and I enjoy the good life because of it. My father's philosophy when it came to money was, when you have it, you spend it. My father was very generous, both in picking up the tab at the cabaret and helping out someone who was down on his luck. Money was fuel to be used. But it was never to be hoarded or, God forbid, lorded over somebody else. I've never worried about money in my life. I always knew that I could lose everything tomorrow and still land on my feet. That's why if I have five dollars and you need two, you can take the two. If you need five, take it. I'll get another five. Some people may have taken advantage of me in the past because, like my Dad, I have to make everything right for everybody. But I adhere to his philosophy, especially when it comes to my family and those who are close to me: "Either we all go or nobody goes."

But in those first months as a clerk, it was hard for me to wait for my chance to prove myself as a trader. Luckily, I only had to wait a few more months. In September 1981, I got my seat at the Exchange to trade gold. But it wasn't the best time to be getting into the gold market. Volume was drying up and, to make matters worse, I only had about $5,000 in my trading account. To be a successful trader, you need much more than that—preferably 10 to 20 times that amount—to allow you to trade enough contracts to make a profit and to give you a cushion in case of a bad run. I was filling orders and I was trading, but I wasn't making much more than my $3,000 a month lease on my seat.

Capitalization is one of the key concerns in trading, whether on the floor or at the PC. When I started out, a young trader needed nothing more than a trading account and someone to vouch for him. Today, the exchange rules are more stringent. I recently put up a $50,000 T-bill to back a young floor trader I have been training to supplement his $10,000 trading account. Plus, you have to figure that a novice won't make any money the first year. All tolled, including the lease on a seat and living expenses, it costs about $250,000 a year to back a trader. For those trading professionally off the floor, I believe you must have a minimum of $50,000, even to trade one-lots, particularly in a volatile market like S&Ps. This provides an adequate cushion not only to cover potential margin calls on overnight positions, but to provide insurance against losses.

Futures are a leverage game. One S&P contract has a cash equivalent value of $250,000 in stock. Even trading one contract, or lot, you can net $3,000 in one day. Based on $50,000 in your trading account, that's a 6 percent return in just one day. But leverage works both ways. Losses on one contract can amount to several thousand quickly. That's why money management skills are just as important, if not more so, than market savvy and mastering trading techniques. The 11th Commandment for traders: *Thou shalt not shoot the whole wad.*

I nearly crapped out my first year as a trader. I had little money left in my trading account, and it looked like I wasn't going to make it. Plus, I was plagued with outtrades. In an outtrade, you think you have made a trade—say, selling 10 lots to the guy across the pit, but in fact, that guy across the pit did the trade with the trader standing next to you. So, you think you've sold 10 lots to somebody and, in fact, there's been no deal. Complicating matters, as an order filler, you've made a commitment to your customer that a trade was completed at a particular price. You've got to reach an agreement with another trader on that outtrade and make it up to your customer—a process that often involves thousands of dollars out of a trader's pocket.

These outtrades were devastating to me as a new trader. But, worse than the dollar losses was the fact I was afraid of losing favor with Maury and Jack. The Merc had just launched the S&P contract, which would become its most successful ever. It was long before the bull run that would take the Dow Jones Industrial Average—corrections not withstanding—from under 1,000 to well over 9,000. I saw the S&P pit and I knew I wanted to be part of it. Maybe it was because this new contract would be a new start for me. Or, maybe I just had a gut feeling about the contract. Whatever the reason, I wanted to be part of that action.

But I was struggling in gold and I didn't have any money to get a foothold in S&Ps. Maury and Jack brought another trader on board and it looked to me like I was going to be the odd man out. If I was going to make a go of it in the S&P pit, I had to do it on my own. So, I hooked up with a trader named Marty Potter, helping him out in the S&P pit. Each day, I traded gold until the pit closed at 1:30 in the afternoon. Then, I headed over to the S&P pit to help Marty fill orders, including for his biggest customer, Bache Securities. The S&P pit was the place for me, I knew, and I needed to find a way to trade there full-time. That opportunity came one day when I made the luckiest mistake of my life. Although luck plays a certain role in trading, as it does in life, there is more to success than just fortunate happenstance. You have to be engaged for luck to have an effect; all the luck in the world won't help if you're sitting on the sidelines.

It was during the Falkland Islands conflict of 1982 between Argentina and Great Britain. Gold was making big moves in response to every news item on the wires. I was in the pit, filling orders for customers and trading for my account, under dual trading that was allowed in those days. All of a sudden, the news hit the wires: Argentina had surrendered in the Falkland Islands crisis. Gold dropped $50 in a heartbeat. Then a little while later, the news came out that there was no surrender. Gold rocketed back up $50.

In the middle of the frenzy, I had written down a trade that I sold at the low to another trader named Mike. When I went to check the trade with Mike, he said he had sold at the low to me.

"So we're sell-sell," I said to Mike.

"Yeah, and now the market is $50 higher," he grinned. "So you buy mine and I'll buy yours."

We settled the trade and each pocketed $57,000. In one day, I had made more than enough to get a start in the S&P pit. My trading account was flush for the first time and my future was set. I left the gold pit and went to S&Ps, and I never looked back. As fortunate as that mistake was, the timing was even more fortuitous. I had learned the ropes over the past year and was ready to make my move to the S&P pit. Had that $57,000 fallen into my hands earlier, I could have gone through it quickly with bad trades. In this instance, it was a case of a perfectly timed windfall.

As an order filler for Marty, I quickly showed Maury and Jack what I could do in the S&P pit. My confidence restored, I became one of the best in that pit. I was the odd man out no longer, and Jack and Maury brought me into the fold as a full-fledged trader on the team.

Among my customers in the S&P pit was a major commodity trading firm, O'Connor Partners. When I filled orders for O'Connor clients, I always paid special attention to trades handled for one of its biggest customers: Jim Pierce. Jim was one of the best off-the-floor traders I had ever seen. He had an instinct for the market that was uncanny, and I decided to do whatever he did. So when he would give me an order, such as to buy 500 S&P contracts at the market, I'd execute his order and then I'd buy 20 lots for myself. The market would go straight up. When Jim got out of the market, I sold his contracts and then I sold mine. But what did Jim Pierce, who was sitting in front of a computer somewhere in the Carolinas, see that I didn't? What Jim was doing was studying price charts, looking for key price points in the market for support (where the market was unlikely to drop further) and resistance (where it would have difficulty breaking through). That's when I began to dabble in technical analysis, a pursuit that would become a full-time passion.

Watching the customer orders, I could see that trades gravitated toward certain price points. This sparked an interest in finding out why these price patterns developed and how my customers were using them. From the beginning, I hungered to learn all I could about trading, whether it was charting the markets or doing spreads between futures and options. There wasn't enough that I could learn.

I also began to pay close attention in the pit to floor-order flow. The flow of buy and sell orders onto the floor gives you a sense of the underlying dynamics of the market. But it's more than just selling when the order fillers begin to dump a lot of contracts. It means watching the body language of the brokers who handle the big customers' decks. Are they nervous about executing a big buy order as the market rises rapidly? It also means watching the cash market, in this case the value of the S&P 500 Index itself. When I was a young trader, I was mystified at first when cash S&Ps were going up and the futures were getting hammered. Then, it occurred to me: the portfolio managers were buying stocks, and hedging their positions by selling futures. The two markets didn't always work in sync.

Floor-order flow interpretation is more art than science. There are days when I walk onto the floor, believing that I'm going short. Then, I sense the floor-order flow and I immediately go long. My gut instinct and my floor trading presence were and always will be my foundation, but my understanding of the technical factors behind the numbers is another plus. My strength in combining these two skills in such a way has led to my success—and helped keep me successful.

For me, my ability to read the floor-order flow came with experience and longevity. I had been on the floor for so many years, as a broker and then as a local, that the flow of orders and the shift between bullish and bearish sentiment became palpable to me. In the same way, patterns in trading become evident when you're watching the screen. You see the levels at which trades congregate, the prices at which there is more buying or selling activity. By the same token, computerized trading systems also recognize certain patterns, levels of support and resistance, and prices at which the market breaks out or retreats. It comes with experience and careful study. If you pay attention, the market will be your teacher.

There is another element to trading that is difficult, if not downright impossible, to explain. It is what I call the *intangible*. You could just as easily call it gut instinct. Whatever the name, it is that sense of what the market is going to do. There are days when, watching the tick-for-tick on the screen or standing in the pit, you see more and more sellers come into the market like people piling onto a boat. There will be a point when, just like an overcrowded boat, the market will sink, and sometimes fast. Otherwise, you'll notice that the market is building momentum, turning like a corkscrew until it is so tightly wound that it springs upward. This instinct is developed over time and is honed by experience.

Trading is a profession unlike any other, and being an S&P trader is better yet. What compares most closely, perhaps, is professional athletics. In both arenas, there are the superstars who outperform and outlast everyone; there are the hopefuls who crash and burn; and there are the guys who never make it to the top, but manage to enjoy a great living over a long career. But, across the board, traders—like athletes—ride the emotional highs and lows. Every day that you've won by making money in the pit, it's a great feeling; the days you lose money, you don't feel so great. And then you have a few losses in a row. . . .

There is no security being a trader, and you are only as good as your next trade. There are many times a trader wakes up in a sweat in the middle of the night and asks himself, "What if I lost it? What if I can't trade anymore?"

Trading is a game of instant loss and instant gratification. Luckily for me, I have never been the kind of person who needs a check every week. There are some people who go the safe route, perhaps out of insecurity. I'm not insecure and I never went the safe route my entire life. I was very confident of my ability, so I never worried about where my next dollar was coming from. I always felt in life that I would land on my feet. I knew I would go through ups and downs—and believe me, I have. But I always knew I would survive and, in time, thrive. I learned this lesson from Dad.

My father, Tony Borsellino, could spot an opportunity. In the legitimate business world, I swear he would have put any venture capitalist or corporate raider to shame. But, my father came from a different world. Opportunity had to be grabbed with both fists. For instance, when Dad was driving a truck, he and the other truckers used to shoot craps at lunchtime in a trailer at Grand Avenue and Lower Wacker, the parallel roadway that runs underneath Chicago's Wacker Drive. One day, my father showed up at the trailer where 15 or 20 other guys were making bets and shooting craps. He picked up the dice and said, "I'm cutting the game." That meant he was going to run the dice game for a share of the pot.

"Hey, who made you the boss?" some guy complained.

My father's reply? Boom! One hit and the guy was out cold. "Anybody else want to argue with me?"

From that day on, Dad ran the craps game.

I often wonder what would have become of my father had he been able to complete his college education. Would he have had a career that would have afforded him the lifestyle that he wanted? Would he have taken the straight path? But fate did not deal my father that hand. Dad had to leave Texas Tech after one year when his father became ill. He came home and started to drive a truck.

My parents lived in the old neighborhood after they got married, and I lived there as a small child. After those early years, my father longed for nothing less than the proverbial American dream. He wanted a house in the suburbs for his wife and two sons. So when Uncle Norfe, Dad's brother, moved to Lombard, Illinois, my father was quick to follow. He bought a $23,000 house with $2,000 down in a new subdivision where our neighbors were not only Italian, but Polish, Irish, and German as well. The house was my father's pride and joy: a three-bedroom raised ranch with some 2,200 square feet that felt like a castle compared with our old apartment.

We were only the second family to occupy the house, and my father quickly made it his own, from the *B* for Borsellino in the screen door to the white-stone facade he added to make ours the only all-white brick house on the street. That house was my father's dream, but the mortgage payment of nearly $300 a month was tight on his salary of $150 a week driving a truck. That's where temptation came in. The trucking business gave Dad access to goods that could be hijacked and sold. His first heist netted him about $100,000, his first taste of big money. My father took the first steps down a path he never should have followed. But once he started, there was no turning back.

My father went to work every day driving a truck. He worked hard and he loved his family. If I say nothing else about my father, I must say that again. He loved us all more than anything, more than even his own life, which is why he took the risks that he did.

Early on, I realized that my father was not just a truck driver. Back in the early 1960s when everyone wanted a color television, we had one—and so did my Dad's older brother, Uncle Norfe. The same thing with a stereo or an eight-track tape player. Those little luxuries showed up at the house, but never with a sales receipt. My father's explanation was, "It fell off a truck."

I remember when Joey and I wanted walkie-talkies like the other kids. We wanted the kind made by Mattel. What Dad gave us were walkie-talkies that had a range of up to eight miles, the kind that he and his partners used on "scores." More and more things started showing up at the house.

Mine was not a normal childhood. By the time I was nine years old, I knew my dad was more than just a truck driver. I could tell by the things—expensive things—that we suddenly had at the house. When I overheard my father and his friends talking, it sounded like a game to them. The serious talk was away from young ears. I knew my father wanted us to have the good life, the things he never had. To an adult's mind, it may not make sense, but to me, as a boy who looked up to and loved his father, I could sense what he was all about. He wanted us to have more than he did, and in his mind it was the only way.

Where there is risk, however, there is also fear. Fear cannot be avoided, and it is not a sign of weakness to feel it. The important thing about fear is how to handle it. Mastering fear propels you forward. Letting fear master you paralyzes you.

In trading, there is one common reason why people freeze up: the old deer-in-the-headlights syndrome. It is the fear of losing their money and their possessions. Their things—money, houses, cars, whatever—mean so much to them that they can't really enjoy what they have. They become like the person who is so afraid of getting a dent in his beautiful car that he won't drive it. Their fear is often compounded by the fact that they take on too much risk. They are paralyzed, entrapped by their own fear and insecurities. To be successful in life, especially in trading, which puts your money on the line every day, you can't be a prisoner of your own thoughts.

There are two ways of thinking when you lose money. You can go home and say, "Oh, those guys screwed me . . . ," or you can say to yourself, "You know what? I screwed up. I did this and this and this. . . ." You sit down and you write out what you did and you look at it. Then you go to the gym to work off a little steam, and wait for the market to open up the next day. Why? Because all any trader worth his salt wants to do is *get his money back.*

When you have a bad day, you go back to the basics of what you do: watching the market and executing disciplined trades. At all costs, you cannot afford to lose your focus. In fact, in my early days I never took a day off from work. I stood there, from opening bell to closing. I lived and breathed trading. I studied the market until it was my second nature, and I never lost my respect for it. The worst thing I could ever do would be to assume the market could no longer surprise me. Even after 18 years in that pit, I know the market is a monster that nobody can tame.

This is a tough lesson for some people who are afflicted with what I call the Harvard MBA syndrome. Some very smart guy with an impressive degree says to himself, "My research is telling me that the market is going to bottom out here and then it's going to go there." They get into a trading position and they just sit and wait; however, what happens is the market in the short term moves against them. They are losing more and more on their position until they are belly-up in the water. Guess what happens next? The market takes a turn and goes right to where they said it would. The problem was they tried to predict exactly where, and when, the market was going to move. If I've seen it happen once, I've seen it a million times. All the analysis— quantitative, fundamental, technical, or whatever—won't do you any good if you don't have timing. You let the market have a bottom and jump on the upswing; then, you have to let the market top out and jump on the downswing. Timing is not something that you can gain from a book, a course, or a lecture. It is something that has to be developed; it comes with experience, and is its own reward.

In the end, it all comes down to being in sync with the market. To be a successful trader, you have to see yourself as part of the market. When the markets are wild and crazy, you can trade a little more footloose and fancy-free. The swings are so great, you have a better chance of making money as the market gyrates. But when the market is slow and orderly, you have to trade slowly and orderly. You take on the personality of the market every day.

You take your risks, reap the rewards. Or, when you make a bad decision or the market turns against you, you face the consequences. That's the way it is in life. I saw that as a youngster, at an age when most kids' lives were little more than the playground and Saturday morning cartoons. I saw firsthand what it was to accept risk and pay the price. It shaped me as a boy and as a man.

In 1963 and 1964, we were living high on the hog. Then in 1965, my father was arrested and charged with hijacking a load of silver worth about $1 million. Ironically, the load they were charged with stealing was the one they were never paid for. They had been double-crossed and stiffed on the money they were expecting to make. The FBI got a break when one of the partners in the score was caught stealing in Indiana. While the partner was in jail, he became convinced his wife was having an affair with a neighbor. The thought of it was driving him crazy. That's when the FBI approached this guy with a deal that would get him out of jail and back home to his wife: turn state's evidence and identify his partners. The partner named my father as being part of the crew who made the score.

After Dad's arrest, the FBI decided to try to turn him into a stool pigeon based on his profile—a wife, two kids, and a job he went to every day. What they didn't count on was my father's character to act according to his own code of honor. Being a "rat" wasn't part of that code. He was held in Cook County Jail in Chicago after his arrest in 1965. Ironically, from the prison yard he could see Harrison High School where he had been a star football player years before.

To pressure Dad into turning state's evidence, they put him on murderer's row. He and one of his partners walked into a cell with four beds and 13 guys. The leader of the cell handed my father a blanket and said, "You sleep on the floor in the corner."

"Yeah? Where do you sleep?" Dad asked him.

"I sleep in the top bunk."

"You do, huh?" Dad beat this guy until he was on the floor. "Now I sleep up in that bunk," he said.

Nobody argued with him after that. Two days later, Dad was made an honorary member of the Black Peace Stone Nation and was given a gang member bandana. It helped that he was labeled with "O.C.," for Organized Crime, on his prison jacket. With that mark, nobody wanted to mess with him. But his toughness and sheer will made him a force to be reckoned with as well.

My family didn't hide the fact that Dad had been arrested and, even after he was released on bond, we knew he was facing a trial. The day the jury rendered its verdict, Dad called me into my parent's bedroom where he was putting on his tie and jacket. He sat me down on the edge of the bed. "Lewis," he told me, "I could be found guilty today. And if I am, I'm going to have to go to jail. Maybe for a long time."

I nodded. I was a nine-year-old fourth grader, but I knew what was going on.

"You know that I love you, your brother and your mother," Dad continued. "That's never going to change. But if I go away, I need to know that you'll take care of the family."

"I will, Dad," I promised, so scared that he was going to jail and, at the same time, proud that he thought I could be the man of the family. Then the little boy in me won out, if only for an instant. I asked him the strangest thing: "Dad, if they find you guilty, can I have your wallet?"

"My wallet?" Dad repeated, amused by my request.

"Yeah. Can I have it?" I loved the smooth-leather wallet Dad always carried in his back pocket.

"Sure son, you can have it."

Dad went into the bathroom to comb his hair. When he came out a few minutes later, I had taken his wallet out of the dresser and was emptying the contents. "What are you doing?" he asked me.

"Taking your wallet."

"You don't have much confidence that I'm going to be found not guilty."

"No, Dad," I told him, "I don't."

My father was found guilty of hijacking, transporting stolen goods, and kidnapping the driver of the heisted truck. He was in custody the day he was sentenced. My mother went to court to be there, while all the aunts and uncles gathered at our house—waiting. Aunt Josie was in the kitchen, cooking spaghetti, even though everybody was too nervous to eat. The adults gathered around the television set in the living room, waiting for the news. Joey and I sat down with them.

"What are you kids doing here?" Aunt Louisa asked. She waved us out of the room with her hands. "Go upstairs and play."

I walked slowly up the stairs with Joey, but we didn't play. We turned on the television set upstairs and listened to the news, just like the adults downstairs. We heard someone swear and one of the aunts started to cry when the verdict was announced. Dad was given four concurrent 20-year sentences. On the television screen, I saw Mom walking out of the courthouse beside a man with a jacket pulled over his head to hide his face from the television cameras. I heard the news reporters yell questions to him. "Tony, how do you feel?" "Tony, do you think you can win an appeal?"

When I heard the man yell back at the reporters, I knew it was my father. I recognized his voice.

A cameraman tried to get a close-up of Dad, shoving the camera right in his face. All of a sudden, the camera veered wildly and shot up at the sky. My father had leveled the cameraman with one punch, breaking the guy's jaw.

"He's gonna get you for assault," someone yelled.

"I just got sentenced to 80 years, you dumb [bleep]," my father yelled back, the obvious expletive beeped out by the television station. "What difference does it make?"

What I saw on the television screen that day was burned into my memory. My father was escorted into custody to begin serving his time at Leavenworth Federal Penitentiary. I knew he wouldn't be coming home for a long, long time.

I was playing gin with some friends one night, shortly after my first appearance on CNBC. "Hey, saw you on the television the other day," one of the guys said as he dealt the cards. "You almost sounded like you knew what you were talking about."

"That was a proud moment in my life," I joked back. "You realize I'm the first member of my family to appear on television without a jacket over his head?"

We all laughed at my expense. But, I knew nobody could appreciate that joke as much as my father would have. And no one would have been as proud—with the possible exception of my mother—to see my brother or me on the television screen for a legitimate reason.

I cannot help but wonder what my father would think of me today. At times I can picture my father in my mind, the epitome of charm and style, and the very definition of lean and mean. He was five feet seven inches, with a 32-inch waist that he kept trim with the five miles he ran every day and his regular workout in the gym. I can imagine a smile spreading over his handsome face, looking to all the world like a brown-eyed Paul Newman with a broken nose. I hear his rich, deep voice, which echoes in my own, except for my persistent raspiness from years of screaming in the pit; I hear him say, "Hey, fuck it! We made it!"

My father raised my brother, Joey, and me to be tough and strong, disciplined and focused. He gave us stomachs for risk and the ability to push past the fear. He taught us to look for the worst-case outcome and weigh that against the reward. Without knowing a thing about the profession, Dad raised Joey and me to be traders.

Combat

The trading pit is like no other place of business: Money is on the line, the
action is fast and furious, and everyone is pumped with
adrenaline and testosterone. Traders stand nearly on top of each
other, screaming buys and sells. They jockey for position, trying
to see—and be seen by—the buyers and sellers in the pit. The
fiercest of rivals and the most intense competitors stand shoulder to shoulder or, at most, just a few yards away from each
other. Hands and arms fly in the air. Somebody gets jostled in
the fray. Somebody pushes, and somebody pushes back. To the
outside world, it looks like pure chaos; however, there is an
order to the pit. Everybody has his turf, about one square foot
on which to stand. When you're trading, you defend that turf.

In the business world, traders are a breed apart. Every gain is
instantly recorded; every loss is instantly felt. When you make a
mistake you know it on the spot. Even before you've had time to
get over the anger, you know what the loss is to your bottom line.
Every trade is like having a one-second fiscal year. This is not so
in other businesses, where a mistake today may not be felt until
next month, next quarter, or maybe even next year. This volatility
makes the instantaneous world of trading nothing less than hand-

41

to-hand combat. Sure, the only thing you can lose is your money and not your life. But to many people, their money *is* their life.

In this regard, I believe the only activity that can compare with trading is competitive athletics. On the field, on the court, or in the trading pit, the players are pumped with adrenaline. Mental preparation is just as important as physical stamina, and focus must be 100 percent on the game. For most athletes, however, this kind of mental and physical endurance lasts only as long as the basketball or football game. Professional athletes practice every day, but not with game-time intensity. For traders, the intensity is the status quo, day in and day out.

Against this competitive backdrop, it's easy to see why tempers flare. It's as if the trading pit has been doused with kerosene, waiting for one good spark. As for myself, I have the dubious distinction in my 18-year career at the Chicago Mercantile Exchange of having the most infractions and fines for fighting, using excessive force (i.e., pushing and shoving) to enter and exit the pit, and swearing. No one has to tell me that it is wrong to hit another person; there is no way to justify that behavior. The last thing I want to do is brag about incidents from my days as a young trader when I never looked for a fight, but didn't walk away when someone started trouble, either. But the stories follow me, some true and some outlandish embellishments about this time or that when I punched another trader in the pit. It's all part of the lore of Lewis Borsellino, floor trader. But now, at 41, I roll my eyes when somebody asks me if I really stabbed someone with a pencil one day (true, I must admit) or if I actually punched 14 guys in the pit one day (a gross exaggeration).

Unfortunately, these incidents are the stories that are told and retold about me—with one significant omission. Sometimes people fail to mention that I haven't been successful in the pit because of a brute force, but rather a cerebral one. I haven't made a name for myself in the S&P pit because I was so tough, but because I am very good at what I do.

I did not bring the rough-and-tumble style of trading to the pits. It began with the introduction of financial futures in the 1970s and early 1980s. These volatile, high-volume contracts such as currencies, Treasury bonds, eurodollars, and S&P futures brought a new breed of player into the pit. They were younger and more aggressive, both physically and mentally. Both the Merc and the Chicago Board of Trade have built new trading floors and facilities because of the financial futures and the young turks who traded them. It was a sharp contrast to the old days at the Merc and the Board of Trade, which were once used exclusively to trade agricultural commodities. The atmosphere then was more like that of a men's club with all the courtesies of the old-boy network.

I felt at home in the mentally and physically demanding world of trading, where the pace was fast and the action was competitive. But there was a key difference between the other traders in the pit and myself. The other traders often talked a tough game and conducted themselves as if they had been hanging out on the street corner their whole lives. They yelled in each other's faces, swore and called each other vile names, and pushed one another. It was an elaborate ritual in a game called intimidation. Few were willing to stand behind their tough talk.

I had grown up in a different environment. Although I was a graduate of DePauw University, I had also been trained in the "Tony Borsellino School of Life." To me, my father defined the term "a man's man." He was strong, tough, and loyal, the kind of guy who was fun to be with and, when there was trouble, he was the one you wanted to be on your side. My brother, Joey, and I were Dad's peace of mind. He had to know, even when we were little boys, that we could take care of ourselves and our mother. To protect us, especially when he wasn't around, my father raised us to be just as tough as he was.

When I was in the fourth grade, just before my dad's trial, a sixth grader beat me up as I walked home from school. My father watched the whole thing from the living room window and met me at the door when I dragged myself up the sidewalk, blubbering all the way.

"What's the matter with you?" he asked me.

"I got beat up," I cried. "He's a sixth grader and bigger than me."

I got no sympathy from Dad, only another one of his life lessons. "Let me tell you something," he said, grabbing me by the shoulders. "You go out there and defend yourself, or I'm going to beat you up."

With Dad trailing me, I went out of the house and down the block. I found that sixth grader in his yard. He was half a head taller and at least 10 pounds heavier than I was, but I pounced on him. I hit him again and again until he was on the ground, crying. My father stood back and watched, proud of the way I defended myself. When the boy's father came out of the house to break up the scuffle, Dad settled the score with a right to the man's jaw. My Dad knew the boy was the one who passed by our house in the evenings and yelled in the open windows, "Hey, Mr. Borsellino, how's the hijacking business?" Dad didn't blame the kid. He was only repeating the bad-mouthing he had heard from his father.

I walked home next to my father, his hand gripping my shoulder proudly. I had a bloody lip and a black eye, but I had learned a lesson in my father's school of life. There was no such thing as walking away from a fight.

When Dad was in jail, I stepped into my father's shoes as the man of the family. Even though I was only nine, this meant defending my brother who was only a second grader when Dad went away. Physically, Joey and I are opposites. As kids, Joey was small for his size, with an olive complexion, dark hair, and green eyes; I was stocky with blue eyes and white-blond hair that matched my white-hot temper. But no two brothers could ever be closer than Joey and I.

I remember an incident when Dad had been in jail for two years and I was in the sixth grade. Joey, a fourth grader, was being picked on by "Big Al," an eighth grader who stood about six feet tall. Although Big Al was a crossing guard who was supposed to look out for the younger kids, he took special delight in tormenting my brother every morning. Joey's only revenge was to stop in the middle of the crosswalk and yell, "Fuck you, Big Al," and then take off on his bicycle before Big Al could get him. Then one day, Big Al knocked Joey off his bicycle and broke all the spokes in the wheels. Even though I was only about four feet nine, I had to devise a way to defend my brother against Big Al. I waited for Big Al outside the school door, sneaked up behind him, and pushed him down a flight of stairs. When he hit the bottom, I pounced on top of him. We got caught fighting, and Sister Regina Marie called us into her office. When the whole story came out, she sent me back to class and sent Big Al for the spanking paddle in her office.

From the time I was a boy, I had learned how to defend myself. I knew not to go looking for trouble or instigate a fight. But, if your honor or your integrity was on the line, you didn't back away from a confrontation. When I arrived at the Merc, some of the other traders got more than they bargained for. Guys who were used to throwing their weight around to intimidate someone else found out very quickly that this strategy did not work with me. I drew a line on what I would and would not tolerate from other traders in the pit. Anyone who stepped over that line had to be ready for the consequences of his actions. I was not the kind of guy who was going to let someone try to intimidate me. If someone yelled in my face, swore at me, or tried to push me around, I was more than capable of defending myself. And, I wasn't the kind to write up a complaint against someone for swearing at me or pushing me, any more than I would complain to a security guard at the beach because someone kicked sand in my face. If someone took aggressive action against me in my younger days, he had better be prepared to defend himself.

I remember when I was a new trader, still learning the ropes in the gold pit. One morning before the opening, I was scanning a computer printout of my trades from the day before. The records indicated I had an outtrade on five contracts that were part of a 20-contract buy order. I executed the first three trades of five contracts each without a hitch. But the computer printout indicated that I had not bought the last five contracts to complete the 20-lot trade. My records showed that a trader, whom I will call Stuart, had sold me the last five contracts.

Stuart stood about six feet four inches tall and looked like he didn't weigh more than 150 pounds. But he talked like some tough guy. The outtrade was going to cost one of us $4,000. He knew he was in the wrong, but he decided to try to intimidate me to get me to eat the error. "You stupid idiot," Stuart yelled at me. "You don't even know what's a buy and what's a sell. You shouldn't be in this fucking pit. . . ."

At first, I was angry about the way he was talking to me. Then I realized that if he was going to continue with the tough talk, this could work to my advantage. At first, I tried to reason with him. "That was a 20-lot multiple order. There wasn't a problem with the other three parts of the order. So you know what? That tells me it's your mistake."

Stuart kept trash-talking me, trying to make me give in. "You don't even know what you're doing in this pit."

That was it. I had reached the point at which reason was not going to prevail and backing down was not an option. I grabbed Stuart by the throat. "Listen you," I yelled in his face. "This is your mistake. You're going to make good on it. And another thing, if you ever talk to me like that again, I'm going to eat your eyeballs out of your head."

I never went into the pit to fight. I was there to make money, and the war against the market was grueling enough. But at the age of 23, I had endured life experiences that most people only read about. Because of the way I was raised, I believed that walking away from a confrontation would not defuse a potentially volatile situation, but rather make me appear vulnerable. Add to that the brashness of the S&P pit itself, where the oldest trader was probably no more than 30 years old and the stakes of trading were in the tens of thousands of dollars.

In this world, I was a double threat—I was college educated and confident in my ability as a trader; plus, I had a physical toughness that clearly communicated that I wasn't someone you wanted to tangle with. This duality has been both my greatest asset and has made me a bit of an enigma. Had I only been a street-smart kid with brass balls and no brains, I would have lasted a New York minute in that pit. When other brokers and traders saw just how good I was, they knew I was a force to be reckoned with. And, when I was younger, I did not shy away from using force when I perceived it was the only option.

I had been in the S&P pit about a month, filling orders for customers and trading for my own account. I had an order in the deck one day to sell 50 contracts at a half. "Fifty at a half," I yelled, shooting my arms over my head and waving my hands. "Fifty at a half."

Before I could find a buyer at 50, a trader, whom I'll call Ricky, jumped in. He started bidding at 55, 60, and then 70. The sellers rushed to Ricky and the market moved before I had a chance to complete the trade at 50. I pushed my way over to where Ricky stood. "You went through my orders!" I said. "You'd better make good on them."

According to Merc rules, I knew Ricky had to make good on my sell order at a half. But Ricky tried to brush me off. "Fuck you," he said, and pushed me aside.

When reason didn't work, I responded with my muscles. It took five traders and two security guys to break up the fight. Ricky sat on the floor, dazed. He wrote a complaint against me to the Merc's disciplinary committee for hitting him. I was reprimanded verbally, but nothing more came of the incident. I wrote a complaint against Ricky for trading through my sell order, which, in the scheme of things, was a more serious violation.

My actions were certainly not politically correct. In hindsight, I could have simply complained to the exchange that Ricky had gone through my sell orders. But in my younger days, I was concerned that if I tried to walk away from a fight that someone else started, I would become a target for everyone's aggression. When I stood up to Ricky, I sent a clear message to the other traders. The new guard had arrived.

By 1983, I was working one of the biggest decks of customer orders in the S&P pit. One day I had an order to buy 400 contracts for O'Connor Partners. Beside me was my clerk, Bobby Natali, who later became a trader. Behind Bobby stood a bear of a man at six feet four and some 270 pounds, whom I'll call Bru. Bru was trying to fill an order, literally over my head. As he jumped up and waved his arms, he knocked into Bobby.

"Bru," I yelled back at him. "Leave my clerk alone."

"I got an order to fill," Bru barked back. He knocked into Bobby one more time.

While I worked that order for O'Connor, Bru kept pushing Bobby into me.

"Bru, leave my clerk alone!"

Wham. He knocked into Bobby again.

"Bru, leave my clerk alone!"

One more time, Bru knocked Bobby into me.

Finally, I bought the last contract for O'Connor. Bru smacked into Bobby for the last time.

"You asshole!" I screamed and, boom, with one punch I launched Bru out of the pit. I leaped off the step in the pit and onto Bru. I had him on the floor, grabbing him by the lapels of his trading jacket. When I looked up, I saw my brother, Joey, who in those days was still a clerk, running to my aid, just like when we were kids.

Harry Lowrance, better known as Harry the Hat, grabbed me by the shoulders to pull me off Bru. Suddenly, Harry was out cold on the floor of the Merc and my brother was standing over him. Oh, no! I thought to myself. My brother had just decked one of the most revered brokers in the business. After that fight, I was given a cease and desist letter from the Merc, but was not fined. It helped that I worked for Maury Kravitz, who was very respected and politically connected, through his association with both Leo Melamed and Jack Sandner. My association with Maury kept me out of a lot of trouble. But there was still the matter of my brother, a young clerk, hitting Harry the Hat.

The next day, one of Harry's clerks approached me in the pit. "Harry wants to see you," he said.

Harry was sitting at one of the desks on the floor where clerks answer the phones and take customer orders. In Harry's hand was my brother's clerk badge. It had fallen off in the fight. "Tell your brother he can't be hitting brokers," Harry said with a smile.

Like the true gentleman he is, Harry the Hat handed me my brother's badge and never said another word about the fight. I was still in my twenties, a kid compared with a man like Harry. But, he showed me the respect of a senior trader.

Now, at five feet nine and a half and 185 pounds, I'm not the biggest guy in the world. In the pit, there are other traders who literally tower over me. So when somebody wants to get aggressive or throw his weight around, I'm usually the target. It was exactly what my father had warned me about years ago. He called it "The Borsellino Curse."

Dad explained that curse to me one night when I came home drunk from a party when I was a sophomore in high school. Dad knew that teenage boys were going to sneak a drink. But he feared that if I got drunk someone would take advantage of me, beat me up, and really do some damage.

"Don't ever let yourself get out of control. Don't get yourself into a situation where they can take advantage of you." Dad paced the living room while I slumped on the sofa. "Lewis, you've got the Borsellino curse. I've had it all my life. If there's a person who is going to start trouble, you're the person they are going to start with. Maybe it's the way you walk into a room. Maybe it's the way you carry yourself. Then again, we're not the biggest guys in the world. People who want to start trouble want to start with the smaller guys. To make matters worse, you're popular. You're the kind of guy people want to take down."

There were many times in my younger days when Maury Kravitz, my friend and mentor, and Jack Sandner, his associate who was also chairman of the Merc, would lecture me for my own good. They'd encourage me to stay calm and not lose my temper. Their aim was to smooth out some of my rough edges. But there were times when they used those rough edges of mine for a strategic advantage. Whether it was the look in my eye or my physical presence, I conveyed a sense of confidence that, frankly, could be intimidating. Coupled with my ability as a trader, this made me a one-man strike force. That's what Maury knew when he sent me into the eurodollar pit.

By the mid-1980s, I had made a name for myself as one of the best order fillers in the S&P pit. Under dual trading, which was allowed in those days, I traded for both my customers and myself. The big, roiling market known as S&Ps and I were made for each other. But Maury wanted me to go into the eurodollar pit. He had tried to establish a presence in eurodollars, but each time a broker was sent in there to trade, he came back bruised. Maury was literally shut out of eurodollars because the major players in that pit refused to trade with his brokers. So Maury turned to me, knowing that I wouldn't let anyone push me around.

"I want you to go into the eurodollar pit," Maury told me one day.

"I'm not going to eurodollars," I told him firmly. "I trade S&Ps."

Maury looked at me over the top of those glasses of his, fixing me with a stare that told me he wasn't too happy. "Lewis, I need you to do this."

Maury had once done a kindness for my family that will never be forgotten. When my father was up for parole from Leavenworth, Maury wrote the $1,500 check to hire a lawyer for my father. My mother was working as Maury's legal secretary in those days, and he knew all about Dad's legal battles. Because of what he did for my family, I am loyal to Maury to this day. So I agreed to do what I could for Maury in the eurodollar pit, but I wasn't giving up S&Ps, either.

"Here's what I'll do," I told him. "I'll trade eurodollars at the opening at 7:30, and get us established there. But when S&Ps open at 8:30, that's where I'm going—and I'll be there for the day."

Maury shook his head. He wasn't sure if one hour was going to be enough to get a foothold in the eurodollar pit.

"Don't worry," I assured him. "I'll do what I have to do. But S&Ps is where I make my living."

The next morning, I went into the eurodollar pit. The most prominent trader there was a guy named Dick, who had a large deck of customer orders. I walked right up to him and said, "Hey, Dick. What's going on? I'm going to be standing here." I looked at the traders to my left and my right. "And nobody here is going to throw me out of the pit. Now if you want to start something, we'll start."

In eurodollars, as in any pit, traders each had their own spot to stand on. So when I took a spot in the eurodollar pit near our trading desk where the customer orders came in, a lot of other traders had to make room for me. I was certainly no stranger to them, and they knew why I was there. They were worried, no doubt, that I could solicit their customers to fill their orders in eurodollars, especially the clients we already serviced in S&Ps. They weren't about to make me feel at home on their turf. As trading began, the guy next to me knocked into me. "What's going on?" I asked him.

"They pushed me," he answered.

I looked down the row of traders. Somebody was pushing somebody else, starting a chain reaction that ended with me. The object of this game, I knew, was to shove the new player out of the way.

"The next time you knock into me, you're going out of the pit," I told the guy next to me.

"It's not me. Somebody else is pushing me." He motioned to the trader standing to his right.

"Then you're both going out of the pit."

He was knocked into me again. I grabbed him by the lapels of his trading jacket and threw him out of the pit. I launched the guy standing to his right a few seconds later. That sparked a brawl in the eurodollar pit. Traders were punching brokers and clerks were jumping into the fray. Security was called, and I had to appear once again before the Merc's disciplinary committee. The committee didn't impose a fine, but I was warned that any further incidents within six months would result in a penalty.

At this time, Maury was a partner in an order-filling business with another trader named Jimmy Kaulentis. Jimmy, who was a pork belly trader, also had an interesting sideline, backing young fighters including James "Quick" Tillis who fought for the world heavyweight title. When Maury and Jimmy heard about the eurodollar brawl, they decided I should have an assistant. The next day, as I took my place in the eurodollar pit, there was a familiar beat-up face with a smashed nose grimacing among the crowd of clerks. It was Johnny Liara, a former lightweight boxing champion who had been a contender for the world championship. I had known him when I was a kid, working out in the gym and doing a little boxing myself.

"Lewis, you let me know who's messing with you," Johnny told me. "They won't bother you no more." I appreciated my friends' efforts, but Johnny had a very short career as a clerk.

In the end, Maury had his beachhead in eurodollars. Every day, I worked an hour or so in eurodollars and then another broker would relieve me. I'd announce on my way out, "I'm leaving. But if anybody messes with him, I'm coming back."

There were times when my aggressive style of trading was a double-edged sword, particularly when my background came into play. Rumors and innuendos have trailed me most of my career. Because of that, I was overly sensitive to any reference to organized crime or even jokes about Italian-Americans and the Mob. For me, it wasn't a laughing matter. When I was just starting out in S&Ps, I had a dispute over an outtrade with a guy who grew up in Melrose Park, Illinois, a predominantly Italian community that has a tough reputation to this day. Our discussion over the outtrade grew heated, but no threats were made or punches thrown. But I did say in anger, "You make this right or you're dead."

You're dead. If anybody says that during an argument, nobody takes it seriously. It's something we've all said in the heat of anger. But in my case, this trader reported me to the Merc's disciplinary committee for making a threat. "Lewis knows people who would have my legs broken," the trader told the committee. Then I was put in the humiliating and unnecessary position of having to explain to the Merc that I did not threaten this guy. It was not the last time that I had to face these allegations.

I know people said these things about me because of my father. But I would never deny him or distance myself from him. In my youth, I was shaped by my Dad's character. To this day, he remains a powerful influence in the background. He's the one who gave me the edge that made me a fearless trader—but not so fearless that I ever accepted unlimited risk. That internal risk limit, ultimately, has been one of the keys to my success. Because of my father, I learned at the age of nine that I could do whatever I intended to do. Because of him, I grew up knowing he loved and supported me unconditionally. And because of him, I was forced to grow up faster than my peers.

My father's life has been my greatest strength, but also my Achilles' heel. You see, no matter how many appearances I make on CNBC, no matter how many articles are written about me and my success as a trader, certain people will only think of me one way. To them, I will always be the hot-tempered guy whose father was involved in organized crime. Since high school and college, regardless of my successes—whether on the football field or in the trading pit—I've always come up against one question in people's minds: Am I or am I not involved in organized crime? As much as I hate that question, I have to face it. The short and only answer is no. I am not now nor have I ever been associated with organized crime.

The question too few people ever ask themselves is why I would ever want to become involved with organized crime. Because of that element, my father was in jail from the time I was in the fourth grade until I was a sophomore in high school. Because of the Mob, I had to grow up with my Dad "away," seeing him only once a year and then just briefly in the visiting room at Leavenworth. My brother and I never followed the path my father did. It was never an option. Dad had made that clear from the start.

Dad's gift to us was far greater than any damage he might have done to our reputation. He gave us heart, character, and values like integrity, love of family, and responsibility for ourselves and others. And when we were wrong, we took responsibility for that as well.

There have been plenty of times when I have had to face the fact that there was an outtrade and I was the one responsible.

Every morning, before heading to the pit, I'd check with Joni Weber, a broker who took care of all my outtrades. "Lew," she'd say, "do you remember a trade yesterday with So-and-So?"

"Yeah," I'd reply, searching my memory. "I think I traded 15 or 20 lots with him."

"You did, huh? Well, you didn't write it down."

Maybe that outtrade was a $40,000 or $50,000 loser. I'd kick myself all the way to the floor to find the other trader. "Lewis, what happened?" he'd asked me.

"I forgot to write the trade down. It's not your problem. It's my problem." Then I'd settle the outtrade and pay him the money I owed.

There's an unspoken rule at any exchange that everybody knows all the winners but nobody wants to know the losers. Somebody will say, "I just don't remember that one. Why don't we split the loss?" But I couldn't do that. If I knew the outtrade was my fault, I ate the error. I didn't like paying out $30,000, $40,000 or $50,000 from my own trading account. But if the mistake was mine, I took the responsibility.

Trading is predicated on giving your word. Think about it. In what other business can you do thousands of trades a day, representing millions of dollars, with nothing more than a nod and a hand signal and no lawyer? When you make a commitment on the trading floor, your word is your bond. For brokers who are filling orders for customers, there is no such thing as long-term loyalty, and certainly few contracts of commitment are ever signed. A broker keeps his business by keeping his customers happy.

By 1986, I was part of the predominant broker group in the S&P pit. Our group consisted of Maury, my brother Joey, Bobby Natali, a friend named Louie Falco, and myself. I affectionately called us four Italians and a Jew. We were the best in the S&P pit and I was the point man, filling orders of 50 contracts or larger. Our group had a large deck of major clients, a virtual who's who of brokerage firms like Smith Barney, E. F. Hutton, O'Connor Partners, and Bache Securities. While the S&P pit grew, so did the competition for business.

Because the S&P pit was based in Chicago, it attracted quite a bit of attention from the rival city of New York. After all, most of the big stock portfolio managers were based in New York. But the Chicago Merc had the foresight to go after the S&P 500 to launch a stock index. The S&P 500 was the benchmark for stock performance, even more so than the Dow Jones Industrial Average. The S&P contract took off and quickly overshadowed a stock index launched by the New York Futures Exchange. So, it was only a matter of time when a New York–based trader came to Chicago to get in on the action. That trader was a man I'll call Doug.

He was as brash as the city he came from, and parlayed his New York contacts to land some business with some major brokerage houses. That pissed off more than a few people in the S&P pit, who resented this New Yorker on their turf. My only real dispute with Doug was over a price at the close of trading one day, which would have cost me a few grand. I had a buy order to fill at the close. But at the last minute, Doug reported a late trade at a price that was higher than the market. I didn't want the price to be included in the record. The minute Doug reported that price, he jumped on the phone with his customer, bragging about what he had accomplished.

"Hey, the market was closed. Take that price out," I yelled at Doug.

He ignored me and kept talking on the phone.

I grabbed the receiver out of his hand and said, "He'll call you back," into the mouthpiece. Then I told Doug to his face that I was disputing that price. I wanted him to go with me to the pulpit (i.e., to the podium above the pit where trading is monitored and prices are recorded) to settle it. Doug refused to go. He turned to me and said in his New York accent, "I don't give a fuck what you say."

I grabbed him by the lapels of his trading jacket and brought him to the price podium. "Tell them to get the price out," I demanded.

Doug struggled to get away from me. I tightened my grip. "Tell them to take the price out," I repeated.

"The market was closed," Doug gasped. "Take the price out."

I was given yet another cease and desist letter from the Merc's disciplinary committee, but the price was taken out. Doug's aggressiveness in getting customers eventually was his undoing. He was slapped with a trading violation a few months later and suspended from the floor for six months. The lesson for Doug, whom I later befriended, was that Chicago had its own way of dealing with outsiders who trespassed on our turf. That's why it was no surprise to me that the Merc's Compliance Department took exceptional care to ensure that Doug adhered to every letter of the law.

Competition for customer business was so fierce among the order fillers in those days that brokers cut their commissions again and again to try to get business. Brokers were getting $3 per contract to execute a customer trade. But not all that money ended up in the brokers' pockets. Maury, for example, charged me $0.50 for every contract that I filled in the pit because the business came from his customer deck. So, in effect, I was being paid $2.50 per contract. Then brokers started to fill contracts for $2.00 and then $1.75. To stop the erosion in brokerage commissions, there was even talk of unionizing the floor brokers. But standardizing commission rates raised antitrust concerns, and the idea of organizing the brokers never progressed beyond the talking stage.

The commission discounts also gave Tom Dittmer, president of Refco, a leading clearing firm, an idea. His genius was a plan to slash commissions to $1 per contract and to pass the savings onto his customers. To offer such low commissions, he put house brokers into the pit, instead of using independent brokers like me. The problem was, many of these house brokers were undercapitalized, inexperienced guys. They were attracted by the idea that, even at $1 per contract, they could make as much as $20,000 a month. But if they made a trading error, they had to make good on their own mistakes. With errors and expenses, much of that $20,000 a month evaporated. As a result, the S&P pit was becoming populated by young brokers who did not have sufficient capital behind them. And God forbid you should have an outtrade with one of these guys because quite often they didn't have enough money to settle the mistake.

We were all pissed after Refco cut commissions, and we took it out on the Refco house brokers in the pit. As fate would have it, the Refco brokers stood two traders away from me in the pit, and I took particular pleasure in making their lives miserable. When they had a market order to sell, we'd push the market down with aggressive offers, forcing the Refco broker to execute the trade at a lower price than he wanted. When they had a market order to buy, we'd race the market higher with bids, forcing the price up.

Then one day this guy in a suit came down to the trading pit to show these Refco brokers how this was done. He stood right behind me and, as he was trading, he kept nudging me. I told him to knock it off several times, but he persisted. Finally, I had enough. He nudged me for the last time. I turned around, planted my hands on his chest, and pushed him out of the pit. He scrambled to his feet and came running back into the pit to trade.

A little while later, one of the other brokers came up to me. "Do you know who you pushed out of the pit?" he asked me. "That was Tom Dittmer."

"So what?" I replied. Tom Dittmer wasn't going to tread on my turf. But I respected him for coming back into that pit after I pushed him and never making an issue of it. As much as we all resented his house brokers, he didn't sit back in some office and bark orders at them. He had come to the floor to show them what to do.

Nobody has to tell me that you don't go around hitting and pushing people. I don't wake up in the morning wondering who I can punch out that day. I'd much rather go the route of reason. Or, at the risk of perpetuating a stereotype, you might say that I've become less like Sonny and more like Michael. *Godfather* fans will recall that Don Corleone's sons were as different as the approaches they took. Sonny was hot-headed and blew up at the slightest altercation, which later became his undoing. Michael, the strategist, had ice water in his veins.

I have learned to walk away from trading disputes on the floor. A broker who is offering 50 contracts may later claim he didn't see me, even though I yelled, "Buy 'em!" five or six times. Perhaps he didn't. Or maybe another trader jumped in between us, snatching those contracts out of my grip. There is little that I can do beyond complaining about the trade to the broker, then to go about my business. And that business, of course, is trading. In this arena, I have outlasted many of my competitors and most of my detractors. My best weapon is not my muscle, but my intelligence and my ability. In this, I have surprised even some colleagues who failed to recognize both my trading ability and my business acumen.

I remember the day I told Jack Sandner, who was then chairman of the Merc, about my idea to offer catastrophic outtrade insurance for traders and brokers. True to my word, after two years of thorough study and diligent work, I brought an outtrade insurance product to market through AIG, the leading U.S.-based international insurance company. People were shocked that I not only thought up this product, but that I landed AIG as my partner.

For brokers and traders, outtrades are the bane of our existence. Every year there are stories that circulate about large six- and seven-figure outtrades. The fear that an outtrade of this magnitude could happen to them should be enough, I figured, to encourage brokers and traders to buy the insurance. But the product did not succeed, in part because clearing firms and exchanges did not require brokers and traders to carry it. Or, as a friend of mine explained to me, the insurance was marketed to the ants instead of the anthill.

Although outtrade insurance did not succeed, I do not consider that it was a failure. It was an idea that I conceived, nurtured, and launched. Looking back, I see how it could have been marketed differently. But that only gives me insight for the next project that I undertake. I take my losses and move onto the next thing, taking responsibility for what I did right and what I did wrong. In the end, that's what being a successful man is all about.

CHAPTER 4

A Competitor's Heart

I am a born competitor. Although the outcome is certainly important to me, I thrive on the game itself. Whether on the football field, on the golf course, or in the trading pit, competition drives me. It is my primary motivation, one that I got from my father.

If I had been a high school football coach or an attorney, it would have been the same. Competition makes me rise above the rest, pushing beyond my natural limitations. Don't get me wrong. I thoroughly enjoy the fact that my wife and I both drive a Mercedes and we own a couple of homes that could be featured in *Architectural Digest*. Still, money is merely a by-product of what I do. It is the reward for making the equivalent of the home runs and touchdowns of my business.

The S&P market was down 2,000 points in after-hours, electronic trading on Thursday, August 27, 1998. The Russian financial crisis and concerns that Boris Yeltsin would soon resign had panicked the markets overseas. I pulled up to the parking lot across from the Merc, jumped out of the car, left the engine running, and bolted across the street before the attendant even gave me a ticket stub. My clerk was waiting for me with my trading jacket in his hand. That white jacket was looking pretty grimy after what had already been a grueling few days in the pit.

I traded from the short side most of the day as S&Ps smashed through support levels. The market whipsawed, but not like in 1987, when it could free-fall because there were no trading limits. Yet, the intensity was just like those days after the Crash of 1987. I sold 90 contracts at one point, then watched S&Ps rally 500 points in my face, before nose-diving again. Even after 18 years, it still takes every bit of my physical and mental energy to trade a market like this. But wild markets are big opportunities, especially for an experienced trader like myself, who can take on the big moves and the big risks that go with it. I traded three hours in the morning and two more in the afternoon. I went back to my office, dog-tired and bone-sore, with a hefty six-figure profit for the day.

The prize, though, is the satisfaction that I, an "old" trader at 41, can still battle the market. I can take the pounding in the pit as well as the young turks. You can't imagine how grueling it is to stand in that pit, amid the noise, the pushing and shoving, the spit, and the sweat. After five or six hours, I feel like a punch-drunk boxer. Some days I wonder if I can still do it and on others I wonder why I still want to. My solution has been to trade increasingly off the floor, not just because of my age, but because of the new opportunities presented to me. But on the big and volatile days, I still have what it takes in the pit. I haven't lost the one attribute that has served me throughout my life and is my best asset as a trader and in my new arena as a fund manager: *heart.*

Outside of sports, it's hard to define this term. When a player has heart, he lives and breathes the game. He has the dedication and pure willpower to go beyond his own physical limits. No obstacle will stand in the way of a player with heart, the guy who will play injured and push his body and mind beyond the pain.

Heart, stamina, and a tenacious personality have been the keys to my survival and my success in sports and as a trader. I remember getting a rude awakening as a freshman at DePauw University in Greencastle, Indiana, when I realized that I had coasted through high school without learning much. I was a classic underachiever: I was smart and did well enough to get by, but I had virtually no study skills. At DePauw, I was on my own. To compensate for my lack of academic foundation, I spent three to four hours in the library every night, reading and studying. Nobody had to tell me to do this. I knew it was the only way I was going to make it.

I applied that same drive and determination on the football field at DePauw, which was a Division III school. I had been a pretty good player in high school, but at DePauw, which had given me a partial football scholarship, I was up against very talented athletes. I couldn't imagine what it would have been like for me had I gone to a Division I school.

I certainly wasn't the biggest player on the varsity football team at DePauw. But the defensive coach, Ted Katula, once described me as the most tenacious player he had ever seen. I remember when I was a freshman on the varsity squad and I wanted to run with the first team. I said to the offensive coach, Tom Mont, one day, "Give me a chance to run with the first team. Let me show you what I can do."

Coach Mont was taken aback by my directness, but the next day when we were doing half-speed drills, he wanted to see what I could do. I was up against George, six feet three inches, 235 pounds, and dumb as a box of rocks. "Hey, Borsellino, you call that a block?" the coach called out to me.

"Coach, we're doing half-speed drills," I protested.

"You still think you're better than the other running backs?" he baited me.

I looked at George. "Put in your mouthpiece and buckle your helmet, George. I'm coming at you full speed," I told him.

"Now you're going to tell the players that you're going to block them?" the coach yelled out.

I stood up and faced Coach Mont. "Yeah, I am. And every time I go out to block, I'm going to knock him on his ass."

I ran toward George and faked like I was going high. He stood up and—boom!—I went low and cut his legs out from under him. The second time, I faked that I was going low. He crouched down and I ran right over him. The third time, I faked low and faked high and I nailed him.

Being a kid and pumped with adrenaline, I shot my mouth off. "I told you I'm better than any of your other running backs," I yelled at the coach. But he wouldn't give me the time of day.

Luckily for me, Coach Katula had seen what I could do and immediately recruited me for his defensive team. What I lacked in physical stature and natural ability I made up for with heart. By my sophomore year, Coach Mont had me back on the offensive team as the starting running back. I remember one game against Valparaiso University on a cold, rainy day. The ball was snapped at the half-yard line. I got a lucky break from the mud that took down a lot of the opposing defensive team. I took a swing pass in the flat, cut around a few guys, and ran for a touchdown—99.5 yards—and a record that still holds at DePauw University and the State of Indiana. The thing I remember most about that play was seeing my father and two of my uncles running down the sidelines in step with me. Of course, I must also admit that, true to Coach Mont's form, we ran the same play the next time we had the ball. The defensive team was ready for me and I was knocked out cold. . . .

Whether heart is an attribute that is inherited or learned, I got it from my father. Although Dad suffered from rheumatic fever as a child and was hospitalized for nearly two years, he trained himself to be an athlete. He swam and dove, boxed, and played softball. He was a star football player at Harrison High School in Chicago, where games in those days would attract huge crowds at Soldier Field. Even when he was in his forties, my father ran five miles with ease and worked out in the gym on a regular basis.

Heart, physical and mental discipline, and competition—these skills of the athlete were what my brother and I derived from my father. These attributes were his code of survival and what distinguished him from the rest. In Leavenworth, Dad used these skills to survive. He did whatever he could to keep his mind occupied and to better himself. He took the Dale Carnegie course and won awards for public speaking, and even organized a blood bank in prison. To keep his body in shape, he exercised every day and played handball, eventually becoming the prison champ in that sport.

Dad had been in prison a few months when we went to visit him for the first time. I remember sitting in the waiting room as he walked in. His salt-and-pepper hair was cut short and he was tanned. Other than being a little thinner than before, he looked about the same. He had on the standard prison uniform, white pants and a white shirt. But as always, Dad took pride in the way he looked. He had paid the tailor to fit his shirt and cut the lapels. His pants weren't just washed and pressed, they had a razor-sharp crease and his shoes were spit-shined. Under his tailored shirt was the St. Jude medallion he always wore.

"You see this?" he asked, fingering the tip of his collar. "Cost me a pack of cigarettes, but it looks good." Dad didn't smoke, but cigarettes were like currency in prison. "The press on these pants? Cost me another pack."

I didn't realize it at the time, but looking back I know why my father had his prison uniform altered. In a system that tried to institutionalize men by literally making them numbers, my father fought to keep his individuality. The cut of his lapels and the crease of his pants were his signals to the guards and every-one around him that he was still his own man.

Sitting in the visiting room, Dad didn't complain to us about being in jail. On the contrary, his biggest concern was us. He entertained us with stories about the other guys in jail, making us laugh. "There isn't a guilty guy in the whole place," he joked, winking at Mom. "It's amazing. Everybody in the whole place is innocent."

Finally, I spoke up. "Dad, it sounds like you're having fun in here."

Dad stopped laughing and told me just how it was. "Let me explain something," he said. "Jail is not hard. These people can't get to me. But I'll tell you what is hard for me: being away from you, your brother, and your mother. The only way they can get to me is if they get to you. So you have to be better than the rest."

Better than the rest. It was praise and a push all in one. Looking back, I know my father saw clearly what he wanted for Joey and me. He wanted college educations, legitimate careers, and professional success for his sons. He wanted us to rub elbows with the right kind of people, to be accepted in the white-bread world, and not lose our street smarts. He wanted us to use the skills of both worlds. But, as I saw so many times in my life, this duality put both worlds on guard.

Even though he was in prison, Dad communicated those hopes for us, not so much by what he said, but with his love for us. Joey was only seven when Dad went to jail the first time. Because he was so young, my parents decided not to tell him where Dad was going. As far as Joey was concerned, Dad was in the Army. But on that first visit, when Joey looked around the visiting room at Leavenworth, Dad couldn't lie to his youngest son.

"Dad, are you sure you're in the Army?" Joey asked.

"Does this look like the Army, son?" Dad replied gently, with a question.

"No."

"It's not the Army. I'm in prison, son."

My father could have told Joey anything, including that he was "in college," another favorite euphemism that people used for jail. Or, he could have told Joey that he went to prison because somebody had made a mistake or that he was framed. He could have told us just about anything. As a father, myself, I wonder what it was like for him to tell his seven-year-old son the truth about himself.

"I'm here because I did something wrong. But, I still love you. Do you still love me?"

Joey put his arms around Dad's neck and kissed him. "Sure, Daddy."

Some people believe that the old do-as-I-say,-not-as-I-do theory doesn't work. They believe that children emulate everything that their parents do. My brother and I prove that theory wrong. My father made it clear, from the beginning, that Joey and I were never going to go the way that he did.

My brother and I grew up to be successful men, who kept our word in business, took care of our families, and were involved in our children's lives. I attribute these qualities to the fact that we knew Dad loved us and that Mom kept our family together. She could have left Dad when he was in prison. When he was first given four concurrent 20-year sentences, Dad told Mom to divorce him. "You'll have no life," he told her. She was only in her early thirties then. But she was, and remains, Tony's devoted wife.

I've often said that I hope I can be half the father to my children that Dad was to Joey and me. Some people don't understand that or, worse, they seem shocked by it. "But your father was in prison," they tell me. "He was involved in organized crime." My father's love for us had nothing to do with the life choices he made. If he had been a banker or a minister, he could not have loved us more.

The second year that Dad was in prison, money was getting tighter by the day. We could afford only the essentials. There was nothing extra to pay the $90 fare for each of us to go to Kansas to see Dad in prison. One Sunday, two of our uncles called Mom aside. "Tootsie, how long has it been since you went to visit Tony?" they asked her.

"Almost three months," she told them.

"And the boys? When was the last time they saw their father?"

"About eight months ago."

Uncle Gus and Uncle Mimi reached into their pockets and took out about $200 each. "Tootsie," they told Mom, "take yourself and the boys to see Tony."

I only saw my father on a few occasions from the time I was in fourth grade until I was in the seventh. It wasn't just the money that kept us away. I learned years later that Dad had told Mom it was too hard on him to see us for a few hours and then have to say good-bye to us all over again. Then, finally, after three years of legal battles, Dad won an appeal for a new trial. He was back home again and in charge.

He tried to make up for the three years he was away from Joey and me by immersing himself in our lives. I had begun to play sports, particularly football, which had been his game in high school. Dad showed no favoritism between Joey and me when it came to sports. In fact, he wouldn't even let me play football in seventh grade unless Joey, a skinny kid two years younger than I, could also play.

"Your brother doesn't play, you don't play," Dad told me one morning.

"It's not fair!" I protested. "He doesn't weigh enough. It's not my fault."

"He doesn't play, you don't play."

"But Dad . . ."

"Figure something out." When Dad said that, I knew the case was closed.

The day Joey weighed for the team, I'm glad they didn't check his pockets. They would have found the weights I put on him to get my brother on the team.

Joey and I are as close as brothers can be. While we are independent, our lives are intertwined. He stands in the S&P pit beside me, but we trade our own accounts. He has made his fortune in the market, and yet he asks me for my business advice. When I went through a painful divorce, my brother was my strength. My father would have it no other way. He could have made us rivals, vying for his attention and playing us off each other in some skewed effort to make us stronger. But my father loved us equally. He wanted us each to be independent, to be our own men. The stronger we were as individuals, he believed, the better we were together. To toughen our bodies and minds, he encouraged us to play sports.

When I played football in junior high school, my father came to every practice and every game. He sat on the bench, applauding me when I did well and chewing me out when I screwed up. He was tougher than any coach. When the game was over, he critiqued me all the way home. Over and over again, I heard the same thing. There was no such thing as quitting.

He made Joey and me into fierce competitors, never wanting us to lose the edge that, in his world, was the difference between survival and extinction. So when he told me to give it my all as a seventh-grade football player, despite a sore knee, I knew he wanted me to be tough. When he told me to prove myself as the best, to stand out among my teammates, I knew he wanted me to be the one whom everyone feared and nobody could take down. He wanted me to be like him. I had to be strong. I had to be tough. I had to look my competitor in the eye and stare him down. And I never, ever, could give in to fear.

With the adversity that I have faced in my life, my competitor's heart has kept me strong, not only in sports, but in the trading pit. It gave me the courage to fight and to win, and the guts to rise from my losses.

By mid-1985, our group dominated the S&P pit because of our skill in executing customer orders. But there was one noticeable absence in our customer deck: Salomon Brothers. Being a competitor, I wanted a clean sweep of all the major houses. But the Salomon business belonged to two traders, including a man I'll call Bob. Bob stood three people away from me, and although he was my rival, I had the utmost respect for him. Like me, he was a hot-headed Italian with an in-your-face style. As a trader, he could do it all: execute the orders, trade the spreads, and move a few hundred contracts with ease. As much as I respected his ability, I still wanted to take a little of that Salomon Brothers business from him.

Matt Wolf ran the Salomon desk on the floor of the Merc. He was just a few feet from where I stood in the pit, so I knew he was well aware of what I could do as a trader. But Matt didn't want to give me any of the business. Bob was his man. Matt was loyal to the people he worked with, and when he gave his word in business, he meant it. It took a bit of chivalry toward one of the few female brokers in the pit to help me land that business, and then an ugly rumor would briefly take it away from me.

Jennifer Gordon stood in the male-dominated S&P pit, trading small lots for customers. She was a good kid, and it pissed me off that some of the other traders harassed her. One day, I saw her crying. "Jennifer, what's wrong?" I asked.

"Nothing," she said, turning her head.

"Come on. Tell me what's going on."

Jennifer pointed to some brokers across the pit. "They're giving me a hard time. They think it's funny to get me flustered when I'm doing a trade."

"Who's doing this?" I demanded. Jennifer told me their names.

I walked up to the brokers who were bothering her. "You think you're such tough guys, picking on a woman," I yelled at them. "Listen up. If anybody messes with Jennifer, they mess with me."

From that day on, Jennifer and I became good friends. Whenever someone gave her a tough time, all she had to say jokingly was, "I'm going to get Lewis," and her trouble disappeared. At the time, Jennifer's romantic interest was Matt Wolf. When they began dating (they later married and have two children), I kept telling Jennifer to put in a good word for me with Matt. "Tell him I'm not a bad guy," I'd say, half-joking—but also half-serious. "Tell him to give me a little of that business."

Then one day, after Jennifer pleaded my case to Matt for weeks, my clerk brought me an order to buy 200 contracts at my discretion. The customer was Salomon. I filled the order well, impressing Matt with my ability. I began to get a little of Salomon's business, but Bob was still the major broker on that account.

Then Bob and another broker were charged with a major violation for allegedly making a prearranged trade. They were accused of arranging a trade ahead of time, with one broker bidding for 1,000 contracts and the other executing a 1,000-contract sell order. Although it appeared that the trade was made in the pit, it was allegedly choreographed in advance. This violated the open-outcry auction environment of the pit, where every bid and offer must be made publicly.

After that incident, Bob lost the Salomon business, and I was given the majority of it. Then, I had every major brokerage house in my deck. As for Bob, the incident soured him on trading. He later retired and started up another business. It was a fortuitous move. He took his business public and earned well over $200 million.

The Salomon business was a victory for my competitive spirit. But it also made me a bigger target. Since the day I went to the Merc, I have had to deal with the rumors and innuendos about my father and organized crime. Over the years, anonymous letters have been written to the Exchange, claiming that I was associated with organized crime or that I laundered money. Under the Freedom of Information Act, I have obtained FBI files that showed I was the target of investigations. The IRS has pulled my bank records several times. But no wrongdoing on my part has ever been found. It was just like what my father had told me when I was nine years old: because of my background, I had to be more accountable than the rest.

That's what happened when the FBI paid an unofficial visit to Salomon Brothers. Looking back, this should have been a tip-off that federal authorities were beginning an investigation into trading at the Merc, resulting in a sting operation that would come to light in 1989. But there was no hint of that when the FBI spoke to Ira Harris, who managed Salomon's trading business in Chicago. After speaking with the FBI, Ira Harris placed a call to Matt Wolf. This is the conversation that was repeated to me much later:

"Who's this Borsellino guy who's filling our orders at the Merc?" Harris asked Matt.

"He handles some of our S&Ps," Matt told him. "He's one of the best."

"Well, the FBI contacted me," Harris went on. "They say Borsellino's father was in the Mob. They believe Borsellino may be washing money for the Mob in Chicago."

Luckily, out of respect for Matt I had told him about my father. I didn't want him to hear the story from someone else, and I knew from bitter experience that people could use my father's history against me. Matt never believed that I would launder money, but he had little choice when Ira suggested that maybe the Salomon business ought to be handled by someone else. Matt was genuinely upset when he told me what happened.

"Don't worry about it," I assured Matt. But inside I was seething. "Don't get involved with this, Matt. You can't get yourself in trouble at Salomon on my account."

But Matt wasn't going to let the matter rest. Without my knowing it, he placed a call to a Salomon director, Stanley Shopkorn, in New York. Shopkorn listened carefully to everything Matt had to say about me.

"Has this guy been indicted for anything?" Shopkorn asked him.

"No," Matt replied.

"Well, then, I'm not going to take the business away from him. It doesn't matter what his father did. I'm not going to do this just because his name ends with a vowel."

I never had a chance to meet Shopkorn. But if I ever have the opportunity, I would thank him for what he did for me some 15 years ago. My gratitude to Matt extends far beyond any monetary value of the Salomon business. He stood up for me and my integrity, and put his own professional reputation on the line. In the business world, where true friendship is rare and nearly every action is motivated by the bottom line, it was an act of kindness I'll never forget.

The Salomon Brothers incident brought home to me, once again, a lesson that I learned much earlier in my life. No matter how well I did, there would always be those who would try to take away from me what I had legitimately earned. I had learned to deal with disappointment and responsibility, carrying a weight that was meant for someone far older than I. But part of being a competitor is the ability to shoulder more than your part of the load. It was another of my father's life lessons.

After Dad won his appeal, he and his attorneys decided to forego a second trial and, instead, cut a deal. My father pleaded guilty to hijacking charges in return for what was likely to be a lighter sentence with credit for the three years he already served. We hoped and prayed that the judge would put him on probation. The last thing we wanted was for Dad to go away again. It had been eight months since he left Leavenworth.

Joey and I sat with our mother at the sentencing. I looked around at the wood-paneled courtroom where the lawyers in dark suits snapped open their briefcases and pulled out files and legal pads. I remembered to stand straight like my Dad wanted me to when the judge entered the courtroom. At the crack of the gavel, we sat down. Joey and I stared at the judge with our hands folded in our laps. We knew better than to fidget.

"Your honor," Dad's attorney began, "you know me. And you know I don't normally bring children to a sentencing hearing." He gestured toward us. Joey and I sat up a little straighter.

"But Tony Borsellino is not like the rest of the defendants who come through this courtroom." The lawyer briefly related the story of my father's life. He was a truck driver who went to work every day, but got involved with the wrong people. He had already served three years at Leavenworth for his crime, during which time he was an exemplary prisoner. He told him how Dad had taken the Dale Carnegie course, ran the blood bank, and wrote for the prison newspaper. My father even helped to get guest speakers to visit Leavenworth, including Rocky Marciano.

"Your honor," the attorney concluded, "this is a man who clearly can be rehabilitated."

The judge looked down from the bench and folded his hands. "If Tony Borsellino is everything you say he is," the judge sneered, "why would I want to deprive the institution of such a fine man?"

The judge sentenced my father to 13 years in prison, giving him credit for the 3 years he already served. With 10 more years on his sentence, I knew I would be 22 years old when he came home again. It seemed at that moment that my father would be in prison for the rest of my life.

The next morning, there was a glimmer of hope. My father's attorney called to say the judge had arranged another meeting for Monday morning. We got our hopes up that perhaps the sentence would be reduced. Instead, the judge agreed to give Dad an A-number, which meant he would come up for parole on a regular basis. But my father was ever the realist. Despite that A-number, he had another code—OC for organized crime—on his prison jacket. With that OC, Dad knew the A took on another, different meaning. It could mean he would have to serve *all* of his time.

I didn't cry those first months after Dad went to prison, and I made it through the holidays without him. I endured his first parole hearing after six months when he was turned down, and I lived through the next parole hearing a year later and the next six months after that. Life continued on at home. Mom worked as a legal secretary for Maury Kravitz, and then took a second job as a waitress and later as a fitness instructor at a health club her friend managed. From junior high school, I went to Montini Catholic High School in Lombard. Entering high school, I began to grasp just how long my father had been away and how much of my young life he had missed. My freshman year, my father came before the parole board and, once again, was turned down. This time it hit me harder than before. When I heard the news, I went up to my room and cried my heart out. My mother tried to comfort me. She had never seen me cry so hard before. But there was little anyone could say. Dad was in jail and we didn't know how long he would be away. I decided at that point that I would never cry again because my father was away. I would live in my head, just as I knew he did, and develop a mental toughness that blocked out the pain.

In the meantime, I knew the best thing I could do was what Dad wanted of me. I went to school every day, did what my mother asked me to do, and made the high school football team. Playing sports made me feel close to my father while he was away. I never got involved in drugs. Not only did I not want to disappoint my parents, but I considered drug use to be a sign of weakness. I was part of the jock crowd at high school, and I played other sports in the area. In that I was just like my Dad. I was an athlete with friends in a lot of different circles. I could mix with the upper-middle-class kids at Montini and the Italian kids from the wrong side of the tracks in nearby Cicero, a community with a tough reputation.

In time, I proved that I could shoulder the responsibility my father had placed on me as the man of the family in his absence. I remember the day I came home from my summer job after my freshman year in high school and immediately sensed that something was wrong. Mom's car was in the garage, but I couldn't find her. I walked through the house, calling for her. I went upstairs. The bathroom door was closed. "Mom?" I yelled through the door. There was no answer. "Mom?" I yelled a little louder and knocked.

I opened the door a crack and yelled again. "Mom?"

I found my mother semiconscious in the bathtub, hemorrhaging. I got her out of the tub and put her in the car. Even though I was only 15 and didn't have a license, I drove her to Elmhurst Hospital where she underwent an emergency hysterectomy.

My father was in jail and my mother was in the hospital. I had no idea how close to death she had come. But I couldn't let my fear rule me. I had to get in touch with Dad, but prisoners weren't allowed to receive phone calls on a regular basis. Now, they can call collect every day if they like. But in those days, it was different.

Joey and I went to Aunt Josie's house and called the prison. After some effort, we got in touch with the priest who was the prison chaplain and explained the circumstances. Finally, Dad came to the phone.

It was so good to hear his voice, but I hated what I had to tell him. "Dad," I said, "there's something really wrong with Mom. I came home today and I found her bleeding in the bathtub. I took her to the hospital."

My father was only allowed to talk to me on the phone. That was the rule. But Aunt Josie, his sister, had to let Dad know that everything was going to be okay. "Don't worry about your kids, Tony," she yelled in the background, loud enough for Dad to hear. "They're with me. I'll take care of them, Tony. Don't you worry about them."

"You tell Aunt Josie I heard her," Dad replied. "Tell her I won't worry because she's watching out for you."

After Mom's operation, there were other worries, including the fact that my mother didn't have any health insurance and we had virtually no money. Luckily, the social worker at the hospital helped us get financial aid and food stamps. Mom was too embarrassed to have us shop with food stamps, so she found a grocer who would swap $50 in food stamps for $40 in cash. Dad, for his part, did what he could to help and to thank the hospital for the care Mom received. Because he was in charge of the blood bank at Leavenworth, he arranged for a large shipment of blood to be shipped to the hospital.

While Mom recuperated, she had to stop working. We were broke and I knew I had to do something. Because it was summer vacation, I asked one of my father's friends, named Chuck, if I could get a job with the riggers' union, setting up the big displays at McCormick Place, the convention center in Chicago. Chuck didn't have a job for me. But two days later, I got a call from a man my father knew at the Teamsters' Union. Chuck had called him and explained the situation. He told me to show up for work Monday morning.

At McCormick Place, the teamsters set up and tear down for the exhibitors who come to the various trade shows and conventions. Not a box nor a piece of freight gets moved at McCormick Place without a teamster. That summer, I received a very valuable education. I learned to play liar's poker with the serial numbers on a dollar bill. I learned to shoot craps. And I met some of the best guys in the world, men who were the real salt of the earth.

I got one of my first jobs on the site from a man I called Uncle Lou. He stood five feet eleven inches, with a barrel chest, dark hair, and a blue-black beauty mark between his eyebrows. Uncle Lou ran around McCormick Place on a scooter and whatever he said was done. He stationed me at the loading dock one day with explicit instructions: "Don't let any of the exhibitors park here. We have to keep this area clear. Tell them to go to the parking lot."

As soon as Uncle Lou took off on his scooter, an exhibitor pulled up in a brand new Cadillac. I spoke up: "Excuse me, sir. You can't park here."

The guy locked the door and ignored me.

"Sir, you can't leave your car here," I repeated.

"I'll just be a minute," the guy said, waving me off.

When Uncle Lou came back a few minutes later, there I was—and there was the Cadillac, parked in the same place. "Lewis!" he yelled. "What did I tell you? The exhibitors can't park here."

"I told him that. But he didn't pay any attention to me."

Uncle Lou's face, which was darkened by his heavy beard, turned red with anger. "And you didn't cork him?" "Cork" was part of his private vocabulary meaning, in this instance, to punch.

"No, I just told him he couldn't park there and he ignored me."

"Get the forklift!" Uncle Lou yelled.

I started up the forklift, the one with the long tines that could lift the biggest pallets.

"Pick up that car and move it to the end of the loading dock."

I hoisted that brand new Cadillac in the air with the forklift and dangled it over the edge of the loading dock. When the exhibitor finally came back, he couldn't believe his eyes. "Put my car down!" he demanded.

Uncle Lou looked at the guy calmly and explained. "Didn't the kid tell you not to park here?"

"Goddamn it! Put my car down!" the guy shrieked.

"If we say you can't park here, then you can't park here." Uncle Lou turned to me. "Lewis! Drop the car off the loading dock."

"No!" the guy screamed, running toward the forklift.

"All right. Give the kid fifty bucks and he'll put your car down." Uncle Lou ambled over to the exhibitor and towered over him. "Next time somebody tells you not to park some place, don't park there."

I was eventually banned from the forklift crew after I accidentally put one through a window and backed another into the wall. But I had other talents as the man at the door, checking the bill of lading and managing what the exhibitors brought in and out of the building. Here was the standard drill: An exhibitor would come to the gate with a load of boxes that had to be brought to his booth by one of the teamsters. I'd flip through the bill of lading and then look at the boxes. "I don't see those boxes on here," I'd say. "I'll have to weigh them for you."

The exhibitor would hem and haw a little bit, as I looked officiously at the clipboard. "Tell you what," I'd say. "I'll put down the minimum weight if you give these guys a little something extra on the side."

Despite the occasional hi-jinx, I worked hard that summer—sometimes too hard for the old-timers who had been around for 20 years or more. "Slow down, kid," they'd tell me. "Don't work so hard. This is an all-day job."

And, sometimes, some of the guys would help themselves to a few of the goods that just happened to be left unattended. I remember setting up a fashion exhibit and passing a mannequin on the floor that was dressed in men's slacks, a shirt, and a sweater. The next time I went by, the sweater was missing. A little while later, the shirt was gone. I passed by again, and the pants had been taken. And then the mannequin was dressed again—but this time in old jeans and a work shirt. Out on the loading dock, Johnny was dressed to the nines in new clothes as he directed freight.

Then there was Solly, one of the best forklift drivers I'd ever seen. He drove that thing 40 miles per hour, picking up freight, spinning around pallets and boxes, and never dropping a thing. I said to him one day, "Solly, you have great peripheral vision."

Solly looked at me. "Why can't you just call me a jerk like the rest of these guys?"

"Solly," I explained, "that means you have great eyesight."

"Oh," Solly said, and drove away on the forklift, still mystified.

I have never forgotten the men I worked with that summer, and every summer after that through high school and college. Then finally, I could step down as the man of the family. When I was a sophomore in high school, Dad came up for parole again. Maury Kravitz, who has always been a friend of our family, knew all about Dad's legal battles. He called Mom into his office one day and handed her a $1,500 check to hire an attorney named Peter Lamb, out of Washington, D.C., who specialized in parole hearings. "Take the check," Maury told Mom, "and bring your husband home."

Dad was paroled in January 1973 and, after three months in a halfway house and spending only weekends with us, he came home in April of that year. I was a month shy of 16, five feet nine and a half inches, and looking down at him at five feet seven. My brother, on the other hand, was still a little kid in junior high. But every time Dad looked at me, he could see how much I had grown up while he was gone. My very presence reminded him how long he had been away. It was a constant source of sorrow in Dad's life and he continually apologized for missing so much of my childhood.

I had become all that Dad had hoped for me. Like my brother, I was a good athlete, doing well in school, and popular with a wide range of kids. He always wanted us to be among the kids who wore the "white gym shoes," and seeing us he knew he had succeeded. But he also felt a little distant from what we had become. I remember the day I showed Dad the films from my freshman and sophomore football games he had missed. I invited all my friends over, kids who had heard about my father but who had never met him. Dad stayed about 10 minutes and then he said, "I've got to go."

I was hurt that he left early. When I told my mother, she explained that he felt he had been on display. Looking back, I see that he realized he had succeeded in making my brother and me into the all-American kids. That realization struck terror into his heart. He wanted us to get along in the white-gym-shoe crowd, but he didn't want us to buy into that myth. Our power came from being comfortable in both worlds. We needed to have the guts of street-fighters, but the polish of corporate attorneys. He wanted us to walk in both circles, but never be completely immersed in either. It would become the dichotomy of my life, to be comfortable in any circumstance but always to be a little bit apart from my surroundings.

That's why I believe he was so demanding of his sons, particularly me as the oldest. Any time I failed to measure up in his eyes, any time he saw me do something that he felt was immature or, worse yet, damaging to myself, he'd jump on me. And, at the start of my junior year, when I played varsity football at Montini, he'd critique my every play.

I remember one play in which I had to go out and make a tackle. When we got to the sideline, the guy was already down. So I headed back to the line of scrimmage. Dad pulled me aside. "Hey, what are you doing? You run over there and hit the guy."

"But Dad, he was already down."

"I don't care. You've got to let these guys know you're out there and you mean business."

In his mind, at that moment on the football field, I had bought into the white-bread American way of life, in which we all shake hands and act like best friends while trying to stab each other in the back. To survive, you had to be tough. You had to be on guard. You never could let anyone think you were weak. You always were a competitor.

It must have been difficult for Dad to adjust to suburban life after Leavenworth. His first job after he was paroled was given to him by a man we met in Lake Geneva. He hired Dad to go around to the different grocery stores to set up displays. Dad did so for three or four months, visiting his parole officer on a regular basis and trying to do everything by the book.

But, as grateful as Dad was for that job, he hated every minute of it. He was bothered, I think, that Mom made more money as a legal secretary than he made with his job. More important, Dad, who commanded respect, hated the way the store managers treated him when he tried to set up a display. They'd get in his face and yell, "Hey, you. You can't put that there." All the while, my father bit his tongue, trying to save the job for as long as he could. Finally, one too many store managers shook his finger in Dad's face. This guy started chewing my father out over nothing. Dad flattened him with one punch and quit his job.

He got a truck and called on his friends in the trucking industry, men like him who had once been drivers but were now business agents. He made a deal with a long-distance trucking company to handle its city work in Chicago. I was a junior in high school by this time, and Dad was back in the driver's seat of his life. But the trucking business also put Dad back on the street. It wasn't long before certain people paid him a call, and he was back in touch with an element he should have stayed away from.

As an adult, I can understand how my father's life progressed through a series of responsibility and opportunities. Before my father went to Leavenworth, he was a free-wheeling guy who was not adverse to seizing an opportunity. Even though he wore the OC label on his prison jacket, he had not been part of the organized crime hierarchy. But, while he was in prison, my father earned the credentials that made him valuable to that element: He was tough, and honorable, as well. He had done his crime and taken his punishment after he was caught. He never squealed on anyone. He showed he had the intestinal fortitude to handle risks, relying on no one but himself. But that acceptance of risk also made him vulnerable.

I remember the night two guys came over to the house to talk to Dad. I didn't know who they were as they sat in the kitchen, laughing and joking for about two hours. When they left, they shook hands and called my Dad "partner." From that day on, our financial situation improved. We were living the good life again. My father never hid from me what he did, although he spared me the details of names and particulars. And, he made it clear that he could see no other way for himself. He was an exconvict who had been labeled "organized crime." He saw himself with two choices: scrape by with some menial job or go back to doing what he knew best—living by his wits and his balls, taking risks, and making a score.

Organized crime gets that name because it is organized. There are tiers of authority, or management, and a certain structure of operations—just like in a corporation. As in any company or organization, there were rules of operation. If someone had a score, some of the profit had to be funneled back into the organization. In the case of stolen goods, they had to be fenced through an approved operation. In the Chicago Mob, loyalty was judged on ability and not blood ties, as in the New

York Mafia. But, being part of that organization means you have to buy into the rules and believe the scenario that you will be protected. To get by, my father—the ultimate competitor and the consummate risk taker—had to accept that belief. He had to put his trust in an element that eventually would be his downfall.

Yet, I lived a different life. In high school, I was a star athlete, my picture in the newspaper for my accomplishments on the football field. As a junior, I was all-area, all-conference, and nominated for both all-state and all-American, earning honorable mentions. When my senior year rolled around, I was voted the most valuable player in the conference and named all-area. Once again, I was nominated for all-state, and Jack Lewis, coach of Immaculate Conception High School, nominated me for all-American after I made 17 solo tackles against his team in one game. At Montini Catholic High School, where I was the first guy ever to be named all-area two years in a row, my teammates told me I was the obvious choice to be the school's most valuable player. I even let myself believe it.

The night of the football banquet, I sat with my teammates, but my eyes were on my dad. He didn't try to hide his pride for me as the awards were handed out. When they named me the most valuable player, I knew it would be a big moment for both of us.

The coach took the microphone. He made a little speech about sportsmanship and team spirit. The guy next to me nudged me in the ribs.

Then the coach announced the winner of the most valuable player award—our quarterback, who hadn't even been named all-conference. The quarterback shot me a look of surprise. "It should be you, Lewis," he said, as he got up to accept the award.

All of my friends on the football team got up and left the banquet in protest. As I walked out with them, I saw the color drain out of my father's face. He knew why I hadn't won that award. It had nothing to do with my ability on the football field. And it had nothing to do with our quarterback, who was a good guy and a fine athlete in his own right. It was personal and my father knew it.

I never saw my father look so hurt as he did that night. It was as if everything he had dreamed of for us, his sons, had been shoved back in his face. An honor that should have been mine was taken away from him, and he was at a loss to make it up to me. My father followed me out of the banquet. I was shocked to see the tears in his eyes. He was so hurt because one of his sons was bearing the brunt of an insult aimed at him. "I'm sorry, Lewis," he said. "This wasn't about you. That coach did this to you to hurt me. And it hurt me because it hurt you."

My teammates tried to make it up to me, giving me a bracelet the night of the senior prom that was engraved "most valuable player." Still, the issue did not end there. A family friend, who was a big supporter at Montini, did a little investigating of his own. The story, in time, came out. The coach had told one of the assistants that he was never going to give me the most valuable player award, regardless of what I did on the football field. The coach couldn't bring himself to give me that award because he didn't approve of my father.

It was the first time I witnessed what my father meant when he spoke about "us" and "them." The "them"—society at large and the white-bread world—judge the rest of "us." No matter how hard we try, it will be hard for "us" to belong.

It was a small comfort, but at least we knew the truth. And in time, I had a bit of satisfactory revenge. Revenge, as the saying goes, is a dish that is best eaten cold. It took years, but I had my say. You see, today I am one of the biggest supporters of Montini. I arranged a successful football reunion at the school, and I'm in the midst of a $2 million fund-raising campaign. My motivation is my love of the school and my gratitude for men there like Brother Michael Fitzgerald, who let me stay at Montini even though we couldn't pay the tuition for two years. When Brother Michael learned where my father was, he told me not to worry. "Your father will pay me," he said, and he never mentioned it again.

But there was a special reason I made another donation to the school, the scoreboard in the gymnasium. You see, I know that every time my old football coach goes into the gymnasium, he has to see that scoreboard that has my name on it. And I imagine he must remember that football banquet when he decided to pass me over for an award just because of my father. That coach figured that I would probably never amount to much. I'd end up a loser, or probably in jail.

But, my life didn't turn out the way my old football coach imagined. I remained a true competitor, playing in the legitimate world of business where my father's toughness and discipline have been pillars of my success. I didn't go the way my father did, but I embraced the life lessons he taught me.

The score is in my favor.

CHAPTER 5

The Down Times

Nobody goes through life unscathed, and I am no exception. I've faced my share of setbacks, traumas, and losses: death of a parent, divorce, self-doubt that nearly paralyzed me. When I was in the pit of my personal hell, the only thing I wanted was to get out. If it were in my power, I would do anything to erase those events from my life. But because I cannot, I am left with only one option: to try to gain some insight from what I've suffered. As a trader, there have been invaluable lessons in all of it: Losses happen; they are inevitable. The secret is to keep them from destroying you.

Traders don't like to think about losses. But, nobody is right every single time. Nobody makes money on every single trade or even every single day. We all have a bad day now and then, or maybe a string of bad days. When that happens, you can't let it shake you. Give into fear, and you might as well hang it up. Of course, you can't go to the opposite extreme and believe that you're invincible. I've seen a lot of traders crash and burn because they believed that the market would go *their* way.

To survive the down times, in life and in business, you have to go back to the fundamentals of who you are, where you come from, and where you're headed. You must rely on your own strength. If you're lucky, you may also have the support of a few people around you. But, unlike the high times, when you have an abundance of fair-weather friends, the down times have to be faced alone.

In the high times of 1987, I made $4.5 million, solely by trading my own money. I earned no investment fees or commissions. Every dollar I earned was the profit I made by trading my own money. I was among the fortunate ones who made a lot of money in 1987. Many traders got burned that year and gave up trading. Others were wiped out and never got a second chance to make it back. Despite the profit I made that year, I believe the Crash was the worst thing that could have happened to the market. Sure, the chaotic free fall allowed me to make more than a million dollars in less than a minute. But, I feared that 1987 would be what killed the proverbial goose that laid the golden egg.

It ushered in regulatory scrutiny that slapped burdensome regulations on trading and eventually led to the Merc banning dual trading. After the Crash, the spotlight of scrutiny shined harshest on the S&P pit. The Securities and Exchange Commission (SEC) tried to gain oversight authority of the S&P pit, wresting it away from the Commodity Futures Trading Commission (CFTC). Because the S&P contract is based on an index of stocks, the SEC theorized, then S&P futures should be under its control. But the S&P contract is a futures contract with a cash settlement. You can't hold an S&P contract until expiration and take delivery of stocks in the companies that comprise the S&P 500. The oversight issue went all the way to the Federal Reserve, which referred it back to the CFTC. In the end, the CFTC kept control of the S&P contract, but decided to raise margins dramatically.

Before the Crash, margins on S&P contracts were around $1,500. The CFTC raised them to between $15,000 and $20,000, citing the rationale that higher margins would limit the number of participants in the S&P pit. That, in turn, would reduce the volatility of the market. However, the reduction in participants meant that liquidity was cut, which actually increased the volatility. The more participants in the market, the greater the variety of opinions and price levels that trigger these opinions. This makes for a liquid and efficient market.

As a Merc member, my margins were not as high as those for nonmembers. In addition, because I am a day trader—rarely holding a position overnight—margins were not an issue for me. The only time a trader has to put up a margin is to hold a position overnight. Go home flat, and you'll never face a margin call. But the decline in S&P volume was a major concern, even though I was slow to recognize its impact on me.

After the Crash of 1987, S&P volume was down dramatically. In 1987, S&P volume ranged from about 62,000 to 90,000 contracts a day. In 1988, it dropped to about 30,000 to 50,000 contracts a day. The New York Stock Exchange (NYSE) also saw a decline in volume, but not nearly as dramatic as in the S&Ps. NYSE volume declined from between 150 million and 250 million shares a day in 1987 to between 110 million and 180 million in 1988. It was as if the markets were in mourning for all the investors who bailed out and all the brokerage employees who were let go in layoffs that reduced the brokerage workforce by as much as 30 percent.

While the S&P market had changed, I was still trading the same. That disparity would catch up with me, cutting my annual income for 1988 to a mere fraction of what it had been the year before. I had to look at myself in the mirror—literally—and change the kind of trader I was. I had to get used to the down times, and find my way through the transition years.

By 1987, I had clearly established myself as the largest and most prolific trader in the S&P pit. I was doing anywhere from 5,000 to 8,000 contracts a day, all for my own account. I continued that style of making big trades—sometimes buying or selling hundreds of contracts in a single trade—into 1988. I had made such a name for myself that some fund managers actually instructed their people to watch me trade. They wanted to know what I was doing because of my skill in detecting and analyzing floor-order flow, which gave me the sense if the market was going to turn bullish or bearish. Adding to the attention I was getting,

Dan Dorfman wrote a profile of me, "Ex-Trucker finds his fortune in futures," which appeared in *USA Today* (September 2, 1988, p. 7B). I never intended to become the biggest player in the S&P pit. Whether it was because of my risk tolerance or my trading style, I rose through the ranks to become the largest trader in that pit.

The problem was, volume declined sharply in the S&P pit. Because I traded so many contracts, I was the leading local. That meant when the order fillers had a big customer order to fill—buying or selling a few hundred contracts—they looked to me to take the other side of the trade. On one particular day, I made a large trade at what turned out to be the low of the day with a certain broker. Then I made another large trade with the same broker at what turned out to be the high of the day. These two trades accounted for nearly 300 of the 340 contracts sold at the high, and about 200 of the 250 sold at the low.

This raised the suspicion of the Merc's Compliance Department. Because I had traded at both the high and low of the day with the same broker, he was called in to explain. Compliance was wondering if perhaps that broker had given me those trades. "I traded with the guy who was making the best bids and offers," the broker explained. "I wanted to give my customers the best fill."

The problem for me was I was trading big in a market that had declined in volume. This increased my exposure to risk. With almost every trade I made, I moved the market—sometimes against myself. As a result, I had big swings. I'd be up one day and down the next, and at the end of the week, I'd have nothing but a minuscule profit to show for all my efforts.

At the end of the year, I knew I had to make some changes. I had to face the fact that the market had changed and I, as a trader, had to change with it. As far as I was concerned, 1988 was a losing year for me. Compounding the problem was the fact that, even though I only made $110,000 in 1988, I was living like I still made a few million. Luckily, I had paid off loans on my houses with some of my profits from 1987. And I held that trader mentality to pay cash for as much as possible instead of running up debt.

But the reality was I had to make a fundamental change in myself as a trader. I had let go that I was the biggest player, or more important, that everyone saw me as the biggest player. To adhere to one of my own rules of trading—to always be in sync with the market—I had to change. In a market in which volume was down about 50 percent, I had to cut back.

To use a sports analogy, everybody knows that Michael Jordan is the best player in basketball (although I'm not comparing myself with a superstar like Michael Jordan). But he can't score 55 points every game. He has to take what other people are giving him. There are days when he's going to score just 20 points. When the S&P market changed after the Crash of 1987, I had to become a 20-point player most of the time.

The other lesson I learned during this time was the reality of the dreaded King Midas touch. I say dreaded because it's a fallacy that anyone can really turn every opportunity into gold. Life simply doesn't work that way. But my confidence was boosted by my early real estate deals. I bought a lot in Hinsdale, an elegant, old-money western suburb of Chicago, for $279,000 and sold it six months later for $440,000. I bought and sold houses and properties, renovating some and demolishing and rebuilding others. If I ever strayed from the trading pit, real estate development could have been my second calling. But real estate was the only area in which I was a lucky investor. I broke even or posted a small profit on some investments and was burned on others.

I opened a restaurant, The Tenth Street Cafe, in the old neighborhood. But I learned that unless the restaurant business is your career, it's not a good place for the casual investor. I opened up hand car washes and parking lots, but found to my dismay that nearly everybody who worked there was my "partner" and helped himself to the cash. I lost $10,000 here and $20,000 there, but it was an inexpensive lesson to learn I had to stick to what I did best—trading.

But that didn't stop people from approaching me with more get-rich schemes than anyone could imagine. Some were wild and some made sense. But they all had one thing in common: my money and somebody else's brains. A couple of times I actually went along. Once, I got out in the nick of time.

A friend of mine approached me with the idea of investing in oil wells, as he was doing. I was skeptical at first. "Are we going to make any money in this?" I asked him.

"I have $1 million in it now and I'm getting a return. I'm going to give him $4 million more."

I agreed, a little reluctantly, to put in $200,000, but told my friend I wanted to research this oil well business.

"I guarantee your money," my friend told me. "You won't lose a dime."

But as it turns out, the oil well driller had a Ponzi scheme going. He hooked people like my friend in with a return to get them to invest more. The final word on the oil well driller came from a friend in Las Vegas who was talking to a couple of men from Texas at the craps table. When the oil driller's name was mentioned, the Texans just laughed. "He's the biggest crook in the state of Texas," they said.

It turned out the oil wells he was drilling were nothing but dust holes. This supposed oil tycoon was only making his money setting up the oil drilling equipment, which he owned, and pocketing the $400,000 per well that it cost to drill. Luckily, I got my money out, thanks to my friend who had guaranteed my initial investment. Even though he was down a million on the deal, he was grateful that I stopped him from investing any more money.

I took my losses and faced the music when it came to investments that turned sour or a bad day in the pit. It is all part of the risk-and-reward game known as speculation. I can do this because I know that, in the end, it's only money. I don't worry about taking financial risks because I believe that, going back to what I do best—trading the market—I can always make more. I don't mean to sound cavalier, but that's the reality.

I learned those lessons the hard way by enduring traumatic

events in my life that have left deep scars on my soul. I do not want to trivialize or rationalize what happened to me. But, I know that if you can handle personal tragedy, a monetary loss is nothing. If you can face the most traumatic of setbacks, then even a million dollars down the drain is meaningless. This philosophy is not borne of having money to burn. On the contrary, I learned it long ago when I didn't have more than a few bucks in my pocket.

Everyone has regrets in life. We all have things that, if given the choice, we would do differently. We question, in hindsight, what we would have done, should have done. But we are the sum total of our life choices. We have to live with the mistakes we've made and society's judgment of the actions we've taken. We have to see that certain events, given our upbringing and our core beliefs about ourselves and the world, were inevitable and unavoidable.

Like most twenty-one-year-olds, I thought I was invincible. I had everything going for me. I was on the football team at DePauw. I was working hard to improve my grades to get into law school. I was having fun with the guys and dating the girls. If there is a utopia, it's college for most kids: you can live like an adult, but your parents are paying your way. For me, my college life could not have been sweeter. I saw the beauty of the proverbial American dream, where opportunity—and justice—were for everybody. I was part of the white-bread world that was so different from my father's.

Then, one warm July 4th evening in 1978, when I was home from college between my junior and senior years, it all changed. My father's world and mine collided, and the blinders were ripped off my eyes. I saw the world and its harshness for what it was. In many ways, I haven't been the same since.

The incident was only a fight that began among the teenage boys of the neighborhood. By today's standards of unfathomable violence committed against young people and the senseless terror of drive-by shootings, this fight would not merit the ink on the inside pages of the newspaper. Yet, this neighborhood scuffle escalated out of proportion. On one hand, there was my father's

protectiveness of his sons, which admittedly bordered on para-
noia. On the other, was the legal system, which in my opinion, was
clearly out to get my father. In the end, I was slapped with a felony
assault conviction that has haunted my adult professional life. I
cannot justify anyone's actions that July 4th evening—not my
father's and not my own. I can only attempt to explain why a fight
that should have never gone beyond the street corner became a
raging battle.

I was sitting on the back patio with my parents and their
friends, waiting for the fireworks to start. Suddenly, Dominick,
one of my brother's friends, ran into the backyard. Even in the
dim light, we could see he was bleeding from the mouth.

"They're beating up Joey," he said, and then passed out.

I grabbed Dominick and shook him. "Where's Joey?" I
demanded.

He mumbled something about Joey being on the corner. I
took off down the street, dragging Dominick with me. The
events that followed were like some perverse chain of dominoes.
What started as a neighborhood fight between a bunch of kids
escalated into a lynch mob. A petty dispute over a school rivalry
became a battle in which I was among the casualties.

I found Joey on the corner, surrounded by kids who were
taking pop-shots at him. The instigator of the fight was a neighborhood kid, whom I'll call Smith. A few blows were exchanged
on that street corner until the police arrived to break up the
altercation. But the fight was far from over. When the word fil-
tered through the neighborhood that Smith and his friends were
waiting for us down the street, we answered the challenge. Joey
and I fought Smith and his friends, with Dad right beside us.

Looking back, I see how this incident must have struck terror into my father's heart. To him, this was a matter of life and
death. He survived six years at Leavenworth by knowing that
you could never appear weak. An enemy who wasn't thoroughly
defeated could come back at you another day. Or worse, any
appearance of vulnerability would make you a target from all
sides. He couldn't separate in his mind this neighborhood fight
on a hot summer evening from the mortal threats he had faced

in his life. When he perceived that we were being threatened, the only recourse in his eyes was to make sure a fight that was started by someone else was finished by you.

The next day, a police officer showed up at our door, offering us their protection. Dad looked at the cop like he was nuts. "Police protection? What for?"

"There's a bunch of kids up at the shopping center, threatening to break down your door and drag you and your sons out."

"You have any body bags at the police station?" Dad asked. "Well you bring them down here. Because if anybody comes in this house, you're going to take them away in a body bag."

We were harassed the next day with crank phone calls and firecrackers thrown against the house. Threatening phone calls were even made to our cleaning lady. I had enough. I was going to find Smith and put an end to this—preferably with words. But when Smith spotted my car, he went on the defensive. He jumped out as I approached him and started swinging. He started the fight; I finished it. In the end, Smith was unconscious and on the ground. Someone called the police and an ambulance.

At about nine o'clock that night, the police came to our door again. This time they had arrest warrants. Smith regained consciousness long enough after that fight to say, "the Borsellinos got me." The police arrested my father and my brother, Joey, who were not at all involved in this fight, and me. My mother was beside herself when the police arrested us. "Don't take my sons," she begged the police.

"Don't worry. It'll be okay. I'm with them," Dad yelled to her as the police led us out the door.

We weren't worried, even when the cops brought us to DuPage County Jail. Joey and Dad had not been involved in that last fight with Smith, and I was only finishing what this guy had clearly started. The problem was that it was Saturday night and we were going to be in jail until the bond hearing Monday morning. We sat together on a bench in the cell, waiting.

DuPage County Jail was certainly no Leavenworth, but my father went back to his survival mentality. He stationed himself on the floor in front of the bench. "You two sleep," he told us. Joey stretched out and fell asleep. I tried to stay awake, but nodded off. Dad sat there all night, never closing his eyes, watching out for us.

In hindsight, we did have reason to worry, far beyond the repercussions of a neighborhood fight. What we didn't know at the time was that this fight would be used against my father in an attempt to get him back in jail. That plan would backfire, and instead I would become a target. My vulnerability would hurt my father more than any punishment.

On Monday morning, we were arraigned. A grand jury handed down four indictments against us: aggravated battery, grave bodily harm, permanent disfigurement, and fighting in the public way. We posted bond and went home to headlines that would haunt me for a long time to come: "Mob Overlord and Sons Indicted in DuPage County Beating." Many of my classmates from DePauw, I thought angrily, were from the Chicago area and would read those news stories. Yes, I had beaten up this kid who had started a fight with my brother and then me. But my father and the Mob had nothing to do with this.

Before the trial got underway, we were approached by DuPage County Prosecutor Thomas Knight, who made my father an offer he should have refused. "Here's the deal," Knight told Dad. "You've got two or three years left on your probation. We'll violate your parole and you go back to jail. If you agree to that, your kids go free."

"Okay," Dad said without hesitation.

"No!" Joey and I said in unison.

Dad gave us one look that silenced us. He was ready to take the deal.

After the prosecutors left, Joey and I told Dad he was crazy. "You weren't even in that fight," I pleaded with him. "What am I going to get? Probation? They're not going to send me to jail."

Dad's mind was made up. "If you're found guilty, you're going to have a felony on your record. I don't want that for you." Dad agreed to plead guilty to the assault charges, but at the last minute, that offer was withdrawn by Knight and the prosecuting attorneys.

The memory of how Knight and the DuPage County officials tried to railroad my father never left me. Years later I read with satisfaction the news reports that Knight was among seven law enforcement officials named in a 79-page indictment for concocting and concealing evidence. The case was the infamous trial of Rolando Cruz for the 1983 abduction, rape, and murder of 10-year-old Jeanine Nicarico.

The false evidence led to Cruz being found guilty and sentenced to death for the killing, although the convictions were overturned on appeal. During Cruz's third trial, according to *Chicago Tribune* reports, a key prosecution witness changed his testimony, and the case against Cruz was thrown out. But Cruz by that time had already spent 10 years on death row.

The prosecutor's attempts to pressure my father into a deal opened my eyes to the way the world really worked. I had disputed my father's view that the deck was automatically stacked against anyone with an Italian last name. I was a college student and athlete who was as all-American as the next kid. My brother and I were suburban kids who never got in any trouble with police, never became involved in a gang, and never took drugs. But after this fight, I understood what my father had been telling me all along. The rules did not apply to everyone equally. All the prosecutors wanted was to get my father back in jail, even though he was not involved in the fight with Smith. All they wanted was a feather in their caps for having put Tony Borsellino back in prison, regardless of the innocent lives that would be affected.

That's why I wasn't surprised when a jury dominated by middle-class African Americans acquitted O. J. Simpson on charges of murdering his estranged wife, Nicole Brown Simpson. Regardless of what any of us think about that case, the fact remains that many African Americans know about police harassment firsthand or from the experience of close associates. So, it wasn't hard for those jurors to believe that the investigating officers manufactured the case against us. In my own life, I've seen too many incidents of assumed guilt, instead of the assumption of innocence that is guaranteed by the Constitution. All too often, someone's ethnicity is the only reason they are suspected of being guilty of a crime.

As my father, my brother, and I went to trial on the assault charges, Smith changed his story. He accused another kid, and not my brother, Joey, of beating him up. Joey was off the hook. Charges were brought initially against my brother's friend, but he later proved that he had been out of town that July 4th weekend. A few days later, charges were also dropped against my father. I, alone, stood trial. I was convicted of aggravated battery and permanent disfigurement. After a presentencing evaluation, the counselor suggested I serve five weekends in the county jail because I was a college student. Thankfully, the judge rejected that suggested sentence, and instead, gave me a one-year conditional discharge, with no required contact with the probation department.

The incident left me with a felony on my record, which nearly barred me from the Chicago Mercantile Exchange later. I knew it hurt my chances of going to law school, although I was told it was the kind of incident that could be explained away because it did not involve a crime of moral turpitude. But I had experienced the degradation of handcuffs and strip searches, which showed me the other side of the legal system, and then I got my first real taste of what prejudice was like.

Because of the trial, I was two days late going back to school for the start of football practice my senior year. I saw the stares and heard the whispers. "We thought you were in jail. We didn't think you were coming back," a few of the bolder ones told me. In a school with some 3,000 kids news spreads fast. I had always heard the bullshit about the Mob because of my Italian name and the fact I was from Chicago. But now, based on the news stories about that fight, people assumed that the stories were true. What angered me even more was the fact that I would carry a felony the rest of my life while Smith, who had instigated the incident, was off the hook.

That incident and the rumors cast a shadow on my senior year at DePauw, but I persevered. My father harbored an irrational fear that I would drop out of college, but I assured him that nothing was going to keep me from finishing. Although my grade point average, hampered by poor grades in my freshman and sophomore years, was hurting my chances of getting into law school, I had an above-average score on my LSAT. I decided to enroll in the John Marshall Law School accelerated study program that summer. If I was among the few students who made it through that rigorous program, I would automatically be accepted for law school. I had no doubt that I would be accepted; I had proved to myself that I could accomplish anything if I set my mind to it.

I began to grasp one of my father's other rules about life: The power rested in the hands of those who had money. That raised the stakes for my success in life. Because of my background, few people outside my family and friends thought I would do well in life. I was determined to prove them wrong. I knew that I could not rely upon anyone or blame anyone for my misfortunes. I had to make my own breaks in life.

The day I graduated from college was one of the proudest moments of my parents' lives. Thirty relatives must have come to DePauw for the graduation: my mother and father, my brother, aunts, uncles, cousins . . . Everybody was snapping pictures, and everybody was laughing and crying. Then I saw my girlfriend heading toward us, wiping the tears from her eyes. My parents thought the world of her, and to this day we're still the best of friends. Seeing her on graduation day, crying her heart out, was more than my father could stand. "What's the matter, honey?" he asked her.

Her parents were in the midst of a nasty divorce and her father had refused to sit next to her mother. The problem was the graduation ceremony was scheduled to be held outdoors, but rain was threatening, which would require that everything be moved inside. In the gymnasium, seating was limited and her mother and father would have to sit beside each other. Her father refused. If it came to that, he said he would stay in his hotel room.

I don't know what Dad said to my girlfriend's father. All I know is it upset him that Mr. M couldn't see beyond his own problems to realize he was spoiling one of the biggest days in his daughter's life. Suffice it to say that Dad talked to Mr. M and let him see the proverbial error of his ways. Mr. M didn't raise a fuss. The sun shone after all, and the graduation was held outdoors. Mr. M got to stand where he wanted to.

What strikes me about this incident was how my father put himself out for someone else. That was just the way my father was. If you were part of his life, he cared about you. It was his nature to help people and, in that, I believe I am like him. But that was also his downfall. He had a heart and he had a brain. He couldn't take mindless orders from people. He lived by a code of what was right, and he never wavered from it.

My Dad was very much his own man. He wasn't the type to kiss anybody's ass. He was a very capable individual, who could do anything that was required of him. But he was principled and there were orders that he didn't want to follow. I saw that struggle within my father, and once he talked about it to me. My father was sent to talk to somebody after an altercation at a bar involving somebody's son. When he got to the bar, it turned out the guy who owned the place was someone he had known for years. He sat down with Vince and asked him what happened.

"Tony, that kid was drunk. There were other people in the bar and he got out of line. I asked him to behave himself, and he got out of line again. Then he took a swing at me, so I flattened him," Vince explained.

"I understand," my father told him, and left the bar.

Dad went back to his superiors and related the story. Vince had every right to punch that kid who had gotten out of line and then took the first swing.

"You don't understand," they told Dad. "This kid is So-and-So's son. His father doesn't ever think this kid can be wrong."

Things like this would eat away at my father. I believe that's what made him so insistent that Joey and I always act respectfully toward other adults. He would never have allowed us to mouth off to someone or act rude just because we were "Tony's sons."

We came back from DePauw after graduation feeling nothing less than victorious. When we got home, Dad said to me, "Let's go take a steam together." We must have sat in the steam room in our house for three hours, talking. By the time we finished, I looked like a prune. Dad had something on his mind to tell me and, looking back, I believe he sensed that things were beginning to turn against him and was worried that he was going to be arrested again. But I also knew that Dad had vowed that he would never go back to jail. If it came to that, I wondered, would Dad have to disappear, even if it meant leaving us for a while? I never asked him that question. I sat in that steam room and listened.

"If anything ever happens to me, you have to take care of your mother and your brother," Dad said through the clouds of steam. "Just get on the truck. You've got that to fall back on until you figure out what you're going to do."

Monday passed, and then it was Tuesday morning. Dad and I had breakfast together before he went to work. He came home about two o'clock in the afternoon on Tuesday, took a bath and asked me to rub Ben-Gay on his sore back. "I'm going to take a nap," he told me. "Wake me up at five o'clock."

Dad, who did not sleep well at night, would sometimes nap a little in the day. I went out and returned about 4:30. At 4:45, I went upstairs to his room to awaken him. His bed was empty. I found him in Joey's room, curled up on a single bed. The image chilled me: With his arms crossed over his chest, he looked like he was dead.

"What are you doing in here?" I asked him, opening the blinds.

Dad sat up and rubbed his eyes. "I can sleep better in here. It's darker than in my room."

Dad got dressed to go out. My mother was at home, and I went out to see some friends that evening. At eight o'clock the next morning, my mother woke me up. "Lewis," she said. "Your father didn't come home all night."

I got up immediately. "Don't worry, Mom. I'll start making some calls."

I called a couple of men whom Dad knew to ask if anyone

had seen him, but no one had. I held onto the hope that, maybe, he had been delayed. Even the thought that perhaps he had been arrested was a comfort. At one o'clock in the afternoon, the Lombard Police came to our door. "We've been asked by the Will County Police for a member of your family to call them," they told us.

I got on the phone with the Will County Police. "Can you come to the station? We need to talk to you about your father," they told me.

"Will he need bond money?"

"No, he won't need that."

My worst fears were being confirmed.

Our aunts and uncles came to our house to sit with Mom, who was literally sick with fear. Joey, Uncle Mimi, and I drove to Will County to meet with the police. We were silent most of the way, each occupied with his own thoughts. We sat in the waiting room for a few minutes before one of the officers came to speak to us.

He brought with him my Dad's Christ medallion, his watch, and his wallet. "Do you recognize these things?" he asked us.

"They're my Dad's," I told the police.

"Can you tell us where he went and who he was with?" the officer asked.

"Wait a minute," I piped up. "Is my father here?"

"Yes, he's here," the officer replied.

"Has he been arrested?"

"No, he's not arrested."

"Can we talk to Dad?"

"No, you can't talk to him."

"Is he dead?" I asked finally.

"Yes," the officer told me. "He's dead."

Uncle Mimi passed out cold. Joe and I wrapped our arms around each other and cried.

I never knew exactly what happened to my father, but I could piece together bits of the story. Perhaps somebody in that organization was bad-mouthing my father to the bosses, or perhaps there was a struggle within the ranks that my father was caught in. All I know is my father was a principled, strong-minded man who could not be intimidated. In the end, my father was dead, his body left on a rural road near an Indiana cornfield. His murder remains unsolved to this day. My mother was in shock from the loss of the man who had been the love of her life since she was 14 years old. At 43, she was far too young to be a widow. Like my brother, I was so overcome by my pain, anger, and grief, that I was numb. I went through the motions of making the funeral arrangements and the necessary phone calls, feeling oddly detached from what was happening around me. But when it came to the responsibilities that I faced, there was no running away. Once again, I was the man of the family, stepping into my father's shoes just as I had when he was in jail. This time, however, he was never coming back. At age 22, my life was supposed to be just beginning. Instead, my world had been torn apart.

Once again, I did what my father had asked me to do. I was the man of the family, only this time Dad would never be coming back. I got behind the wheel of his truck and drove it for the most unhappy year of my life until I could figure out what I was going to do for myself and my mother and my brother.

Anyone who experiences the death of a parent at a young age will tell you it changes the course of your life. It's as if you're caught in a bad dream, trying to run but your legs are suddenly paralyzed. You thrash around, trapped and unable to escape an unseen predator. But unlike that bad dream from which you eventually awaken, the helplessness I felt after my father's murder was all too real.

That grief came back to me years later when I underwent one of the most painful times of my life. I married my first wife in 1986, and we had two sons, Lewis and Anthony. Three years later, I left the house and began a bitter divorce proceeding. Death and divorce are similar in that they involve irreparable loss. The divorce took a huge emotional toll on me. No one trades in a vacuum, despite all the discipline and focus you can muster. The divorce distracted me, to say the least, and shook my very foundation. I am not going to rehash the details of that time. My first wife, Diane, whom everyone calls Disa, is a good mother to Lewis and Anthony. No one loves those two boys as much as she and I.

Even though Lewis and Anthony do not live with me full-time, they are part of my life. I love them just as much as Briana and Joey, my daughter and son whom I have with my second wife and former high school sweetheart, Julie. I am blessed to have great stepchildren, Nicole, Jamie, and Nick. But not having Lewis and Anthony in my day-to-day life is a losing trade that I can never reconcile.

CHAPTER 6

The Sting

The trading pit has an etiquette all its own. Amid what may look like chaos and confusion, there is a certain protocol of how contracts are bought and sold with a flash of a few hand signals and a yell across the pit, all in the matter of seconds. It begins with the understanding of who the players are and how they operate.

In the simplest terms, the market is based upon everybody's opinion. Between all the short and long positions, the market reaches an equilibrium. This is not a static point, but a moving target reflecting the level at which the buyers will buy and the sellers will sell, based on a host of variables from interest rates to the latest news across the ticker. In futures trading, there is another variable that goes into the price mix—fair market value. This takes into account the current value of the S&P index and the cost of money between now and when the contract expires. This cost of money is why the futures market nearly always trades at a premium to cash.

For example, in October, the December S&P contract is the front or "spot" month. The price of that contract reflects the current value of the S&P index, plus the cost of money needed to borrow funds until the contract expires. As the December contract nears expiration, the fair market value declines because there are fewer days of interest to pay.

Against the backdrop of variables, the order fillers and locals trade the market. A trade may begin with an order from a retail or institutional customer who has a definite opinion of where the market is going. Based on that opinion, the customer puts in an order to buy or sell the market. These orders go to the brokers, or order fillers, in the pit who must then execute the trade. That's where the locals, or scalpers, come in.

The role of the local is to provide liquidity for the institutional investors. We buy what the order fillers are offering or sell when they're bidding. The trade is made when the price is right. So when an order filler has 100 contracts to buy on behalf of a customer, he may have to bid up the market to get the trade done, say at 1095.50. Once that trade is executed, the local takes on a momentary risk as a seller with a short position, waiting for the market to return to where it was before that order filler began bidding. In this case, the local hopes the market will decline, say to 1095.00, so he can buy contracts at a lower price to cover his short position.

Scalpers, or day traders, like me are the ultimate short-term traders. A scalper has no long-term market opinion and may hold a position for only a few minutes or even a few seconds. We look to make profits amid hundreds of market moves each day. As I've often said, I'd rather make $1 each on a million trades than try to make $1 million on one trade. The profits add up and the risks are minimized by playing the intraday moves.

Futures trading is a zero-sum game. For every winner there is a loser, on each and every trade, and everyone must look out for his own best interest. For the order filler, that means getting his customer the best possible price on a buy or sell trade. For the local, that means making as much money as possible on each trade or cutting his losses. Although this makes for an intensely competitive arena, there is a kind of symbiosis in the pit. The order fillers need the locals and the locals need the order fillers. The result is a fragile relationship between both sides. They love each other and they hate each other, but they need each other to make money.

At the Merc and similar futures exchanges, trades are executed through open outcry. Traders and brokers stand in a pit and literally yell out their bids and offers. We're like hundreds of auctioneers, bidding on and offering contracts. But the pace is faster and more furious than any other arena of commerce. In open outcry, the best bids and offers are the trades that get executed first. Then the market moves as sellers lower their prices and buyers raise their bids to make their trades.

Underlying it all is an unwritten code of conduct on how the pit works. The code encompasses a protocol between the order fillers and local traders. For example, say I'm offering 50 contracts at two and a half, and an order filler buys from me at that price. But he's got another 100 contracts to buy and the market moves up as he keeps bidding. He buys 50 from somebody else at three-even as the market moves higher. With 50 more left to buy and the market now at three and a half, he looks at me and says, "Give me an offer."

His query to me gives me a chance to make up for the 50 I sold at two and a half in a rising market. "I'll sell you 50 at three and a half," I reply.

Now, I hope the market slips to at least two and a half so I'll have a scratch, or break-even, trade on the first 50 contracts, and I'll make a profit on the second. But there's also a chance that the market will keep rallying, adding to my loss. Nothing in the pit is ever guaranteed.

The good order fillers in the pit always know if the big locals are long or short, just by watching what we do. Say I've been buying all the way up in a rising market. Now an order filler has a buy order for 100 contracts. If he's smart, he'll turn to me and say, "LBJ, give me an offer." If he wants 100 contracts, I'll probably sell them to him in one bundle. I made my profit, based on where I bought those contracts earlier, and his customer got a good fill. Even if the market runs higher and I miss a chance to sell those 100 contracts at a better price, I'll never be mad at an order filler for doing that. He gave me a chance to sell and I took it.

An order filler makes a commission of about $2 per contract, so if he executes 50,000 contracts in a month, he stands to make a $100,000 gross profit. But, he also has to pay expenses such as a salary to a clerk and he must make good on any errors, which can cut into his profit. A local, on the other hand, stands to make—or lose—thousands of dollars on a trade. A local's profits for the month could be well into six figures. But keep in mind that locals shoulder enormous risk. They're trading with their own money and not somebody else's. This imbalance of profits on trades has made for a bitter rivalry between order fillers and locals since dual-trading was banned. At the same time, a protocol exists between them. When it makes good business sense, a local will sometimes help an order filler out of a jam.

Virtually every company—whether it's a supermarket with a price special on Diet Coke or a contractor bidding on a job with the state—conducts a certain portion of business for little or no profit. The rationale is you may lose out on some profits in the short term, but stand to earn more money in the future. The supermarket may not make any money on the Diet Coke special, but will draw customers who will load up their shopping carts with other goods. The contractor may only break even on a low-bid contract to pave a road, but will make it up when suddenly a bridge has to be repaired and that job is added to the contract.

The same rationale applies in the pit. Say an order filler has 100 contracts to buy. I offer to sell 20, and we make a trade. Within a few seconds, he buys 10 contracts each from several other traders, and the market rallies 100 points in the process. When I signal the trader to confirm the trade—"We traded 20 at a half"—I see a disgusted look on his face as he tallies up his trades.

"What's up?" I ask him.

"I got 10 more to buy. I only did 90," he tells me.

"Okay. I sold you 30—not 20," I tell him, amending our trade. The whole transaction takes only a few seconds.

With the market rising, I absorb a $2,500 loss on the extra 10 contracts. But as a scalper, I have the ability to play that position through the day. The order filler on the other hand would have had to eat that $2,500 loss. Plus, I've bolstered my business relationship with him for the next time the market takes a turn.

The market may be rising sharply with strong bids when all of a sudden bonds weaken, Fed Chairman Alan Greenspan makes a comment, or news of a company predicting weaker earnings crosses the ticker. The market makes a U-turn and declines—sharply. When that happens, an order filler with 100 contracts to buy at a relatively high price will find himself flooded with potential sellers. It's my hope that because I bailed him out of a jam before, he'll look my way when everybody jumps on him to sell. Maybe he'll sell me 50 of his 100 contracts and dole out 10-lots and 5-lots to everybody else.

Is that a prearranged trade, an illegal practice in violation of Merc rules? Absolutely not. A prearranged trade happens when an order filler has 50 contracts to buy and 50 contracts to sell. So he tells a local, I'll sell you 50 at two-even and buy 50 at two and a half. The trade was arranged between them, and not executed in the pit under open outcry where everybody had a chance. To me, helping out an order filler in hopes that he'll remember me the next time he has a big trade is just good business practice. It's no different than a drug company selling saline solution to a hospital for 50 cents instead of a dollar in hopes of getting a much bigger pharmaceutical contract.

There's also a human side to the pit etiquette and protocol that have developed over the years. As a local trader, I know that an order filler's errors can eat away his profit for the month. While the pit is an intensely competitive place, I don't believe that anyone (with the exception of a few) sets out to hurt someone else. We're in business to make money, not to destroy each other. What comes to mind is boxing. Two fighters may be rivals, but they respect each other as competitors.

Over the years, no one really questioned the pit protocol and etiquette, as long as trades were made in the pit where everyone had a fair chance of getting in on the action. Then came the FBI sting in the late 1980s, and what had been standard operating procedure was suddenly looked at as a potential crime. Traders looked over their shoulders to see what had been going on and who had been watching. They questioned every trade they had made, every corner that had been cut, every rule they had bent or broken.

The FBI sting rocked the insular world of trading at the Chicago Mercantile Exchange and the Chicago Board of Trade. The newspapers were filled with accounts of predawn raids at traders' houses. Accused of illegal trading practices, traders faced the potential of losing their livelihoods, their homes, and their possessions.

In business, there are always a few bad apples who are motivated by greed. They say that in most professions, 90 percent of the profits are made by 10 percent of the people. To try to get into that 10 percent, unscrupulous players may take chances or violate laws outright. In trading, this may mean making a prearranged trade or disclosing a stop order to tip off a friendly trader. These types are invariably tripped up by their own practices, discovered by the computer tracking systems at the Merc and the Board of Trade, and expelled from pits. The FBI sting simply accelerated that process.

At the center of the sting were four undercover FBI agents who posed as traders at the Merc and the Board of Trade. They started out like the rest of us, working as runners and clerks to learn the business. They worked their way up through the ranks and bought memberships to trade. With evidence of alleged illegal trading, including video- and audiotapes, the FBI made the first round of "visits" to several traders' homes in January 1989. There were stories of traders hauled out of bed and questioned in front of their wives and within earshot of their children.

In all, 45 traders and a clerk were indicted at the Merc and the Board of Trade. Ironically, given all the rumors I've faced over the years, I was never among them. I was never served a subpoena and I was never questioned. I knew I had been a target of FBI investigations in the past and was dogged by the Merc's own Compliance Department. I don't mean to take on a holier-than-thou attitude when it comes to pit trading. Under the strictest letter of the law, I would challenge any professional, including myself, to say he's never operated in a gray zone. When the FBI went into the pits, suddenly what many traders saw as standard operating procedures and good-faith gestures were being interpreted as violations of Commodity Futures Trading Commission (CFTC) rules. They were being accused of wire fraud and mail fraud. If traders were found to have engaged in these practices more than a few times, it was seen as an ongoing criminal activity and charges were brought against them under the Racketeer-Influenced Corrupt Organizations Act (RICO).

Stories surfaced later about how the sting actually got started. Journalists David Greising and Laurie Morse in their book, *Brokers, Bagmen & Moles: Fraud & Corruption in the Chicago Futures Markets* (John Wiley & Sons, New York, 1991), explain how Archer Daniels Midland Chairman Dwayne Andreas helped the FBI set up the sting. Agribusiness giant ADM would later face its own legal troubles and pay an unprecedented $100 million in fines to settle a federal antitrust price-fixing case and the vice chairman of ADM, Michael Andreas, would be among those sentenced to jail. But in the mid-1980s, Andreas and ADM agreed to train FBI agents to help them fit in on the trading floor.

"Andreas's continuing frustration with the Board of Trade, his persistent perception that the exchange's trading floor was a rigged market where not even honest members of the exchange could get a fair price, prompted him to complain to the government about conditions in the markets," Greising and Morse wrote. In late 1984, ADM approached the Chicago office of the CFTC, which referred the company to the FBI.

In hindsight, traders' high-living lifestyles amid the 1980s-style greed also contributed to the FBI's interest in commodity trading. As it was explained to me, commodity traders in Chicago attracted a lot of attention in the 1980s. They were, after all, some of the most flamboyant people in the city. Some of the young traders also were spending their money in ways that attracted unwanted attention, including gambling. As the FBI listened in on wiretaps of bookies in town, they heard that some of the big gamblers were traders. In some of those taped conversations, a few traders would boast that they didn't care about losing a bet because they could always make it back tomorrow.

This attitude, I believe, was more tough talk than reality. These traders, who were in the minority, were dealing with bookies and wanted to fit in with that shadowy world by talking like they were John Dillinger. In the white-bread world, a lot of people fantasize about pulling off the perfect crime and even become enamored with the gangster life. They perceive a kind of romance in cutting corners and outwitting the law. But then reality sets in and it's not funny or entertaining any more. That's what happened to some traders when they faced indictments and the possibility of losing everything. It was no longer a joke. The consequences of their tough talk and their actions became a sobering reality.

The FBI sting came as a surprise to the trading community, although in retrospect some people claim there were rumors of Feds on the floor. I did receive a tip-off about the investigation from a friendly source about six months before the story hit the headlines. The source called me in mid-1988 and suggested that we have lunch. I have helped so many people over the years, never asking for anything in return, that occasionally somebody tries to do something for me as a gesture of thanks. For this source, the thanks came as a warning. He told me he had heard the FBI was watching me because of my father. Then he told me something else: There was a sting operation on the trading floor and I was a target.

I kept my mouth shut about what the source had told me until the story hit the newspapers. I appreciated his warning, but I didn't know if it was true or not. There had always been warnings and speculation over the years that the FBI would be in the pit one day. With all this "crying wolf" over the years, I did not take the tip-off too seriously.

As for the FBI watching me, my initial reaction was surprise, followed by anger. My bank records had been pulled by the Internal Revenue Service in 1984, not for a tax audit, but to check the amount of money that went into and out of my account. In 1985, the FBI paid that unofficial visit to Salomon Brothers. Now they were looking at me again, trying to find some link between me and organized crime. I'm telling you, when that happens, you get nervous. Nobody wants to be investigated by the Feds, the IRS, or anybody else.

For two years after the sting came to light, the trading floor was tense as indictments were handed down. Guys who knew each other for life suddenly wouldn't talk to each other. Each feared the other had agreed to testify on behalf of the state. Traders walked around like ghosts, their bodies in the pit but their minds somewhere else. The pit was a hive of suspicion. You'd see two guys walking down the street, their hands cupped over their mouths so no one could hear their conversation. Phone calls were made only at pay phones away from the Exchange. It looked like a scene out of a Martin Scorcese film, only the real-life characters came from a variety of ethnic backgrounds and didn't just have vowels at the ends of their names.

As the indictments were handed down and the investigation spread, some guys whom no one thought would fold, turned state's evidence immediately. Others whom I assumed would cave in at the first pressure stood strong, endured a trial, and were acquitted. Sometimes human nature can be surprising under duress.

Any time a trader with a new-member badge walked into the pit, we'd give him the third degree. "What's your name? Where'd you come from? Who are you?" And then, just to be funny, we'd frisk him. I call this "joking on the square," giving a square-looking guy a good-natured hard time. But, in all our joking, there was a hint of seriousness. You couldn't be too sure just who anybody was or what they would do.

For many traders, the FBI sting was also the end of the good times. Traders worked hard and played hard, amassing a lot of luxuries and "toys." If New York had its high-flying Wall Streeters in the 1980s, then Chicago had its flamboyant traders. Those who had thumbed their noses at the rest of the world from the tinted windows of a limo or the windshield of a Ferrari suddenly felt the glare of the cameras on them. They downplayed their lifestyles, leaving the Rolls and the Mercedes at home and driving their Blazers and pickup trucks to work.

Their nerves were on edge, not just out of fear of what might happen, but their own uncertainty over what they should do. You could read in their faces the anguish of not knowing what they should do if they were questioned by the FBI. Would they turn state's evidence to save their own skins, but have to sacrifice a close friend? Would a close friend give them up to the prosecution? Had they done anything with someone who, in hindsight, really couldn't be trusted? They waffled on what they should and would do. This was during the "me" decade of the 1980s, when everybody looked out for number one, and loyalties didn't last longer than a snap of the fingers. In this atmosphere of distrust and uncertainty, I saw a lot of traders fall apart, their lives ruined, and I watched long-standing friendships crumble.

As for me, I slept well at night. It wasn't that I was such a tough guy who could take on the FBI. My peace of mind came from knowing what I would do if faced with a subpoena. I would answer the questions with the advice of an attorney, but I would never give up a friend or colleague. The way I was raised, there was no other alternative. I could never be a "rat," squealing on someone else. That was a rule of honor that my father had taught me.

Even though I never received a subpoena, when the sting hit the headlines, I took a precautionary measure. I put Tom Sullivan, a former U.S. Attorney who was with the law firm of Jenner and Block, on retainer. It was a kind of insurance policy for me, because no one knew just who was going to be questioned next by the FBI.

Traders who faced indictments sometimes came to me for advice because of my background and my experiences. Some people didn't even want to discuss the sting for fear it could be interpreted as obstruction of justice. But when people are in trouble, they seek out the advice of someone who is strong. For many of the traders, that person was me. My advice was always to hire an attorney and then listen to the advice of counsel. In two instances, I physically brought two currency traders I had known since high school to an attorney. They were too nervous to go alone.

One day, I ran into a defense attorney named Thomas Durkin, who represented at least one of the traders who was charged in the sting. When I was introduced to him, Durkin told me, "I always wanted to meet you."

"Why?" I asked, a little suspicious.

"Because during this investigation, I never heard someone's name mentioned so many times," Durkin laughed. "And you were never subpoenaed."

My name, I was told, pops up throughout the FBI investigation reports, known as Form 302s. When traders were questioned, FBI agents would ask how long they had been at the Merc and what pits they had traded in. When they learned that a trader had spent any time in the S&P pit, the questions would immediately turn to me and a few other big players. The responses, I'm told, were usually that I was the biggest player in the S&P pit. Whatever they said to the FBI, I never heard any more about it. I was never questioned as part of the investigation.

But I learned that I attracted the FBI's attention because I was such a big player in the S&P pit and because I was part owner at the time of a brokerage group known as Associated Brokerage Services Company, or ABS Partners. ABS was founded in the mid-1980s by Maury Kravitz and another trader, named Jimmy Kaulentis. Although Maury and Jimmy were rivals for years, they joined forces to start what eventually became one of the most powerful brokerage groups on the Merc floor.

When I first started trading, brokers would often form associations with a handshake, agreeing to help each other fill orders for customers and share in the commissions. Later these associations became more formalized as brokerage groups spread across the floor. Independents tried to discourage this growth by lobbying for a new rule, which ultimately became a blessing in disguise for brokerage groups. The rule stated that if one member of a brokerage group did not have the financial resources to cover an error or an outtrade, the other members of the group had to make good on it. After the Crash of 1987, when so many brokers went belly-up because of errors, brokerage groups gave assurance to large customers. Soon, the institutions preferred to deal with brokerage groups rather than the independents.

ABS was a who's who of people in futures trading—including Jack Sandner, Maury Kravitz, Jimmy Kaulentis, a broker named Michael Christ, and Mike Gettes, who was part owner of RB&H Financial, a clearing firm. This was a powerful combination of political influence, financial prowess, and business acumen, which made ABS a very tough adversary on the floor.

ABS was able to recruit customer business across all the Merc pits. In return for a contract committing a customer to using ABS's brokerage services, commissions were reduced to well under the standard $2 a contract. While brokerage groups were good business, they were perceived by some to have an unfair advantage because of their size and scope.

The FBI's attention was drawn to ABS after one of the principals and two of the brokers were indicted for allegedly accepting cash in return for trades made with the FBI agents, who were posing as traders. Perhaps ABS brokers were on the take, the theory went, generating a big pile of cash that was split up every month in a scene out of a Las Vegas counting room. For the two years I was part owner of ABS, I can tell you there was no bag of cash.

Because of my association with ABS and the fact that I was such a major player, the FBI tried to get near me in the S&P pit. But the other veteran traders and I had been standing in the same spot in the pit for years. That spot was our territory, our turf that we defended. When you establish your spot in the pit, no one can just walk in and take it from you. That's what I explained to a new local trader one day.

The incident happened in 1987, before the Crash and long before I or anyone else had an inkling of the FBI sting on the floor. When I got to the pit one morning, I found a new trader standing in our spot. "You can't stand there," I told him.

"Why?" the guy asked me.

"Because the guys who stand here have been in this spot for years. That's where we stand. You can't."

Joni Weber, who has been my clerk and assistant in the pit for years, told me that I turned to her that day and said, "That guy looks like an FBI agent."

Honestly, I don't recall saying that. But I do recall that this new local didn't try to break into our ranks again. After the sting hit the headlines, I found out that guy was one of the Feds. Later, I was amused to read that the FBI agents had tried to trade in the S&P pit, but the action was just too fast and too furious. In *Brokers, Bagmen, & Moles: Fraud & Corruption in the Chicago Futures Markets,* the authors explain that the two FBI agents at the Merc started in the S&P pit five months before the Crash. On Black Monday, they were as shaken as everybody else and had suffered some real losses. After disappearing from the trading floor for a while, they came back, but avoided the S&P pit. They headed to foreign currencies where the pace was a little slower.

There were other stories fabricated about me that surfaced during the sting. Someone I knew who was indicted told me that some traders, who cooperated with the FBI, didn't want to testify against a certain trader because he supposedly had "Mob connections." That alleged Mob connection, it seems, was me. I listened with amusement, more than anything else, about how I raised suspicion when I would frequently greet this trader—whom I had known since I was 14 years old—with a hug and a kiss. For two men to greet each other like that, which is an Old World custom I had grown up with, showed that we were "in the Mob," some traders told the FBI.

I suppose there is a risk in telling people that the FBI has been keeping tabs on you. Some might think that perhaps there is something for the FBI to find. But the truth is, I was under scrutiny for two reasons: who my father was and my rapid rise as a successful trader. And face it, being a young Italian-

American with two nice houses, fancy cars, and my own plane, I conveniently fit a certain profile—more a stereotype than anything else. In their view, I had to have some proverbial "godfather" helping me.

I also attracted a lot of jealousy on the trading floor, not only because of my success, but because of my association with two of the most powerful players at the Merc, Maury and Jack. We had more than our share of enemies on the floor. In my younger days—when I lacked a certain sense of, shall we say, tact—I could have been seen as a liability to Maury and Jack. But Maury defended me, not only because of my ability as a trader, but because of his undying loyalty to my mother, who was his legal secretary. Jack, who grew up the hard way on the South Side before distinguishing himself at the University of Notre Dame on a boxing scholarship, recognized a kindred spirit in me. Jack was also loyal to my mother who typed his legal briefs for free when he was a young attorney.

Despite the attention I attracted, the FBI never questioned me in regard to the sting. But they have contacted me for other reasons. I was living in a gated community near Hinsdale, an old and elegant Chicago suburb, when I heard the FBI paid a visit. As I was leaving one morning in my car, I noticed the young woman at the security gate wasn't her usual pleasant self. She looked frightened and edgy. "The FBI was here looking for you," she told me.

"They were, huh?" I asked casually, glancing in my rearview mirror.

"Yeah, but I wouldn't let them in."

"Are you sure they were looking for me and not somebody else?" I knew that a certain former Chicago First Ward politician who had faced corruption charges had moved into our community.

"No, today they were looking for you. They said they wanted me to let them in so they could see where you lived. But I'm prelaw at college. I knew to ask if they had a subpoena. They didn't, so I didn't let them in."

"Good for you," I told the security gate attendant. I thanked her again and drove off.

The next day, I was driving down the highway and talking on my car phone when I noticed an old Chevy in my rearview mirror. When I glanced up again, I saw the driver was holding what looked like a hair dryer with a cone-shaped defuser at the end. When he saw me looking at him, he dropped his hand. I slowed down in the right lane. The old Chevy drove alongside me and then passed me. I jotted down the license plate number. I had a way of checking out who owned the car. I was not surprised to learn it was an FBI vehicle, which confirmed my suspicions. The FBI was tailing me, and the hair dryer was obviously some kind of long-distance listening device to overhear my phone conversation.

Two or three days later, I was driving to work when I was pulled over by an unmarked car. It was a typical-looking sedan with a little red "cherry" light on the dashboard. The guys who got out of the car looked like G-men from central casting.

"We're with the Federal Bureau of Investigation," they told me officiously.

"Really? Was I speeding?" I asked, getting out of my car.

"No, you weren't speeding," one of the agents replied, a little annoyed at my obviously frivolous question.

"Do you have a warrant?" I asked calmly.

"No."

"A subpoena?"

"No."

"Well, then . . ." I went through my wallet to find Tom Sullivan's card from Jenner and Block. "Here's my attorney's name and number. Call him and set up an appointment. I'll be glad to talk with you."

"You won't need your lawyer."

"I want my lawyer present," I insisted. I knew how this all worked because an attorney had explained it to me. FBI agents question people in pairs because it enables one agent to corroborate the statement of another. Once a statement is made to the FBI, a person can perjure himself, which is a federal offense, if he contradicts that statement in the future. While a suspect is read his Miranda rights upon arrest, when the FBI is just asking questions they'd prefer if an attorney is not present. That way they can ask questions that an attorney might think are inadvisable for someone to answer. Most people have a tendency to say too much, hoping to explain away a doubt or deflect a suspicion.

"We want to talk to you," the FBI agents said. "It's about some of your friends."

"Call my attorney," I repeated. "Set up an appointment. I'll talk about whatever you want to talk about." I wasn't trying to be a hard-ass, but I only wanted to talk to the FBI in a structured environment with an attorney present.

One of the FBI agents leaned closer. "This doesn't have anything to do with commodities or the Merc," he told me.

The FBI agents ticked off the names of about 12 reputed Mobsters who had just been indicted. "We want to talk to you about these friends of yours."

"My friends!" I retorted. "Listen, you know that I know some of these names because of my dad. But if you've really been investigating organized crime all these years, you know that I have nothing to do with them."

The agents paused for a moment, not saying anything. Then one of them spoke up, offering what he probably thought would be an enticement for me to cooperate with them. "Do you want to know why your Dad was killed?" he asked me.

"Will that bring him back?" I asked.

"No," the agent replied.

"Then I don't want to know." I got in my car and left. The FBI never called my attorney or contacted me again.

Being investigated is an extremely intimidating experience. But I had certain life lessons that taught me my constitutional rights, and I knew how to exercise them. If the police question someone who is under suspicion, 9 times out of 10 they've already convicted that person in their minds. They just want to know if they can get the charge to stand up in a court of law. I've always remembered my father's wise words: The FBI doesn't ask you a question that they don't believe they already have the answer to. I have seen, since I was nine years old, that when you are the target of an investigation, you can't simply try to explain something to make it go away. In some cases, when you are accused, you can prove your innocence with evidence. But if you are falsely accused and face a fabricated charge, that's when it is the hardest to defend yourself.

These are hard lessons to learn in life, particularly when you are young. But I had to grapple with them shortly after my father's death in May 1979. I was faced with a delicate situation. There were questions that had to be answered and concerns that had to be put to rest. On the one side were the individuals who were responsible for my father's death. They knew how close we were and how Dad had raised his sons. That's why it was no surprise to me to learn that some people thought Joey and I might attempt to avenge our father.

On the other side was the FBI, which wanted to know what, if anything, we knew about Dad's death. Two FBI agents showed up at our door even before Dad's funeral. "We don't have anything to say to you," I told them, not letting the agents get any farther than the mat at the front door.

"We just want to ask you a few questions," they persisted.

"I told you. I have nothing to say." I closed and locked the door, but knew I had not heard the last from them.

I felt so angry and hurt after Dad's death, and I desperately needed someone to talk to, in an effort to understand what happened. I had that chance when one of my father's friends, a man whom Dad said I could trust no matter what, came to see us. He had loved Dad like a father, and there was nothing he wouldn't do for us, and I knew in my heart I could trust him. He had taken it upon himself to vouch for Joey and me in the circle of men that he and my Dad knew. He had given his word that my brother and I would not retaliate. This man made himself responsible for us. In the process, he helped me to deal with my own personal struggle.

My father, you see, never would have questioned what to do if a member of his family had been harmed. He was a one-man army, and he would have taken care of it himself. But what could I, a 22-year-old who had just graduated from college, do? More importantly, what was the right thing to do for my mother, my brother, and myself?

My father's friend sat across the kitchen table from me, one hand folded over the other. I looked to him for strength and guidance, but it was clear that he was deeply hurt by Dad's death. Still, he was there for me, and gave me advice that came from his heart and his experience. "Lewis," he began, "your father's life was *his* life. I know it's hard for you to understand that what happened to your father was just business. It's hard for me to understand that. But we can't do anything about it. What your father wanted for you and your brother was something completely different. We've got our own lives now. We've got to put this behind us."

In my mind, I heard the echo of what my father had said to me countless times: *I do what I do so you don't have to.*

I knew what my father's friend was telling me. Despite the anger that burned like battery acid inside my gut, I had to walk away. "Lewis, if we knew who had done this to your father, I'd be there with you," he said. "But this is something I'll never know because of my relationship with your Dad. And it's something you'll never know. What would we do? What could we ever do?"

"No," I said, but inside I wanted to say "yes" out of my own pain and anger. "I just can't believe that they could do this to him. I can't believe Dad could get set up like this." My father had always seemed invincible to me. Suddenly, I felt vulnerable for the first time in my life.

"Lewis," Dad's friend repeated. "Walk away from this. This is a battle that you can't ever win."

He could read on my face that I was still troubled. "Lewis," he added, "what is more important, where you go from here or what's already happened?"

I knew what he said was the truth. My father's main concern all his life was the future of his sons. That day, I closed the door to my father's former life and locked it forever. Then it was time to bury my Dad.

The day of Dad's wake, hundreds of people came to pay their respects. There were men whose faces were vaguely familiar and others whom I had never seen before. They came in quietly and whispered, "I'm not supposed to be here, but I don't give a fuck. I had to come for Tony." They were concerned, I knew, that the FBI would be watching to see who came to the funeral home.

As the mourners streamed in all day and evening, I saw my friends, my brother's friends, and my old high school football team that showed up en masse. Even guys my father had played football with 30 years before came to the wake. So many people attended, the funeral director had to open every available room.

A young woman approached the casket slowly. She walked on crutches and had braces on her legs, which were twisted with polio. "My name is Patty," she told me. "Your father was a great guy. He gave me a job when I was out of work."

"Really?" I asked, meeting this woman for the first time.

"Yeah. He paid me $500 a week to sit with a walkie-talkie in a car." She gave me a shy smile. "I was the look-out for the crap game he was running."

The day of Dad's funeral, 300 people showed up at the church. Father Phil, our local priest, presided. He had often brought runaways to Dad for some straight talk. Dad usually sent the kids back to their parents with money in their pockets and bus fare. Father Phil never forgot what Dad did.

I had no tears for my father that day. As much as I wanted to go into the next room and cry my eyes out, I decided I had to be strong for my family. The only person I drew strength from that day was Joey. Each time we exchanged a glance, we assured ourselves that we would always have each other.

All around me, my family was grief-stricken. My mother, on tranquilizers that the doctor prescribed, was barely functioning. One of my aunts fainted at the service. I knew that we had to get away. So after the funeral, we went to Florida for 10 days, my brother, my mother, and I, to stay at the home of a high school friend's family. But when we came back, I had to face the FBI.

I was subpoenaed to appear before a grand jury. The FBI

wanted to know what my father had told me about his life and what I might know about his death. To this day, I do not know who killed my father and I can only guess at possible reasons for his death.

Even though my Dad's friend had vouched for my brother and me, when I testified before the grand jury, I had to send the right signal. So I hired an attorney who had a reputation for defending organized crime figures. I didn't know any of the details of my father's death, nor had Dad ever told me anything that could ever incriminate me. But I told Sandy that day that, no matter what the FBI asked me, I planned to invoke my Fifth Amendment rights against self-incrimination. That, I told him, was what I wanted "certain people" to know. I had to protect what was left of my family.

Sandy escorted me to the federal building in downtown Chicago where the grand jury was convened, but could not accompany me inside the room. This was not like some TV courtroom drama. I wasn't a character in some movie, squaring off against the prosecution. I was a 22-year-old kid who was scared to be testifying before the grand jury. When I walked through the doors of the grand jury room, I was facing reality.

"Could you please state your name?" the state's attorney asked me.

"Lewis J. Borsellino," I answered. I watched the court reporter hit the keys to spell out my name.

"Could you please tell us your address?"

"On the advice of my attorney, I respectfully invoke my Fifth Amendment rights."

The state's attorney gave me a sideways look. "Surely, you can't be worried about being incriminated with your address?"

"I respectfully invoke my Fifth Amendment rights."

He asked me who Tony Borsellino was. He asked me who Florence Borsellino was. But I did not even acknowledge my parents' names. His questions became more pointed and his style more argumentative. He showed me photographs of my father with some men. Some of the faces I recognized and some I didn't. The prosecutor questioned me repeatedly, but each time I answered with the same response: "On the advice of my attorney, I am invoking my Fifth Amendment rights."

"Where was your father going the night he was murdered? What did he tell you that night?" the attorney demanded.

The prosecutor could tell he was making me uncomfortable. I tried to appear calm, but was scared on that witness stand, especially over my decision to invoke the Fifth Amendment in response to every question. That's when I remembered what Sandy had told me. If I needed a break, I could ask the court for a moment to speak with my attorney. I excused myself and left the courtroom on the pretense of wanting to talk with Sandy, who was waiting in the hall.

"How's it going?" Sandy asked me.

"The state's attorney is a real piece of shit. I came out here to piss him off a little." Of course, I was scared, but I was talking like I couldn't be intimidated.

I returned to the courtroom and continued to invoke my Fifth Amendment rights in response to every question. Finally, I stepped down from the witness stand. My appearance before the grand jury was over. But the state's attorney and an FBI agent followed Sandy and me to the elevator to get in one last bit of questioning.

"If you're concerned about your safety, we can protect you," they said to me.

I looked at both men. "I'm not concerned about my safety."

"It's certainly your right to invoke the Fifth Amendment, but we can protect you," the state's attorney said. "But if we give you immunity, you can't hide behind the Fifth Amendment anymore."

I knew what the deal was, and it was my biggest fear. If I was granted immunity, I would be forced to testify. If I refused to testify under immunity, then I would go to jail.

"Immunity?" I retorted. "What are you going to give me immunity for?"

"Lewis," Sandy interrupted, "you don't have to say anything."

"It's okay," I told my attorney. "I have something I want to tell them." I looked at the state's attorney and the FBI agent standing with him. "Look, my Dad was in jail from the time I was in the fourth grade until I was a sophomore in high school. Two years after he came home, I went away to college. He got killed two days after I graduated from college. How much do you think I really I know about his life? There's nothing that I can tell you that can help you. Why don't you just leave me, my brother and my mother alone and let us go on with our lives?"

The elevator opened, and Sandy and I stepped inside. When the doors closed, it was the last time I had to face the FBI about my father's murder. But it would not be my last brush with them.

Looking back, I suppose I could have conducted my private life differently to avoid the spotlight that has been on me over the years. I didn't have to have a Porsche and a Mercedes, but I did. Perhaps I was too visible in my younger days, hanging out in the cabarets, rubbing shoulders with the young movers and shakers and sometimes having a drink with a Wise Guy on the wrong side of the law. Maybe I should have turned down an invitation to an Italian-American wedding if I thought the guests might include some people who had been associates of my father. Shaking hands with someone at the reception—while suspicious eyes watched—might have cast doubt on me.

But my father and his associates had a tight fraternity with its own sense of loyalty. Sometimes I'd be in a social setting, such as a wedding, when a man would approach me. He'd shake my hand and tell me, "I knew your Dad for years. He was a great guy." Or else he'd say how they'd been "away at college" together. Then he would tell me some story about Dad from the old days. He'd look at me and say, "So you're Tony's son . . ." Looking at this man's smiling face, I could imagine my father's pride in the success Joey and I had attained. It meant so much to hear these men, who had known Dad for years, to speak so highly of what Joey and I had accomplished. Some of them had been friends of my parents since childhood. And I loved to hear stories about my Dad. For those few moments, it was as if he were alive and with us again.

Although I never turned a cold shoulder to anyone who had been my father's friend, people understood later when I sometimes turned down invitations. I might run into someone who had known my father years ago, whose son or daughter was getting married. "We are inviting you, your mother and your brother to the wedding. We would never leave you out," he'd say, "but we understand if you don't come." And, because my brother and I operated strictly in the legitimate world, it was understood that there were invitations that we had to turn down. We finally realized that we had to step back from this world. Otherwise, even something as innocuous as going to somebody's wedding could raise suspicions. It's a sad commentary that this cloak of suspicion would be cast over a social gathering just because we are Italian-Americans.

It was hard for me sometimes to face some of the people who had known my father. It was a reminder of what happened to him. Sometimes they'd offer what they thought was a bit of comfort, telling me that his death had been "a mistake." They'd hint how somebody fabricated a lie that somehow implicated my Dad. It was all "a mistake," they'd say, and tried to embrace me in hopes of somehow making it up to me.

But there was no making up for what happened to my father. I had always believed that Dad would be there for us, helping us find our way. Then suddenly, he was gone. I was consumed with anger for these low-life scumbags, as I regarded them, who had killed my father. The only way I could avenge his death was through my success and my brother's success. Our best revenge was to become successful in the legitimate world.

I remember when I was a 25-year-old trader, on my way to making my first million, single and living in Chicago. I felt like Frank Sinatra's swinging bachelor character in that old movie, *Come Blow Your Horn*. In the nightclubs and cabarets, I mingled with the power brokers of the city of Chicago, guys who were 10, 15, 20 years older than I was. And I felt very comfortable in that circle, which included businessmen, high-powered brokers and traders, doctors, lawyers, and a few "Wise Guys." The 1970s nightlife brought them all together.

I remembered leaving Faces, the hottest nightclub in Chicago in those days, one evening with my friends. I had just picked up a $1,000 tab for our group and was waiting for the valet to bring my Porsche to the front door. Beside me stood "Gino," one of the Wise Guys who had known my father. "You better be careful, Lewis," he told me, "or the IRS will be all over you."

I knew Gino's warning was well intentioned. The IRS has been a mortal enemy of the Wise Guys since the tax men took down Al Capone. But his words were pointless in my case. "What do I care about the IRS?" I said to him. "I'm legit and I pay my taxes." I had nothing against Gino personally, but I relished every opportunity to rub my financial success in the Wise Guy's faces.

While I enjoyed the party scene, I steered clear of drugs that were so prevalent at the time. Cocaine was everywhere, but it was never my idea of a good time. I never approved of drugs, which scrambled a lot of brains in those days. I remember standing at the bar in Faces with a friend of mine when a beautiful young woman approached us. "You got any 'Blow'?" she asked me.

I looked at my friend. He shrugged. Neither of us had any idea what she was talking about. "Sorry, can't help you," I told her.

She came back a little while later. "Hey," she said to us, "do you have any 'Snow'?" Again, I looked at my friend. We had no clue what she was talking about.

She came back a third time. "Do you have any 'Cola'? You know, 'Coke'?" Then it hit me: She was looking for cocaine. I immediately thought this woman could be an FBI agent and our conversation nothing more than a setup. "Are you talking about cocaine?" I said to her loudly, suspecting that she might be wearing a mike. "Well, I don't have anything to do with cocaine, so get away from me."

It's a sad commentary on my mental frame of reference that I immediately assumed this girl was an FBI agent trying to set me up, instead of just a party girl looking for a good time. But I knew I couldn't be too careful.

There were times in my younger days when I wished that I didn't have to face these risks and life lessons. Sometimes, I'd even daydream and wonder what my life would have been like if I weren't Italian-American. I suppose I felt sorry for myself at those times. But those lessons have served me well, especially during times of crises, such as the FBI sting on the trading floor.

I'm sorry for what happened to some very good traders who, in the midst of the sting, faced trumped-up charges that destroyed their lives. I feel badly for the good guys who, because of their own stupidity and greed, got caught making some foolish trades that saved them a few bucks but ruined their lives. As for the truly bad apples who were scamming the customers, the investigation merely weeded them out more quickly. As I said before, I believe the Merc and the Board of Trade would have caught and expelled these traders anyway.

As for me, during this time, I relied upon one of my key abilities as a trader. When the rest of the world panics and falls apart, I have the ability to keep my cool and my focus. I was not distracted by the investigation or any worry about what the probe might uncover. I kept trading because I knew myself and I knew what I would do under any scenario. The sting was one time when I could be nothing but grateful for all the controversy in my life. I relied on the strength of having been through the fire.

In time, the FBI investigations faded from the headlines. The press, however, did not play up the acquittals and criticism of the investigation with the same splash they used when the news of the sting first broke. Life eventually went back to normal in the pits. But there was a new concern now. The Crash of 1987 followed by the sting shed unfavorable light on the futures trading pits. Regulatory concerns were raised that caused another kind of controversy on the trading floor. It would escalate into another battle, this time a political one, pitting the factions at the Merc against each other. Once again, I was in the middle of it all.

CHAPTER 7

The Metamorphosis

If the market were a living thing, then change would be its heartbeat. Every moment, countless variables make the market rise and fall, charting out a jagged line like a cardiograph. That change, that volatility, is what makes opportunities in the market for buyers to find bargains and sellers to reap premiums. Without change, the markets would be static. In a static market, traders would have no way to make a living, investors would have no way of making profits, and CNBC would be left with not much to air except reruns of the Clinton grand jury testimony.

On a personal level, we all cope with change, for better or for worse. The key, I believe, is to embrace change, to stay ahead of the curve instead of being swept along by the current. Like everyone else, I have gone through my share of changes. Although I believe the core of who I am has not been altered, I have expanded both my abilities and my perceptions.

As a trader in the pit, once I learned the ropes, I wanted to go beyond just scalping between the ticks. I wanted to know what made the market work, why certain things acted and reacted the way they did. The more I learned, the more I wanted to know. As I grasped concepts of market dynamics and technical analysis, the more I changed as a trader. I'm still a day trader at heart, making moves intraday. Even as a money manager, I take a day trader's approach. When we trade client money, we enter and exit virtually all of our trades within the same day. We believe this approach reduces risk, while giving us solid returns.

The volatility of the market is what allows us to day-trade. There are plenty of moves within one day that provide an opportunity to make a profit. At the same time, given the extreme forces in the world, day trading is the safest approach. Exiting all trades by the close of the day—or going home "flat"—eliminates the potential risk of an adverse market move overnight due to the latest economic news out of Russia or Asia. And, as a day trader, I—and my clients—know where the accounts stand at the end of any given day.

Yet, although I'm a day trader in practice, I take a macroview of the market. I consider not only the fundamental factors, but also the technical ones, to form an opinion of how bullish or bearish the market is. My view goes from the long term (this year, this quarter, this month) to the short term (this week, this day, this hour, and, even, this minute). The market sentiment affects not only the long-term trend line, but it is reflected in every tick. If the market is declining, but the overall sentiment is still bullish, I know we're in a retracement. The market will test certain lows before finding a support level. Then as momentum builds, we'll move higher again, meeting resistance on the way up until we break through those temporary ceilings to reach the highs.

My journey from a 23-year-old order filler to a 41-year-old money manager has been a long one. I didn't just start out trading 100-contract lots, controlling futures contracts that, today, represent $25 million worth of stock. I went through a metamorphosis as a trader. Progressions are gradual by definition, one step following the other. They say you have to crawl before you walk, and walk before you run. Perhaps this is even more important in the trading pit, one of the few venues in society in which a person can become a self-made millionaire based on ability alone. And it's one of the few places in which education is not a requisite for success. It's all on-the-job training. You can't learn everything from a book or even a mentor.

The key is knowing how you respond to both your winning trades and your losses. Success can be as cruel as failure. The worst thing that can happen to a rookie trader is two weeks of winning trades. The temptation to believe you're invincible is too great. Then you risk too much capital on a reckless trade, and the market moves against you. I've seen traders wiped out by moves like that.

Back in 1996, when I started backing NASDAQ Small Order Execution System (SOES) traders, I wondered if there was a certain personality type that excelled at trading. The idea was sparked by my father-in-law, who ran a successful business and found that 10 percent of his salespeople accounted for 80 percent of his sales. Not surprisingly, those top salespeople had similar personalities. I used the Meyers-Briggs exam, which categorizes people into 16 personality types. I took the test myself and gave it to my brother. He and I had the same personality type, as did the top-performing SOES traders. I don't want to discourage anyone who has a passion for trading by telling them the personality type. But, maybe I should disclose that to trade successfully, you have to be a little crazy. . . .

I do believe that to be a successful trader, you must be an independent, spontaneous thinker, and you can't be averse to failure. You have to love the losers as much as you love the winners. Certainly, every trader wants to make money instead of losing it. However, the losers are inevitable; the advantage is to use them as opportunities to see what you did wrong and to analyze your trading process. You can never let a losing trade get the best of you. Rather, you have to consider those losers to be loans that you made to somebody else in the market. You'll go back again, a little smarter and more experienced, and get your money back. Remember, futures trading is a zero-sum game— for every loser there is a winner.

In many ways, I had an advantage when I went into the pit that young traders at the Merc don't have today. Under dual trading, I was allowed to fill orders for my customers and trade for my own account. This education of studying the customer deck and applying the lessons to my own trading was an invaluable one. For one thing, by filling customer orders, I became confident. There was no fear of pulling the trigger for my own trades, because I had been screaming buys and sells on behalf of the customers. I was already handling 10-, 20-, and 30-lots, then 50- and 100-, and even 1,000-lots. So, when I began to trade for my own account, the moves seemed natural. I was already in the market flow.

In sports, players talk about being in the "zone." They are literally part of the game. They're at the top of their performance and their moves appear automatic, effortless. The same thing happens when you're trading. You are part of the market flow, which, in the S&P pit, centers around the biggest players, myself included.

Like most traders, I started out trading 2-lots for myself. My goal was to make $500 a day. As I improved and gained confidence, I traded 4- and 5-lots and hoped to make $1,000 a day. Then, I graduated to 10-lots and a goal to make $2,000 to $3,000 a day, and then $5,000 a day. But as my goals increased, so did my potential losses. You can't increase one without the other.

As an order filler, I managed a customer deck: The top half of the deck included all the sells and buy stops in ascending orders. In the bottom half were the buys and the sell stops. I executed those orders as the market rose and fell. That deck provided not only an income for every month, but became my market textbook.

In the pit, I saw that orders from different brokerage houses tended to move in concert. All of a sudden, a 20-lot order, then a 30-lot and a 5-lot order would come in from Merrill Lynch, all from different customers. Then, the same thing would happen with Smith Barney. All these orders would be within 50 cents of each other, and you knew the brokerage houses and their customers weren't talking with each other. I knew these orders didn't just materialize at the same price. Some kind of market analysis was triggering them.

Other times, buy and sell stops would come in from a customer, which were way off from where the current market was. But, more often than not, the market did move to those price levels in time, and those buy and sell stops would convert into market orders and be executed as trades. (Interestingly, just as some customers were nearly always right when it came to putting in buy and sell stops, some were nearly always wrong!)

Watching these patterns of trading, I learned to use these buy and sell stops as a barometer of sentiment. Now, I want to be clear that this is a far cry from trading in front of the customer orders. Not only is trading in front of the customers illegal, it's also a bad idea: If the market isn't gravitating toward a certain price level, all the pushing and prodding won't help. I've seen greedy, unscrupulous traders get hurt trying to move the market to set off their customers' buy and sell stops. They ended up with a short or long position they really didn't want when the market suddenly went against them. Eventually, they'd be caught by the customers or the exchange and be reprimanded or suspended from trading.

When I looked at these buy and sell stops, I used it as a gauge of whether the tone of the market was bullish or bearish. But beyond that, I wondered what market analysis these customers were using that I, as a trader in the pit, was not. What sense of the market did they have that I lacked? Looking at charts of the market, I gained the first clues. I recognized the points at which the market dipped to a key support level and found footing to rise again. I saw the levels at which the market tried to break through the high from the previous week and, failing to do that, began to weaken. It was my first taste of technical market analysis.

Contrary to what most people believe, the markets do have a flow and rhythm to them. Occasionally, the market gets wild and crazy, but there is usually an order to the movement, even in a volatile futures contract like the S&P. Among all the gyrations, rises and falls, support and resistance, breakouts and fake-outs, there are price levels at which the buys and sells tend to gravitate. These prices are key technical levels that, if they pose resistance, will send the market lower, and if they are breached, will propel it higher. Once a trader can identify these price levels using technical charts and analysis, they become like a footprint diagram to the tango. You follow the steps and you're dancing with the market.

I began reading books on markets, looking at the patterns in the previous prices to see where the high and low points were, where the market built up momentum to move higher and where it hit a brick wall and fell. I learned day charts, weekly charts, five-minute charts, and one-minute charts. I saw that the market could be sliced and diced a dozen ways to reveal the short- and long-term dynamics that governed the market.

Studying technical price patterns, I also learned to trade more effectively using stops. For traders starting out, the use of stops is an important lesson. Stops are not only a safety net to get you out of the market when it turns against you, but are really the foundation of money management rules. In plain words, using stops will help protect a trader from losses that eat away capital. In theory, there is no real difference between the stops used by a customer and those used by a pit trader. In both cases, the stops are used to cut losses on a trade to a predetermined level. You believe the market is going higher when you buy, but you pick a price below the market for your sell stop, just in case you're wrong. For customers, these stops are orders given to a broker. For a pit trader, the stops are mental reminders to yourself.

Because of the low commissions on trades that I pay as an exchange member and a floor trader, it's very economical for me to make numerous trades. I'm moving quickly in and out of positions, initiating trades, cutting losses, taking profits. As the market rises and falls, you move in and out of the market, always cognizant of your long and short position. The rules are second nature: add to winning trades, but cut the losers quickly.

Here's how stops can be used effectively: Say, you bought 10 contracts at 1087 and the market rallies, rising 10 handles—or 1,000 points—to 1097. Your sense of the market, the strong bidding from buyers, and the technical price charts all tell you that the market is going higher. But you want to protect yourself in case of a quick reversal. So you put in a sell stop order at

1092. If the market suddenly declines to that price, your 10 contracts will be sold and you'll have a 500-point profit. An important assumption here is that your stop order was actually filled at that price. In a wild market, in which the buyers or sellers suddenly disappear, an order can't be executed if there is no one to take the other side of that trade. Good brokers will do the best they can to fill the order, but they can't perform miracles. The sell stop order at 1092 won't be executed if, as you had hoped, the market rallies from 1097 all the way to 1100 or so. You take your profits and cancel the sell stop.

But let's say you bought 10 contracts at 1087, believing the market was going higher, and then suddenly negative news causes a quick decline, and all the sellers rush in. You get out with a small predetermined loss—400 points—because you had a sell stop in at 1083. Based on your risk level, you were willing to risk 400 points, but saved yourself from a freefall.

The key to successful trading—whether you're a two-lot trader or a fund manager—is timing and money management. You may believe that S&P futures are headed back to 1065 from 1050, but the question is when to initiate that trade. Based on price alone, you could buy at 1060 in hopes of the market going immediately to 1065. But you don't know what external forces or breaking news might suddenly push the market down to 960, before it rallies back and eventually hits 1065. Even with all the technical analysis in the world, there is no way of knowing for certain how the market will perform. The best policy when a trade is initiated is to put a stop order in—with a broker if you're trading off the floor or in your head if you're standing in the pit—as protection in case the market moves against you.

It all sounds so simple on paper. But there are many complicating factors. There is the unpredictability of the market itself, which can make the bravest trader quiver. And then there are the human elements. On one hand, there is greed, which all but the most saintly of humans must deal with. The potential for making money is so great that greed can overcome judgment. At the same time, to be a trader, you know you will have losses—and sometimes substantial ones. This acceptance of the inevitability of loss runs contrary to human nature and the greed factor. It would be like telling people that, if their performance at work was poor one week, they would have to give their bosses a portion or all of their paychecks. For traders, the market is our boss, and it doesn't ask for the money—it just takes it.

A trader I know was seeing a psychiatrist to help him in the pit. Every week they went over the ground rules of discipline, handling risk, and so forth. The psychiatrist couldn't believe that, based on what he was hearing, trading was so difficult. So my trader friend told the psychiatrist to set up a trading account and come down to the floor one day. That's what the psychiatrist did, and within three months he had emptied that trading account. He practiced psychiatry with a newfound respect for traders.

Rookie traders make the same mistakes over and over again. They buy a two-lot at 1097 even. The market drops 400 points and then rallies up to 1098. In the end, they've made $500 on the trade, but they faced a potential loss of $2,000. They're so happy that a loser turned out to be a winner that they miss an important point. When you're scalping profits, the risks and the rewards are supposed to be equal. Had the traders used mental stops, they could have exited a losing trade with a small loss of a few hundred—before it turned into a few thousand.

Instead, they held onto a losing position, wishing and hoping that the market would turn their way. In trading, there's no such thing as wishing and hoping—only the sometimes bitter reality of the market. In this case, they broke a rule, but got away with it, which only reinforces a bad habit. And, remember the old saying, you can break the rules and get away with it, but eventually the rules will break you.

I have a friend who, after he sold his business, decided he would try floor trading. He was supposed to be in the pit with me, learning to scalp. Instead, one day when I wasn't around, he bought one contract outside the pit. The market immediately tanked. What did he do? He bought another contract, figuring that the market had to be near the bottom and he'd make a profit when it rose again. But the market kept falling until he was out $15,000 on a two-lot. In the end, the market finally bottomed out. My friend bought yet another contract and, after the market rallied a little, he got out of the whole mess with about a $2,000 loss, which could have been far worse. He broke another rule of trading, adding a losing position in a practice called "averaging." But, it's a dangerous practice that, in time, will catch up with you.

"I'll tell you, Lew," my friend later confessed to me, "when the market was going down, all I wanted to do was find the Merc computer room and pull the plug on the place."

Stops can also be used to initiate market positions. If the technical price charts indicate that 1087 is a neutral area with no real direction, you don't want to trade there. This is what the television market commentators mean when they say investors are on the sidelines. But, if the market hits, say, 1091, you want to be in the market for what's likely to be a rally. So you put a buy stop order in at 1091. When the price rises to that point, it becomes a market order. Again, if 1087 is neutral but at 1083 the market turns bearish, you put a sell stop order in at that price to go short.

And, speaking of going short, this is the one strategy that most professional traders cling to once they learn it. There is a belief among many traders that the market goes down faster than it goes up. A trading card is divided in two, with a column for the buys—marked in blue—and one for the sells—marked in red. I know traders who never write on that blue side unless it's to take off a short position. I am a contrarian in this regard. I like to be a buyer and, if you look at the charts, this has been a 200-year bull market (give or take a few corrections). I believe prices rise just as quickly as they crash. If you disagree with me, remember that quiet Thursday afternoon, October 15, 1998. It looked like the market was going to do nothing in particular all the way to the close. Then the Federal Reserve unexpectedly announced a quarter-point cut in the discount rate. The market took off like a rocket. Traders who were caught short scrambled to cover their positions in a market with no sellers. S&Ps shot up 52 handles—or 5,200 points—in five minutes without a single down tick, a move that we believe was unprecedented in the history of this contract.

This was one of those few times when a buy stop wouldn't have helped a trader with a short position. When the market explodes upward, there's nothing a broker can do to execute a stop order until the sellers start offering again. The only hope is to have good money management skills so that you never risk so much capital on one trade that you face a potential wipeout.

A volatile market, like S&Ps, allows you to trade smaller quantities and reap profits that are commensurate with those netted with large positions in a less volatile one. For example, you can buy 10 S&P contracts at 1087 and sell them 100 points higher for a $2,500 profit. I remember when I traded eurodollars for a while, the average move was 10 or 12 points. It wasn't uncommon for large institutions to bid 93.00 for 12,000 contracts and offer 7,000 at 94.00. To make that same $2,500 profit, you'd have to trade 100 eurodollar contracts—each worth $1 million in U.S. dollars on deposit in Europe. I was accustomed to trading large, so that kind of position didn't scare me. Then, one day I realized I was long 3,000 eurodollar contracts—a position worth $3 billion! In this low-volatility market dominated by large institutional players, it was no trouble to buy and sell 3,000 contracts. But I had a huge risk exposure if, for example, the Federal Reserve should suddenly cut interest rates. That risk far outweighed the profit I was poised to make. I exited the position with a scratch, or no profit, went back to S&Ps, and never traded eurodollars again.

My discipline and the technical knowledge I developed over the years made me not only a better trader, but an expert order filler as well. By the mid-1980s, I was the lead broker in the S&P pit, and customers would often ask me to rely on my own judgment to fill their orders. I began to get disregard tape (DRT) orders from customers. That meant they wanted me to buy or sell contracts based on my discretion, rather than what the market was doing.

One day, Jimmy, a floor trader in the pork bellies pit, was trading from the short side in the S&P pit. But, to protect himself, he had placed a 50-contract buy stop above the market to exit the position in case of a rally. "Do you want me to work that buy stop for you?" I asked him.

"Sure," he told me, and headed back to the pork bellies pit.

S&Ps hit his stop price, but at that point, a lot of sellers came into the market again, and I decided not to execute Jimmy's buy order. The market turned and headed lower, eventually making Jimmy a $75,000 profit.

Later that day, Jimmy asked me about that 50-contract buy stop. "I didn't execute it," I told him. "I felt the market was going back down."

Jimmy thanked me profusely. He couldn't believe I would have worked that order for him when all he had asked me to do was keep an eye on it. I did a good deed for a fellow trader, and I earned a friend for life. There were some customers, however, who didn't, in my view, appreciate my skill. That was the case with "Vince," a retired pit trader, who traded exclusively off the floor. He and I had several acquaintances in common, but had never met. I knew he was a very disciplined trader, using strict buy and sell stops. He was very technically oriented, relying on price patterns as his guide rather than a gut-level sentiment about the market.

I worked a few orders DRT for Vince, which he appreciated because I was able to give him better fills than he expected. Then one day, in a wild and choppy market, I had a buy order from Vince, say at 87.00; however, the market had rallied up so quickly, I couldn't find a seller to execute the trade until 89.00. That was the best fill I could get for him. Vince wasn't satisfied, however, and he demanded the time-and-sales record. Time and sales is the Merc's reconstruction of every trade made during the day. But, the record is two-dimensional, showing prices at various times. In reality, what we traders experience in the pit in a wild and chaotic market can be very different from the time-and-sales record. On this day, the time-and-sales record showed the price rising steadily from 87-even to 87.30, 87.50, a brief down tick to 87.30, then a rise to 87.60, 87.80, 89.00, and on up. Seeing that record, Vince thought he should have been filled on the down tick at 87.30.

The RB&H desk manager was nervous when he passed on the bad news to me: Vince was demanding a $10,000 adjustment out of my pocket on the trade. I called Vince and tried to explain the situation, which he, as a retired floor trader, knew well. There was no way I could get a fill at that down tick, and I was lucky to have pulled it off at 89-even. Vince wouldn't hear a word of what I had to say and, in the end, I paid the $10,000.

After that, I never worked another order DRT for Vince. I gave him exactly what he asked for and, when he wanted something worked at the market, I didn't put myself out for him. Vince noticed the difference immediately. "What's going on with my fills?" he complained to me.

"What was going on with that $10,000 adjustment?" I replied coolly. "Look, if you don't want to use me, that's fine. But if you do, you have to know I'm filling orders the best I can. You didn't complain when I got you better fills than you asked for."

In late 1986, I gave up the customer deck and became purely a local, trading only for myself. I was making an average of $1 million a year by this time, but only about 10 percent of my income was coming from order filling. I knew the deck was more of a hindrance than a help, and I could see the writing on the wall—the Merc was moving increasingly toward banning dual trading. A few months before, I had given up much of the deck, parceling out the orders to the other brokers with whom I worked. I had kept only the Salomon business, largely because I had such a great relationship with the desk manager, my friend Matt Wolf. The other reason was, as an order filler, I could stand on the top step of the pit, which, at five feet nine and a half inches, was a valuable vantage point for seeing and being seen.

Then the Merc instituted the top-step rule. Only brokers who filled customer orders and did not trade at all for themselves were allowed to stand on that top step. The locals and the dual traders had to stand further down into the pit. I made my move—literally—stepping down to the second step and giving up the deck. Then came 1987, my first full year as a local, when I was part of history—although I missed Black Monday—and made $4.5 million, solely by trading my own money. I was fortunate to reap the benefit of unprecedented market moves of a magnitude that was not seen again until late 1998. In terms of percentage of the market value, however, nothing has yet compared with the Crash of 1987.

As a local, my interest in charting and technical analysis grew. I wanted every advantage I could have to become a better trader. That advantage was knowledge. The more I could learn about what made the markets move, the better prepared I would be. In 1988, I had an opportunity to invest in the original rights of legendary market chartist and technical William D. Gann. Gann was, and still is, market wizard, guru, and mystic all rolled into one. I was fascinated by Gann and jumped at the chance to own his charts and overlays.

Gann was a stock and commodity trader whose theories on technical analysis of the markets are still used—and debated—today. He was also a lecturer and an author, sharing some, but certainly not all, of his insights into the markets. Some of his rules were seemingly simple. In his book, the 1951 edition of *How to Make Profits in Commodities* (Gann Financial Classics Library, Chicago, Illinois), W. D. Gann lists the "qualifications for success": knowledge, patience, nerve, good health, and capital. As basic as those attributes sound, they are truly the foundation of any successful trader.

I believe, as Gann did, that you can never know too much about the markets. Knowledge, as they say, really is power. Patience is the backbone of what I call knowing when to pull the trigger. It takes experience and discipline to know when to trade and when to wait. Or, as Gann wrote, "You should learn to trade on knowledge and eliminate the fear and hope. When you are no longer influenced by hope or fear, and are guided by knowledge you will have the nerve to trade and make profits."

Nerve—without guts in the pit, there's no chance for survival. You need what I described earlier as a competitor's heart, the dedication to go the distance and the drive to overcome the obstacles. Good health is a necessity because of the physical demands the pit places on you. It takes stamina to stand in an open spot for hours on end, yelling your lungs out. I've come back from the pit some days feeling like I've been through a triathalon. As for capital, nobody makes it long-term if they are undercapitalized. Had I not made that advantageous error in the gold pit that netted me $57,000, I don't know what would have happened to me as a trader.

What I extrapolated from reading Gann was his philosophy—that every part was related to a larger whole. And every whole was, in turn, part of a larger whole, and so on. This Zen-like concept of everything being part of a greater whole was the foundation of his mathematic principles. Because, in Gann's view, everything was related, he believed it was possible to apply mathematical ratios and constants to virtually anything. He charted and studied hundreds of markets from silk to black pepper, wheat to cottonseed oil.

I invested in the Gann charts with two icons of the trading industry, Jack Sandner and Les Rosenthal, a former chairman at the Chicago Board of Trade. Les, who headed Rosenthal & Company, which later became Rosenthal Collins, had been a great trader in his day. Our idea in 1988 was to use the Gann charts to form an IB, or introducing broker, business in commodities. Although I went along with the business plan, my real interest in the deal was to have access to the Gann charts. In addition, I wanted to be associated with successful men like Jack and Les, from whom I could learn more. In meetings, I often sat with my mouth shut, just listening, trying to pick up ideas through osmosis.

One of the most important lessons they taught me was about investing in other businesses. All traders, in time, look for a business venture or investment to serve as a stable source of income, to supplement the profits they reap in the pit and offset the losses. These ventures also help provide for the day when traders finally leave the pit. With the amount of money that traders make, it's easy for us to be lured into investing in other ventures. There are always plenty of people with ideas looking for investors with capital. The problem is that even the most promising businesses cannot possibly post the same kinds of three- and four-digit returns as trading, and they take time and energy away from what we traders do best.

After a few months, it was clear that the retail business in commodities had dried up after the Crash of 1987, and we agreed to disband on a friendly basis. Still intrigued by the Gann charts, I bought the rights from the other investors and hired our technician to work for me.

Many traders on the floor subscribed to charting and technical analysis services, which provided a report every morning. With a technician working full-time for me, I had access to market analysis that was updated continually. I used a runner to bring me messages from the technician whenever the market neared a key point. Then, when pagers were introduced, we used them to communicate. He'd send me a numeric message right into the pit, signaling me about a key technical level.

Although I have the utmost respect for the market technicians I've worked with over the years, I know that you can't rely on the charts and computer systems alone. Market technicians are experts in reading the market, but in most cases they are not good traders. All that market knowledge and analysis is insightful, but you can't have too much of a good thing. There comes a point when you have to stop looking at the charts and stop analyzing all the ticks and pull the trigger to execute a trade. Perhaps, they are too intelligent and their thoughts get in the way. They try to factor in one more price or examine one more trend line, looking to nail down the last variable before making a decision. Then the market makes another move.

Today, my clerks and I use wireless phones to communicate between the pit and the upstairs office, giving us an instantaneous link between the charts and the trading floor. I have also moved from strictly charting to using computerized trading models. It began when I hired a technician in the early 1990s who was versed in artificial intelligence, which enabled a computer to read the market and identify certain key price levels based on a host of variables. Over the years, trading systems were developed that looked at price patterns such as moving averages, Elliot wave theory, candlesticks (an intricate form of bar charting), breakouts, stop-reversals, and momentum. What artificial intelligence allows you to do is combine all these variables—and a host of others—into one trading system. My company has a proprietary, state-of-the-art computerized trading system that combines 18 programs into one. The computer literally picks and chooses among the variables to identify key price points for trades to be executed. These sophisticated systems can generate high-probability trades that may be executed only a few times a year or a few times a month. Others identify more numerous day trading opportunities.

The technical analysis I use has become increasingly sophisticated, but I never strayed from my own fundamentals—market sentiment and floor-order flow. This combination of the trading floor and technical analysis has been my hallmark as a trader. Even today, while I move increasingly to computerized trading, I believe you cannot underestimate the insights gained from reading the trading floor. The technical price charts serve as a kind of navigation guide, but they are not the complete picture. Standing in that pit, you can sense the mood of the other traders. You watch the order flow from the brokers, which gives you an indication of the underlying fundamentals. And, there is simply the gut instinct that I've developed over the years.

Technicians I have worked with sometimes refer to me, affectionately, as "the gypsy." There are times when I execute a trade based on my instinct and experience—and not based solely on technical analysis (although I do not ignore it). After 18 years of trading, I have simply developed an ability to read and interpret the market that can't be traced in any chart, bar graph, or computer program.

I have always been more than a scalper. I traded with conviction, a belief in where the market is heading. There are scalpers in the pit who never trade with an opinion, who do very, very well. They make six-figure incomes by trading tick-to-tick. They wait for the big customer orders that temporarily knock the market out of equilibrium. They jump in, buying the momentary lows or selling when the market ticks a little higher. The profits per trade may be small, but they are consistent and add up quickly, and the risk is relatively low. This is the analogy I use to describe this kind of trading: It's like you're some kind of Gumby baseball player, able to keep your left foot on first base and stretch your right leg all the way around the bases to home plate while a fly ball is in the air. When the ball goes over the fence, you take your foot off first and snap back to home. You scored, but you were safe all along.

That was never my style. I started developing opinions about market direction and sentiment. While I still scalped profits, I would trade with a bullish or bearish bias. My conviction and my track record for reading the market correctly attracted the attention of other major players in the pit, traders for the big brokerage houses or who worked for money managers like Paul Tudor Jones. Days when the market had no apparent direction, I'd be in there bidding or offering aggressively. Brokers would report the market activity to the desk managers, who wanted to know one thing: Who was bidding or offering? Very often that reply would be "LBJ."

Much of the conversation on the trading floor is done with hand signals, facial expressions, and lipreading. The place is too noisy to be heard more than a few feet and you certainly can't leave your spot in the pit to yell in somebody's ear. So, when a desk manager asks "Who's bidding?" he signals the question. The reply from the broker on the floor is often a signal. For Merrill Lynch, the signal is a clenched fist with index and little finger raised to make the horns of the bull—Merrill's symbol. For E. F. Hutton, the signal was a tug on the ear. ("When E. F. Hutton talks, people listen. . . .") For me, the signal was to hold my breath and puff out my cheeks. I don't know what that was supposed to mean. Maybe they thought I was a windbag. I never asked anybody how that facial expression was associated with me. Then again, maybe I don't want to know. . . .

Other traders began to shadow me, buying when I bought and selling when I sold. So I had to develop a few tricks along the way to disguise what I was doing. Say, I wanted to go short or to exit a long position. I knew if I started selling, then a lot of people would jump on my bandwagon, pushing the market lower, and it would be harder for me to sell at a high price. So I'd use brokers to sell my contracts. For example, I'd put in orders to sell 10 contracts at 70, another 10 contracts at 80 and 20 contracts at 90. Then I'd starting bidding as if I were going long. If the market was at 50, I'd begin bidding 55. Other traders would join in, bidding at 60. Then, I'd bid 60. Then, they'd bid 70, and my first sell order would be executed. Once that trade was done, I'd bid 70 and someone else would bid 75 and then 80, and my other order would be filled. Then I'd bid 80 and somebody would bid 90 and the last of my contracts would be sold.

Although I've enjoyed a successful career as a trader, including more than a decade as a local, I have not done it all myself. I have worked with some very good people over the years, many of whom have gone on to become successful traders themselves. I would be remiss if I did not salute one person in particular, Joni Weber. Joni, who has been a clerk, a broker, and a trader at the Merc since 1969, has worked for me for about 15 years. She used to stand beside me for years in the pit and keep track of my trades. She tells the story that, back when I first began in the S&P pit, she had to be talked into working for me. I was so arrogant and brash that there was no way she was ever going to work for me. Finally, as a favor to my mentor, Maury Kravitz, she agreed to work part-time for me and then became my full-time assistant.

When it comes to rectifying outtrade, straightening out errors, and reconstructing trades, there is nobody better than Joni. And, over the years, I have had complete trust in her ability and her judgment. More important, when I went through my difficult times, including when a traumatic divorce proceeding sometimes took my mind off the market, Joni was the one person outside my family in whom I could put my complete trust. The highest praise I can give her is that I always knew we were a team, that her best interest and mine were the same.

For years, Joni assisted me in the pit. When the Merc said that only members could stand in the pit, I bought an additional membership so she could stand beside me. While I traded, fast and furiously, Joni kept track of my cards. In my early days, traders and brokers were allowed to turn their cards in at the end of the day. Then, the rules became more stringent, and we had to turn them in within a certain time frame. Then, the cards had to be numbered in sequence and the name of the trader printed on the top. Because I can sometimes make several trades in succession, buying or selling 10, 20, 30, or even 100 contracts, keeping track of the cards slowed me down. That's where Joni came in.

Seven specific things are required to be written down on the card for every trade: the commodity, the month, the quantity, the price, the time bracket, the badge ID of the other broker or trader on the deal, and his clearing firm. I was notorious for putting down only the bare minimum of details on the cards and then handing them to Joni, who by watching my trades, could fill in the blanks and decipher my hieroglyphics. But, sometimes there would be a scribble or a scrawl that even Joni couldn't figure.

"Hey," she yelled at me, using one of her pet-name expletives for me. "What is this supposed to be?" I'd squint at the card and give her the details.

Or else, after buying 20, then 33, and then 10, and selling 7, another 6, then 15, 30, and then 5, I'd turn to her and ask, "So where am I?"

She'd keep a running tally of the buys and sells, and let me know if I was short, long, or flat.

Together, Joni and I instituted a lot of innovations in pit trading. We hired a clerk just to help us check trades. Say, I sold 30 contracts to a broker. My clerk would then go over to him and confirm that he bought the 30 contracts that I sold. At first, some of the other traders and brokers resented this practice, but then it caught on. Now, virtually everybody has a trade checker in the pit. We all find that it reduces costly outtrades and enables us to address mistakes and errors immediately.

Although nobody can master the market, I learned how to be in sync with it more often than not. The secret comes down to one word: *discipline.* Traders must discipline their bodies and their minds just as athletes do, until certain behaviors become automatic. It's like the football players who practice and practice, and when they walk on the field the plays are second-nature. Golfers practice continually until they can step up to the tee and just swing (a skill that I have yet to master). It's all a matter of muscle memory.

Traders have to train their brains to bring them through each trade. With every win and every loss, traders must examine their behaviors and reinforce the elements of a winning strategy. Trading has to become so second-nature that it's done without thinking. As with the athletes, this kind of trading ability comes only through discipline. I had learned to train my body when I was a kid. But when it came to training my mind, that was a lesson that was brought home to me in college.

For most 18-year-olds, away from home for the first time, college is a major transition point in their lives. For me, it was something else. DePauw University, a school with very high academic standards, was a rude awakening and the biggest transition of my life. When I was a high school football player, I was convinced that I could play pro ball (regardless of the fact that I was only five feet nine and a half). But as a freshman at DePauw, a Division III school, I was among some really great athletes. Within this crowd, I was an average athlete, and only my determination distinguished me. That experience also confirmed that if I wanted to succeed in this world, I needed a good education.

Academically, there was no more just "getting by" for me. I realized I had to make a concerted, conscientious effort to get an education. I was determined to succeed at college if it killed me; I owed it to myself and to my parents. It was like a day of reckoning for me. In my father's words, it was time "to put up or shut up." I didn't want to disappoint my parents, especially my father who had been forced to leave college after one year. I wanted to go the distance.

My life consisted of classes, football practice, and then three to four hours a night at the library, trying to absorb what I didn't know. If I was going to truly make something of myself, I had to discipline my mind as well as my body. I began to read the newspaper for more than just the sports scores. When the Middle East conflict dominated the news headlines, I wanted to know why. I took a course on the history of the Middle East. Perhaps the most important lesson I learned was that there was more than one way to look at anything. The world was not black and white as I had always perceived it; there was a lot of gray.

I was a political science major because I planned to go to law school. But, by nature, I gravitated toward economics, which was headed by Professor Ralph Gray, who had been an advisor to President Eisenhower. The economics department was the toughest on campus, so I stayed away until I was a junior. Then, I took Professor Gray's introductory course. His opening line the first day of class was, "Look at the guy next to you. He's either going to drop this course or fail it." Keynesian economics, supply and demand—it all made sense to me. The only thing that I scratched my head over, laughingly, was a term that kept popping up: widgets. Company X makes widgets . . . Company Y buys widgets . . . What, I wanted to know, was a widget?! Now, I know a "widget" is just a term for a hypothetical product. But, I didn't want to deal in the hypothetical; I wanted real-life examples.

Years later, when I was at the Merc, somebody tapped me on my shoulder in the trading pit. There was a fellow trader, who had also graduated from DePauw, standing with none other than Professor Gray. "Hello, Lewis. I hear you're doing very well," my old professor said. "It's good to see you."

Seeing him instantly brought back my college days when I was learning economic theories. Much of what I learned then I could see played out every day in the market. I pointed to the mob of chaos around me. "You see all these traders? They understand supply and demand," I told Professor Gray. "But I have to tell you. None of these guys has ever seen a widget!"

There was more to my education at DePauw than just the academics. My world, which had been largely viewed through the eyes of an Italian-American from Chicago, suddenly broadened. Looking back, this transition is comical. A rough-talking guy from Chicago, I was like an alien from some distant planet as I walked a college campus with the sons and daughters of some of the wealthiest families in the Midwest as well as farmkids from Indiana.

When I arrived at DePauw, I didn't know what a Hoosier was, and I sure as hell never played "euchre." The whole world looked as foreign to me as, truthfully, I looked to them. Thankfully, I hooked up with a kid named Jay from Morgan Park, whose father was a Chicago cop, and another Chicago kid named Nick, who was the son of a dentist. Then came the "rush" to join a fraternity. The three of us decided to stick together and join a house that would accept all of us. That turned out to be Phi Gamma Delta, or FiJi for short. While each of the houses was known for something—a home for the Preppies or the Jocks—FiJi was dominated by football. There were 60 guys at FiJi, about 35 of whom were on the football team, and half of those 35 were from the Chicago area. But, many were from Winnetka, Lake Forest, and other preppy places, which were a far cry from the blue-collar suburb where I grew up.

After settling into the FiJi house, it was time for the first mixer—a kegger—and a chance to check out the coeds. I was 18 and had honed my social skills at the clubs on Rush Street in downtown Chicago. So I put on my tight Sicily jeans, my nick-nick shirt, and three tiers of gold chains. I stepped into my platform shoes and blew my hair dry for about 40 minutes. When I walked into the party downstairs at the frat house, I knew I looked good. Everyone else stared at me as if I had stepped off a spaceship. All around me were kids with straight-legged jeans, Izod shirts, clogs, and Topsiders. Beyond looking like a guy from Mars, my way of speaking—very rough, very Chicago—was like nothing they'd ever heard before. I saw a few glances in my direction and heard a couple of giggles from the girls. They didn't quite know what to make of me.

I stared back at my fellow students with some of the same amazement. When I spoke, I sounded like a tough guy out of a movie. When they spoke, they sounded to me like the twanging of a banjo. We were all speaking English, but it was sure some other kind of dialect. "Are you Eye-talian?" they'd ask me.

"Yeah. I'm from Eye-taly," I'd reply.

As the night wore on, the differences between me and my fellow students became more pronounced, in direct proportion to the amount of alcohol consumed. A look or a remark became a provocation for one side or the other. "Boy, I'm going to take you outside and give you a whoopin'," somebody twanged in my direction.

Outside? I thought. Where I came from nobody went outside to settle anything. "You don't have to go outside," I replied. Then we rumbled, Chicago-style.

When my Dad came to visit me for the first father-son fraternity house dinner, I pulled him aside. "We gotta go shopping," I said to him.

"Why? What's wrong with the way you look?"

"Dad, take a look around. I don't exactly fit in. It's cramping my style."

Dad understood the importance of that, and took me shopping for straight-legged jeans and Izod shirts.

My father became the toast of the FiJis. I remember sitting around the table with my frat brothers and their fathers, who boasted, "Your grandfather was a FiJi. I was a FiJi. Now you're a FiJi, and I hope some day your son is a FiJi." When they asked my father about his background, he joked, "Me? I was a Phi Gamma Ghetto." They loved my Dad for his humor and his hospitality. Whenever he'd come to visit, he'd ask any of my friends whose fathers weren't there that weekend to join us for dinner. It wasn't uncommon for Dad to take a half-dozen guys out with him.

At FiJi, my pledge father was George, the captain of the football team who had gone to DePauw on the G.I. Bill. While it was George's job to look out for me and teach me the ways of being a good "FiJi," we became friends. He even poured his heart out to me after his girlfriend, Melanie, left him soon after she joined him at DePauw. I was sympathetic to George's broken heart, and I commiserated with him each time he told me he saw Melanie talking to another guy. And I let him know if I saw Melanie talking or walking with somebody. I confess that I was especially diligent in giving George the report if the guy was somebody I didn't like. My real motivation, of course, was to keep George's mind on his life and off mine.

"She was walking with *him?*" George would ask.

"Yes, she was."

"Do you think she's going out with him?"

"I can't say for sure. But it wouldn't surprise me."

If the guy was an offensive football player who had gotten under my skin, I wouldn't spare any of the details when I told George, a defensive player. Those guys could not understand why George was so hard on them at the next football practice. In the blocking and tackling drills, they got the impression that George wanted to kill them.

College also smoothed out some of my rough edges, while not compromising who I was or where I came from. I learned to adapt and to change, to mold myself to my circumstances. That's why, even today, I can be at home at an international investment conference, on the golf course with my buddies, or laughing with somebody from the old neighborhood.

I saw that to adapt was to survive in a Darwinian sense, but also in a Machiavellian one. If I was to distinguish myself, if I was to be a leader and not a follower, I had to learn to accept change to survive and, in time, to thrive. As a trader, this discipline has served me well. Although I have gained confidence as a trader, I know that I can never lose my respect for the market.

Just when you think you have it all figured out and you are clever enough to simply know *where* the market is going and *when,* reality will come along and slap you in the face. It has happened to me, and I'll swear, complain, and kick myself for the better part of a day, and then I'll be grateful for the wake-up call. You go back to the basics, never forgetting to respect the market's own sense of timing.

After nearly two decades in the S&P pit, I've seen some very good traders grow up around me. Today, there is some very stiff competition from traders who truly know their stuff. There is a sort of locker-room respect among traders, even between fierce competitors. The risks that a trader faces each and every day can only be comprehended by another trader. That's why, if I could take a moment to salute anyone, it would be my fellow traders. Whether we're friends or bitter rivals, the good traders respect each other and our abilities.

The S&P pit is like no other. Everybody who wants to trade invariably wants to be part of the S&P, a market too big to be tamed or underestimated. It is truly an animal unto itself. I remember when I was executing trades for customers and I received my first 2,000-contract buy order. I suspected that a buy order of that magnitude would push the market upward, but it hardly budged. Then another day, a 20-lot order cracked the market 400 points. There seemed to be no logic, rhyme, or reason.

Those huge, 2,000-contract orders, however, gave me an interesting insight into how institutional players were using the S&P contract—portfolio insurance. They'd be buying the futures and selling the cash—or vice versa—to hedge the value of their stock portfolios.

The trading lifestyle, the prospect of big money and what looks like a relatively short work day is appealing to more than a few people. But, what they don't often comprehend is the stress level that we have to stomach each time we go into that pit, whether we're trading for our own accounts or filling orders for customers.

I use a lot of sports metaphors to describe trading, but for those outside the profession it may be the closest comparison. In the pit, you're on your own. If you screw up, you don't have anyone to blame—and certainly not the market. On the good days, you feel like a superstar. But, on the bad ones, you want to crawl out of the pit on your belly so you can go unnoticed. Remember that old *Wide World of Sports* slogan? "The thrill of victory and the agony of defeat." Believe me, there are days when every trader—myself included—can identify with that guy who fell off the ski jump.

I can, and do, continue to make a great living trading in the pit. Yet, for me, there is no mental stimulation or intellectual gratification from only pit trading. All you can do is perfect your discipline to the point that you become robotic. Once you reach that point, where reflexive actions take place of real thought, you can become a great pit trader. For me, however, there came a point when trading in the pit was not enough. And truthfully, at 41 years of age, I don't want to be standing in the pit still, pushing and shoving and having guys sweat on me. The time has come to contemplate life out of the pits, although not out of trading, to be assured. But, I'm taking my day trading techniques off the floor and upstairs in a room full of computers.

As the attention in the trading world is focused increasingly on electronic trading, and away from the pits, it is perfect time for me personally and professionally. Just as when I began charting markets or hired a technician to assist me, I had to stay abreast of the change. I always knew I wanted the most market information that I could get my hands on. Now, I'm gathering as much market innovation as I can.

I'm the kind of person who doesn't worry about making a living. I don't want to sound boastful or cavalier. Believe me, I have plenty of things in my life to worry about. But, when it came to making money, taking care of my family and myself, I was determined to do well. Unfortunately, too many people in this world end up getting pigeonholed in a job, doing the same thing year after year. It's not because of a lack of skill nor, I believe, because there aren't opportunities. What holds most people back is fear of failure. I have never feared failure, not because I think I'm *always* going to succeed. I've been in plenty of business ventures in which I lost money, wasted my time, or both. The difference for me is that I am not devastated by setbacks. Perhaps this trait is what separates a lot of successful traders from the rest. I've never looked at a setback like it was a catastrophe. In the same vein, you can't look at a losing trade like it was a disaster. You take your loss, process what happened, and then go back to the fundamentals. Otherwise, you might as well hang up your trading jacket.

I still put on my trading jacket, although not as often as in the old days. My trading firm and I will have a presence on the floor as long as the pit exists. But, the balance is shifting. When I was a full-time pit trader, I used the computers and charts to confirm what I saw happening in the pit; today, I'm trading increasingly by the computer, and using the activity in the pit as the confirmation. No longer trading only for myself, I am managing client money. It is a natural extension of what I have been doing for the past 18 years, and an opportunity for clients to capitalize on my expertise. It is nothing more, or less, than the next metamorphosis in my life.

CHAPTER 8

Trading Goes Electronic

There was hardly a sound in the Italian trading room except for the click of the computer keyboard and muffled voices of traders talking with each other. It could have been any financial office except for the unmistakable tension in the air as traders focused intently on their computer screens, watching the markets. As I watched, traders bought and sold lira and Italian stock futures, entering orders on the computer screen by maneuvering the mouse and tapping on the keyboard. If I didn't know better, I would have guessed the traders in that Milan bank's trading room were doing nothing more than sending e-mail or surfing the Internet. But, as I watched the men and women at the computer screens in the trading room of that Italian bank, I knew I was getting a glimpse of a new breed of trader.

When I went to the Chicago Mercantile Exchange 18 years ago, I learned to trade in the pit. This physical world of pit trading, where brokers and traders scream bids and offers at each other, is largely the realm of the young and the physically fit. And, no sexism intended, the vast majority of players in the pit are men. But in that Italian trading room and in offices in Switzerland and elsewhere in Europe, I saw the next generation of traders. For them there never was nor would there ever be a pit, a physical place where they went to trade. All they needed was a computer, the right software, and a live connection to the market. It didn't matter if they were in Milan, Paris, London, Zurich, Brussels, or anywhere else. For the first time, I saw clearly that the futures exchange could be brought to the traders.

As I saw on that recent trip to Europe, electronic exchanges do not require a physical locality, merely the technology to trade. If electronic trading expands in the United States, the same will be true for American traders—regardless of age, gender, or physical stamina. Whether they are trading U.S. futures contracts electronically or, if U.S. regulators allow it some day, accessing European electronic exchanges, it won't matter if they are in Chicago or New York, Seattle or Atlanta, or any place in between.

For the sake of those outside the futures industry, it may be necessary to draw the distinction between an electronic exchange and computerized trading. An electronic exchange is an automated system that allows buys and sells to be matched without a human interface to complete the trade. This "black box," as electronic exchanges are sometimes called, replaces the trading floor entirely. Computerized trading, on the other hand, simply means that a trader sits at a screen instead of standing in the pit. When I'm trading S&Ps off the floor, I watch the tick-by-tick action on the screen, which reflects the price at which contracts are being bought and sold on the Merc floor. The ticks on the screen are not trades that are made electronically; rather, they reflect the action in the pit in which buyers and sellers come together in a display of pure capitalism.

Perhaps the biggest difference between an electronic exchange and open outcry is that electronic trading provides a playing field in which all participants have the same vantage point and pay the same commissions. There is no human emotion in the electronic market except your own. On the floor, traders and brokers have a bird's-eye view of the order flow. That advantage is what comes with the price of membership to an exchange. In an electronic venue, however, buy and sell orders are entered anonymously and executed without any-one—except the two parties directly involved—knowing who was doing the bidding and offering. Although proponents of electronic trading favor such anonymity, I believe it runs against the grain of one of the basic tenets of futures trading. The trading floor is an open auction in which all bids and offers are made publicly for all to see and hear.

As a floor trader, this transparency was especially important when a major economic report, such as U.S. unemployment statistics, was due to be released. Traders on the floor tracked large orders executed by brokers on the floor, knowing that institutional players were taking position in advance of the "numbers," as we refer to these reports. Clearly, some institutions analyzed trends such as unemployment figures and made their own projections. But the question was always raised in our minds: Did someone have access to the numbers a day or two in advance? If that were to occur, it would be easy enough to follow the trail from the broker to the brokerage house to the customer. But what would happen under the cloak of secrecy provided by the anonymity of an electronic system? Would such a cover allow, or even encourage, someone with access to the data in advance to place a trade, knowing that it would be hard to track in such a system?

When it comes to futures trading, I have the bias of being a veteran pit trader who has spent 18 years on the trading floor. I have been a fierce defender of open outcry and the need to pre-serve both liquidity and open access to the market. But my per-spective is changing. I no longer see the pit as the only place to trade, although I do not believe open outcry will be silenced any time soon. Rather, I think we will see a hybrid marketplace in which more futures contracts are traded on a side-by-side basis, meaning both electronically and via open outcry. We've seen side-by-side trading in the Board of Trade's Treasury contracts and with a scaled-down electronic version of the Merc's S&P contract—the E-Mini—which trades during the day while the S&P pit is open. The Merc will soon launch side-by-side trading in eurodollars, and I imagine currencies will be close behind.

In time, I believe every futures contract will trade side-by-side. This will give customers the option to pick what they believe is the most efficient market. Some contracts may eventually become all-electronic, especially highly liquid and low-volatility markets such as eurodollars, bonds, and currencies (although I have some serious concerns about the ability of an electronic marketplace to accommodate a sudden rise in volatility). Agricultural contracts like soybeans, corn, cattle, and pork bellies, which at times are illiquid and volatile, may be offered electronically. But I believe these contracts will continue to favor the pit, in which locals can more easily provide the necessary liquidity when the institutions come to hedge their positions.

Side-by-side trading allows both the futures exchanges and their customers to test-drive electronic trading. Customers can see if electronic trading suits their needs, without weaning themselves completely from the pit—particularly if volatility suddenly increases. The exchanges, themselves, also will be able to address critical issues, from liquidity to latency, while protecting the integrity of our markets. Although I believe the pit, in some fashion, will still have a role in the future, U.S. futures exchanges cannot stand still while the rest of the world forges ahead into electronic trading. Even those of us who have spent our entire careers in the pit must adapt to this new world.

The debate over electronic trading goes beyond the question of whether traders stand in a pit or sit at a computer. By the same token, the issue of a purely electronic marketplace versus open outcry has nothing to do with tradition or the preservation of the livelihoods of a few pit traders. It all comes down to the best means with which to execute trades efficiently and expeditiously, while preserving equal access to the futures markets.

There is a misconception that floor traders are afraid of computers. Some people perceive that pit traders are like a bunch of blacksmiths shoeing horses, who think the automobile will never catch on. That couldn't be further from the truth. Even under open outcry things have not been static. We have come a long way from the earliest days when bids and offers were written in

chalk on a blackboard. Exchanges have become more sophisticated, both in clearing and monitoring trades and in making
order filling more efficient. At the moment, the single best use of
advanced computer technology at the futures exchange is to
speed the delivery of orders to the pit, cutting the time between
a customer's decision to trade and the execution of that trade to
just seconds. This evolution of pit trading technology will continue because the customers—and the pit traders and brokers—
demand it.

When I started out as an order filler, a customer would call
his broker with an order. The broker would then call the desk
manager on the exchange floor, who filled out an order and
handed it to a runner. The runner brought the order to a broker
in the pit, who executed the trade. Then, certain large customers
were allowed to bypass the brokers and call the desk managers
directly. The desk manager would then write the customer's
order down and hand it to a runner, who brought it to a broker
in the pit. Then came the practice of arbing, or using hand signals, to flash customers' orders into the pit. The desk manager
would arb the order to the broker, who would then execute the
trade. Often, the whole process occurred in a few seconds, while
the customer was still on the phone. Today, technology is being
implemented to speed the order delivery process even further. I
can see the day when every trader and broker in the pit has a
small computer—a little larger than a Palm Pilot personal orga-
nizer—instead of a stack of trading cards. Brokers would receive orders on the screens of these miniature computers, which
would preserve the security of the orders.

These devices also could be used to report a trade instantly
without using a trading card. But, this is no panacea, either. A
broker with a handheld computer cannot compete with the speed
of an experienced trader using traditional trading cards. I can
execute several trades, including buys and sells, in rapid succession, then scribble the bare minimum of details on my trading
card. I hand the card to my clerk, who then fills in the rest of the
details to be reported to the exchange. With a handheld computer, a trader would have to enter all the details of the trade or

else hand it off to a clerk to enter the time, price, quantity, and the badge ID of the person with whom the trade was done.

From the decision to trade to the execution, which I call the front end of the trade, no handheld computer device—even with preprogrammed "hot keys"—can compete with a pit trader using trading cards, I believe. Granted, once the trade is executed, the speed of reporting and clearing the trade is vastly improved using a handheld computer instead of the traditional trading cards. There is an advantage to expediting the back end of the trade from reporting to clearing. This will allow outtrades to be settled more quickly and alert clearing firms to large outstanding positions held by customers that require additional margin commitments. In futures trading, positions are settled before the market opens the next day. In stocks, it may take two or three days for a position to be settled.

This instantaneous reporting of trades using a handheld computer, however, does present another drawback. It becomes difficult, if not impossible, to make an on-the-spot correction in a trade. Say, for example, a broker in the pit is selling at the market and I'm bidding to buy. "Sold you 27, LBJ," the broker signals me. Then a second later, as he mentally tallies up the contract he has sold, the broker signals me, "No! Sold you 24—not 27." The correction is noted on my trading card and reported as a 24-contract trade. With a handheld computer, however, the trade would have been instantaneously entered as a 27-lot, and I would have to do an offsetting trade to reduce the amount of contracts I bought from 27 to 24.

Despite some problems that must be addressed, the efficiency of using a handheld computer to speed order flow undoubtedly outweighs the inconvenience of using it in the pit. Just as we've seen over the years, traders are an adaptive bunch. We adjust to rule changes, sometimes begrudgingly, and we've adapted technology like pagers and wireless headsets to our best use. As I see it, the best feature of handheld computers is the ability to expedite order flow, which will help preserve the competitiveness of open outcry as we move increasingly toward side-by-side electronic and pit trading.

When looking at electronic futures trading, the model is Eurex, the European all-electronic exchange. From its beginning in 1987, Eurex, which was formed by the merger of Frankfurt's Deutsche Terminborse and Soffex of Switzerland, was destined to succeed. For one thing, it was founded by several of the largest banks in Germany that were prominent users of futures to hedge interest rate and currency risks. Say, for example, a large, multinational company goes to a bank for financing of a large transaction, such as a contract to buy raw materials in a foreign currency. Interest rate risk is assumed by the bank when it provides financing over the next several months or years. To offset that risk, banks turn to the futures exchanges to hedge their foreign currency and interest rate risks by taking offsetting positions by buying and selling futures contracts. With the banks behind Eurex, it is little wonder that the main futures contract listed on that electronic exchange was the 10-year German bond, or the Bund. When Eurex launched the Bund, it was also trading in an open-outcry format at the London International Financial Futures Exchange (LIFFE). That presented an arbitrage opportunity for speculators, who took advantage of momentary price discrepancies in the Bund quote on Eurex and LIFFE. Eventually, Eurex became the dominant market for the Bund, and today it accounts for all the trading in this contract.

The Bund contract was successful on Eurex not only because of the backing of the major banks that used this contract, but also due to improvements in technology. In addition, an increase in the number of participants made the market more efficient. That had a twofold effect: The spread between the bid and ask—the prices at which to buy and sell—narrowed, and the liquidity increased. Contrary to the belief of some Eurex supporters, the most important factor, I believe, is the underlying low volatility in interest rates and the relative stability of the world economy. This allowed institutional users, in particular, to educate themselves in the workings of an electronic market without the risks associated with a volatile and unpredictable market.

Given the success of the Bund on Eurex, you could easily imagine that similar types of contracts would also trade efficiently in an electronic forum. Contracts such as eurodollars and currency futures seem like good candidates for electronic trading because they are liquid and dominated by institutions, meaning trades could easily by made from customer to customer, or from order filler to order filler. But serious questions remain when it comes to implementing electronic trading. What happens when an orderly market suddenly turns volatile? When more traders come into the pit at an exchange, the floor gets a little more crowded—and noisier. We're shoved shoulder-to-shoulder against each other like a New York City subway car during rush hour. But there are physical constraints to just how many brokers and traders can crowd into the pit.

What happens when there is suddenly a large influx of orders on an electronic exchange? Theoretically, at least, a virtually infinite number of participants can be connected to an electronic trading system, whereas the trading floor has physical constraints. How can an electronic system handle a sudden spike in orders being entered into the system? Anyone who has ever logged onto the Internet knows that when there are a lot of users on-line, the system slows down. The analogy, while simplistic, raises the question about electronic trading. In the pit, 1 dozen or 100 dozen bids and offers can be shouted out simultaneously. Could an electronic exchange give the same access to a rush of bids and offers without a bottleneck that slows trading? And, as more users plug in to the electronic exchange, can computer networks be expanded quickly and smoothly to handle a sudden rush in trading traffic? What happens when the computer network goes down?

In April 1992, an underground wall was breached, allowing the Chicago River to flow into the communication and service tunnels underneath several buildings in downtown Chicago. The Chicago Board of Trade was flooded, but trading was not stopped, although the clearing and reporting of trades was interrupted when the computer system went down. To solve the problem, the Board of Trade used portable computers to record and clear trades. With an electronic exchange, if the black box were suddenly hit by a flood or some other kind of pestilence, would trading cease? What would happen to open positions, particularly in a market that suddenly becomes volatile because of world events?

And, on a philosophical level, as I'll address later in this chapter, futures exchanges must ask themselves what their responsibility will be to the legions of new on-line day traders who want to trade futures on their lunch breaks. What is the industry's responsibility to educate this new player, who may not realize how addicting the adrenaline rush of trading can be—that is, not until it is too late?

Among all the issues to be addressed in electronic trading, perhaps the most critical is volatility. Often a market turns volatile when something unexpected happens, such as a surprise rate cut by the Federal Reserve Board, as we saw on October 15, 1998. The best way to control volatility is to ensure there are ample participants in the market, each with a different opinion based on price levels and fundamental and technical analysis. Having 200 or even 500 customers trading a contract does not help curb volatility if everybody has the same opinion, or if they are all institutions using similar models to gauge how to best hedge their positions. When there are participants with varied opinions, including professional speculators who will take the other side of a trade at the right price, liquidity is ensured and unnecessary volatility is curbed.

Some contracts, such as eurodollars, are dominated by institutions to the near exclusion of the locals. With such large volumes being traded in eurodollars, which has a $1 million face value per contract, many locals are not able to compete. The capital requirements have outgrown the ability of many of the locals to trade large enough lots—often in the hundreds of contracts—to attract the attention of brokers filling orders for institutional clients. Eurodollars tend to be a highly liquid, but low-volatility contract. For example, on one quiet Monday morning, the front month in eurodollars traded in a 6-tick range, with each tick worth one-half point. But, when the Fed cut rates on

October 15, 1998, eurodollars soared, trading in a 40-tick range that day as hedgers and speculators scrambled to buy near-term contracts.

That day, the market participants were undoubtedly grateful for the locals in the eurodollar pit who provided the necessary liquidity to handle the sudden influx of orders. Without the locals, who knows how high eurodollars would have risen. This then begs the question: In a purely electronic forum, would those local participants have been present? Or, would an electronic marketplace, in which buy and sell orders are matched, squeeze out the locals? That would be dangerous, even in a seemingly quiet market like eurodollars, because without sufficient participants price swings become even more exaggerated. The rate cut incident, I believe, illustrates the true value of an open and liquid marketplace. When conditions suddenly become volatile, the integrity of the market is preserved by having a broad base of participants. With ample participants—including speculators and hedgers—the volatility becomes manageable.

Sustained volatility certainly is not a problem in eurodollars because of the low inflationary environment in the United States and the relative stability of interest rates. But, we cannot assume that will always be the case. History teaches us one thing: It repeats itself. When I began trading, the price of gold was $800 an ounce, inflation was around 15 percent, and short-term interest rates topped out at 21 percent. I remember when we sold our house in Lombard, Illinois, we netted a $200,000 profit, which we put in a one-year CD earning 17 percent. That generated $34,000—more than we needed to cover our household expenses for a year.

Who knows what future global economic calamity will cause double-digit inflation or a worldwide recession? Not even Nobel Prize–winning economists could forecast the extent of the Asian financial crisis, the Russian debacle, and their impact on the world. Therefore, we must be assured that an electronic market can handle a surge in both volume and volatility as easily as the pit.

When it comes to the current state of electronic trading, we look to Eurex and its Bund contract as the example. But for the future of electronic trading, we must look to the S&P contract, a highly liquid, volatile, and untamable market that institutions have not—and cannot—dominate. The dynamics of S&Ps are unlike any other, in part because it is based on the stock market, which reacts to anything from a change in interest rates to a warning by a major company about its quarterly earnings—all against the backdrop of a flood of new speculative capital into the market. The S&P contract is unpredictable, making it impossible to determine just how the market will react on any given day to the prevailing fundamental and technical factors.

During my career, I've seen a 2,000-contract order—a lot so large that you'd expect a sharp rise or fall in the market—executed within 20 points. On another day, I've seen a 20-lot trade break the market 400 points. When I began trading, a 20- or 30-point move in the Dow Jones Industrial Average was a notable event. Today, the Dow moves 200 points and nobody blinks. Similarly, the S&P may see a 2,000-point move in any given day. Because of this volatility, a purely electronic forum, I believe, would not be able to accommodate a contract such as S&Ps.

Certainly, there are some people who welcome an electronic forum in S&Ps. Currently, the Merc offers the E-mini, a scaled-down version of the S&P contract valued at $50,000, while its "big brother" contract in the pit is valued at $250,000. Although the E-Mini has been successful in attracting smaller professional participants, the market still favors the liquidity of the pit. This foray, however, into side-by-side trading thanks to the E-Mini illustrates the shortfalls that, in my opinion, will prevent S&Ps from ever becoming a totally electronic contract.

Consider what happened to E-Minis when the Fed cut rates on October 15, 1998. The full S&P contract shot up 5,200 points without a down tick as sellers disappeared and buyers flooded the market. But S&Ps did not trade above 1075 on the floor of the Merc that day. E-Minis, however, went all the way to 1128. In fact, at one point, with an absence of sellers in E-Minis, the computer ticked all the way up to the limit of 9999. The Merc later stepped in and nullified trades that were conducted at 1128, and made 1082 the E-Mini high. As for the sky-high quote of 9999, that price—which was not valid—would have netted some lucky trader an $11 million profit on a one-contract trade! This underscores the shortcomings of the E-Mini due to a lack of liquidity. Without enough participants in the market, liquidity suffers and price movements become exaggerated.

Even on Eurex, liquidity and volatility are concerns in the German stock futures contract, known as the DAX. One European trader told me recently that he refrains from trading more than 20 DAX contracts at a time because of the lack of liquidity. Where liquidity is a concern, the trading pit will continue to dominate the action, even when an electronic alternative is offered. That is why I believe—particularly in illiquid markets or in markets that are liquid, but highly volatile—we need to couple the most sophisticated electronic forum with the traditional open-outcry system.

I'm not saying good-bye to the floor where I have traded for nearly two decades. But, electronic trading continues to make inroads because of the relative ease of point-and-click technology and the ability of sophisticated computer-based exchanges to handle large volumes. Technological breakthroughs will only increase the efficiency of the market. Then, pit traders will have to face the music, whether it's a call to action or a requiem for the trading floor.

Over the years, various arguments have been raised by proponents of electronic trading, such as the ability to reduce trading costs by eliminating floor personnel. Others have cited competitive pressures and, more recently, a perceived need to give open access to all players in the futures market, including retail customers. While electronic trading is in our future, I believe there is a real danger in abandoning our past. The integrity of our markets, which is predicated on open access to all players, cannot be undermined by an attempt to leverage expensive technology across a broader range of products. Real issues still exist that must be addressed before electronic trading can be adopted with complete confidence.

One major issue is latency. In theory, latency levels the play-ing field by assuring that all players, regardless of where they are located, access the trading system with the same speed. Take, for example, GLOBEX, the Merc's after-hours electronic trading system. Latency allows a trader in Asia to place his orders—which in an electronic system are filled on a first-come, first-served basis—as quickly as someone with an office in the exchange building. But not all electronic systems, I'm told, offer the same access to all players. The Board of Trade's Project A supplemental electronic trading system, I have learned, allows traders and brokers located with offices on premises to connect to the system via the exchange's local area network (LAN). This LAN connection, I'm told, sometimes gives these players within the Board of Trade building a two- to seven-second advantage over traders and brokers located elsewhere.

Another concern, from my perspective, is how multiple bids and offers are handled under Eurex's first-come, first-served method of filling orders. Here's an example of something that happens countless times a day in the S&P pit. Say a broker has 300 contracts to sell, and 20 people jump on him to make the trade. He may dole out these contracts to, say, the first 7 people he sees. "Sold! A hundred! Fifty! Fifty! Fifty! Twenty! Twenty! Ten!" In a second, the broker has traded with 7 different people virtually simultaneously. If you're among the traders who were spotted by that broker, you get a piece of the trade; otherwise, you're shut out. But, in either case, you know instantaneously if you've bought some or all of those 300 contracts or not.

In an electronic system, it's an entirely different game. Again, say an order to sell 300 contracts attracts dozens of eager buy-ers, all clicking on their computer screens at once. To keep a competitive advantage, these technotraders are likely to enter their bids as market orders, meaning they'll be executed at the prevailing price. Most likely, to save time, traders will use pre-programmed hot keys on their keyboards to bid at the market. The bids are filled on a first-come, first-served basis and, within a few clicks the market orders are filled. But what happens to the remaining bids on that 300-contract offer? Bids that were entered as market orders are still live in the electronic system and cannot simply be cancelled. They remain market orders that tick higher and higher until they are executed.

As I've said before, execution and recording of a trade is undeniably faster in an electronic venue. But electronic trading cannot compete with the split-second speed of making a decision and executing a trade in the pit. Also, it takes time to load a trade at a specific price in an electronic system. A trader must type in the contracts they are trading, the amount, the price, and so forth. This can take far longer to set up than simply turning to another trader in the pit and yelling, "Sell! 20!"

Another worry about electronic trading is the potential for technical errors. It's probably a safe assumption that all of us, at one time or other, have experienced the frustration of a computer that doesn't seem to be responding. We can't open an e-mail or a file, so we click the mouse again and again and again. . . . Finally, we have 12 copies of Microsoft Outlook open and the computer has frozen up. The same thing can happen in electronic trading. A rumor circulated in November 1998, which was also reported in the press, about large volumes traded in error on Eurex. One story said a trainee accidentally entered an order for 100,000 contracts, thinking he was only practicing and not trading live. What really happened is unclear. But, it raises the concern that too many clicks on the keyboard by a novice could result in a huge—and unintended—position in the futures market.

Just consider the fate of Griffin Trading, which went bankrupt in December 1998 after suffering losses on unauthorized overseas trading. According to the February 1, 1999, edition of the *Financial Times,* in an article by Vincent Boland, entitled "Futures Traders May Seek to Recover $2.7 Million Tied to Griffin Trading Collapse" (published by Dow Jones & Company, Inc.), Griffin was shut down after an independent trader who used the firm to clear his trades incurred $10 million in losses by investing in futures on German government bonds. This incident makes it imperative that Eurex and other electronic exchanges set up safeguards against huge, unauthorized positions being taken in the market. In an anonymous, order-matching system, what would stop two traders from agreeing to enter simultaneously huge offsetting positions—say, a buy and a sell order for 10,000 contracts each—knowing that they would be matched automatically? The traders would split the profit on the winning trade, leave the clearing firm liable for the loser, and then head for some South Pacific hideout with no extradition laws. It's clear to those of us who are veterans in the business that the clearing entities at electronic exchanges must educate themselves on managing risks just as the traditional futures exchanges have done. In open outcry, large trades are very conspicuous.

When I was a partner in a NASDAQ Small Order Execution System (SOES) room, one of our traders put in an order to buy 1,000 shares of stock. When he didn't get a confirmation right away, he hit the button again. There was still no confirmation, so he hit it again. By the time he stopped pressing the button, he had inadvertently bought 15,000 shares of stock.

It may seem fairly simple to prevent these clicking errors with a simple rule: Don't do it. But when the market is moving fast and furiously, you're trying to execute a trade and the computer doesn't seem to be responding, there is a temptation to think there is something wrong with the machine. To keep these kinds of keyboard incidents from becoming catastrophic losses, controls must be built into electronic programs. Traders should not be allowed to trade beyond their limits. It may be up to the trading firm or clearing operation to set that rule. But, it must be in place to protect not only the traders, but the clearing firm that could be liable for the losses should a trader go belly-up.

As much as floor traders over the years have complained about the threat of electronic systems, at the Merc in particular, we have ourselves to blame. Currencies and eurodollars, for example, are institutionally dominated contracts, thanks in part to the low volatility of the market, which has led to a narrow spread between bid and ask prices. An order filler standing on the upper ring, or top step, of the pit with 1,000 contracts to buy can often look across to another broker with 1,000 contracts to sell. There is virtually no incentive to turn to a local who is offering 200 contracts when a trade can be made easily from order to order. This activity has squeezed out the locals, who often do not have sufficient capital to make large trades with institutions.

The dominance of the institutions in eurodollars was reinforced by hard feelings between many brokers and traders at the Merc after dual trading was banned. As a result of the ban, some order fillers lost as much as half of their annual income. This rift prompted some order fillers to avoid trading with locals whenever possible. The plight of the locals in the eurodollar and currency pits prompted the formation of a special "local committee" at the Merc in the mid-1980s, composed of independent futures and options traders. Because of my prominence as a local, I was asked to join the committee. One of the first things the committee did was commission a study of order flow in the pits. The results were astounding. In currencies, about 75 to 80 percent of trades were made between order fillers, excluding the locals. In eurodollars, the percentage was as high as 90 to 95 percent. Surprisingly, locals are involved in roughly one-half of all trades in the highly volatile and liquid S&P contract, which explains why institutions have not been able to dominate this market. This goes to the basic tenet of futures trading: locals are needed to provide liquidity.

After this study came out, a meeting between locals and order fillers was called to forge a peace among the players. I remember Jack Sandner's sobering message at this gathering: "If you want to make a case for these contracts to be traded with the black box, then you keep doing what you're doing and freeze out the locals," Jack chastised the brokers.

In the futures industry, we have known for well over a decade that electronic trading was on the horizon. Today, it is here. Trading has been revolutionized by technology. My firm, for example, uses computer models that employ artificial intelligence to signal trades. These tools allow me to stay in the market long after I want to stand in that pit. But even with the best of technology and in a purely electronic venue, the human element is still crucial in trading. It is the one facet that cannot be replicated by a program or duplicated with artificial intelligence. Intuition and gut instinct are essential for trading, even though they sometimes defy the cold logic of the computer. When it comes to making trades for our clients, we rely on computerized systems to analyze the market and signal the price levels at which we should buy or sell. But, I oversee the execution of the trading, based on my 18 years' experience in the pit. A computer can analyze the market, but only a human being can gauge and predict the psychological factors in the market.

Perhaps it is ingrained in our human nature to fear replacement by the machines we have created, in some twist of the Frankenstein story of the creature overrunning creation. Automation costs jobs, the workers say. Automation improves productivity, management counters. It's an old argument that's not likely to be settled anytime soon. There is also some of this same dynamic in the debate over electronic trading. Even computers with artificial intelligence need a human to program them. But, the exclusivity of the futures industry—you had to be *in* Chicago, New York, London, or wherever to trade—is being challenged by this electronic forum. The players don't have to come to the arena; the game comes to them.

I remember clearly the Merc leadership called a membership meeting in 1987. The announcement came as a complete surprise to me and many others. The Merc was proposing an electronic after-hours trading system—known as Post (Pre) Market Trade, or PMT, which was later called GLOBEX. Both Leo Melamed and Jack Sandner tried to sell the idea to members as a way of preserving the Merc's franchise in financial futures. The electronic trading system, they argued, would actually *save* the trading pit because it would stave off foreign competitors from taking over our contracts. Threats were perceived everywhere.

We only had to look as far as the Chicago Board of Trade, which was concerned about the opening of the Tokyo International Futures Exchange and the potential impact on its leading futures contract, the 30-year U.S. Treasury bond. The Merc had S&P futures locked up because it held the exclusive license to offer this contract. But currencies and even eurodollars, the

Merc leaders claimed, could be traded on foreign exchanges during the hours when the Chicago floor was closed.

The best defense against this perceived threat was an offensive tactic. The only way to preserve the pits was to introduce electronic trading after hours, the Merc leadership told us. Locals and brokers at the Merc did not perceive GLOBEX as a threat because of an agreement that it would be solely after-hours trading for at least 15 years.

To sell the idea of GLOBEX to the trading community, Merc leaders used a powerful incentive: greed. We heard stories of "bucket shops" in Asia, which were nothing more than clubs of investors who traded the S&P contract from delayed quotes, and then settled up in cash among the players at the end of the day. These bootleg operations showed there was demand overseas to trade our contracts. To capitalize on that demand, the Merc leadership envisioned GLOBEX as a revolutionary tool to extend the reach of our contracts during the hours when the trading floor was closed. Greed was instilled with promises that offshore institutions that traded on GLOBEX would access our markets during trading floor hours to unwind or take positions, thus bringing more business to the pit.

GLOBEX was taken to a referendum in early October, just two weeks before the now-fabled Crash of 1987, and approved by a 6-to-1 ratio. "It's unbelievable," Jack Sandner was quoted as saying in an October 8, 1987, *Chicago Tribune* article, entitled "Merc Oks Automated, 24-Hour Mart," by Carol Jouzaitis. The "landslide victory" was "even better than we thought."

In June 1992, GLOBEX went into operation, bringing together the Merc and Reuters Holdings Plc, the British-based news and market data company. The Board of Trade was a latecomer to GLOBEX, and later dropped out in favor of its own electronic Project A. GLOBEX had a slow launch, but it is clearly here to stay as more subscribers join, including Borsellino Capital Management. GLOBEX allows the traders who work with me to expand into night trading, and also enables us to monitor the market on behalf of our investment clients. In that, GLOBEX is another tool to be used by the marketplace.

Just like the technical price charts, arbitrage between cash and futures or futures and options, and all the rest of the market innovations, electronic systems are tools that no trader can afford to ignore.

But electronic trading has made its impact on the exchange floor. Nowhere is this more apparent, perhaps, than in the price of an exchange membership, or seat. As a local trader, my major investments were two memberships at the Merc, which cost me $150,000 for an International Monetary Market (IMM) seat and $150,000 for an International Options Market (IOM) seat. The value of those seats has been a barometer of the value of having locals at a futures exchange. When GLOBEX was announced, the price of exchange seats actually increased. In fact, my IMM seat hit a high of about $950,000 in 1996, while the IOM seat peaked at $400,000. But today, the IOM seat has a cash-price value of between $130,000 and $140,000, while the IMM seat is valued at between $210,000 and $220,000. The reason? Electronic trading continues to make inroads in our industry, reducing the value of having a seat on a traditional futures exchange.

Historically, futures speculators have not been long-term investors. The mentality of a short-term speculator goes hand-in-hand with a day trading philosophy. We only have to look at the advent of the Internet to understand why there are many within the futures industry who welcome the coming of electronic trading. Today, there is a new speculator in the market-place—the individual, on-line investor/trader who buys and sells stocks through a home PC. This influx of new investors into the stock market has caused some in the futures industry to contemplate opening our market, which is still a boutique within the overall financial industry, to a wider audience of players. Just consider the numbers: Some $36 billion invested *worldwide* in managed futures; one day's stock trading activity on the New York Stock Exchange (NYSE) has an aggregate value of $29 billion. A decade ago, studies showed that 400,000 people worldwide traded futures while 40 million invested in stocks. Today, through mutual funds and 401(k) retirement plans, the number of stock investors has at least tripled. Even at the same rate of growth, the number of people involved in futures is minuscule by comparison.

Internet stock trading has shown there is an entire population of speculators, ready and willing to operate from their home PCs. They are no longer buy-and-hold investors who purchase a stock today and keep it for months or years. They are short-term investors looking to turn a quick profit within a few days or even within the same day. This eager at-home speculator, once educated, could trade certain futures contracts, such as Treasury bonds, S&Ps, Dow futures, currencies, and eurodollars. These stock speculators already grasp certain technical factors, such as how changes in interest rates affect the market. This gives them a greater affinity to trade financial futures than, say, more esoteric contracts, such as pork bellies or cattle, which are affected by other fundamental and technical factors. And, in time, it will take only a short study for these individuals to figure out that futures trading, although risky, is a fairer marketplace to day-trade.

For one thing, volatility allows profits to be made quickly in futures. I don't know of a single speculator who buys an S&P contract and holds it for five years. Second, the performance bond, or margin, is $16,000 to trade one S&P contract, which carries a cash value of $250,000 worth of stock. That's a far cry from the 50 percent margin required to trade individual stocks. In addition, although the advent of electronic trading has reduced commissions, on a dollar-for-dollar basis they are still far higher in stocks than commodities. It may cost an investor anywhere from $7 to $20 to buy 100 shares of a $10 stock, which would have a $1,000 face value. But for about $10 in commissions for a round turn—both a buy and a sell—an investor could trade one S&P contract worth $250,000. Futures trading also allows speculators to use leverage to take far greater positions than the cash in their accounts would allow in stocks.

In commodities, when an order is entered, the participant is immediately part of the market. In stocks, when someone wants to trade, he or she must first call a broker. The brokerage house then has the choice of whether to take the other side of the trade.

The rise of on-line stock trading has changed that. There is clear demand for a system to allow greater individual participation in the market, for orders to be entered and traded without a broker. Why else would on-line brokerage E-Trade Group Inc. and investment bank Goldman Sachs Group LP have agreed to buy 50 percent of Archipelago LLC in a rumored $50 million deal? Archipelago operates a system that allows day traders to enter their NASDAQ stock orders electronically using its Electronic Communication Network (ECN). Using an ECN, day traders gain professional access to the NASDAQ, without a broker. Commodities markets have the opportunity now to learn a lesson from this on-line revolution in stocks. Electronic access can easily draw in more participants, particularly individuals with capital and the desire to trade.

But trading commodities is a far different game than trading stocks, even in an electronic venue. Futures trading is predicated on open and equal access to all players. In stocks, customer orders are delivered electronically to brokers who can choose to take the other side of the trade or offer them in the market. Regardless of whether a stock is trading on NASDAQ or the New York Stock Exchange (NYSE), a broker is always handling the transaction and, often, participating in it. This fundamental contrast between stocks and futures underscores why an electronic trading system, such as NASDAQ, could never be adopted as a model for futures trading. For the futures market, which is based upon equal access through open outcry, adoption of a NASDAQ-type system would require a fundamental change in protocol and the very rules of trading.

Still, it's beneficial to examine the evolution of the stock markets as technology was developed and employed to speed the delivery of orders to the floor. At the NYSE, local traders moved off the floor and into upstairs offices years ago. The floor of the NYSE is dominated by the specialists who operate like one-person pits in an open-auction system. The specialists oversee the execution of the buy and sell orders, ensuring that trades are transacted in an orderly fashion. The specialists also have the duty and obligation, in the absence of any orders, to make a market for the public; that is, if the market is declining and there are no buyers, they are obligated to buy sell orders based upon market conditions and the amount of capital their firm has available. If the price of a stock drops too low, a specialist may halt trading and lower bids to attract buyers. Once equilibrium is regained, trading can be resumed. These types of trades result in about 10 to 20 percent of the specialists' activities. Furthermore, when specialists trade for their firms, they can only do so in a way that will not negatively or positively affect the price of the stock—meaning they must only buy on a down tick and sell on an up tick. The premise is that all customer orders from the public take precedence over their own.

The majority of customer orders on the NYSE are delivered via the electronic Designed Order Turnaround (DOT) system. The DOT, which was introduced in the early 1970s, was designed to enable stockbrokers around the country to enter small orders electronically. Since then, the DOT system has been used heavily by stock traders to deliver their orders to the floor and now accounts for the lion's share of the NYSE stock volume. When the DOT system was introduced, it was thought that the specialists would be replaced. Instead, the influx of orders through the DOT has made the role of the specialists even more critical.

The NYSE is essentially a two-tier market, with some orders handled by specialists and large block trades among institutional investors that are matched and executed off the floor. The handling of large blocks off the floor spares the market of the psychological impact of, say, 50,000 shares of IBM being bid for or offered on the trading floor in one lump sum. As a futures trader, this concept of matching buys and sells off the floor runs contrary to the open forum in the futures markets. If I were day-trading IBM stock at my home PC, I would want to be aware of a 50,000-block trade before it happened—not after.

Since its beginnings in the 1960s, NASDAQ has been a totally electronic market. It is a network of broker dealers, and it has never had a trading floor. Rather, bids and offers in stocks are made by market makers and disseminated through the NAS-

DAQ quote system. There are two basic orders executed on NASDAQ:

1. Buy and sell orders that carry a specific price.

2. Market orders to be transacted based on the current price quote.

NASDAQ member firms make markets in stocks by providing bid and ask quotes, and also have the option of taking the other side of customer trades. For example, a customer calls a NAS-DAQ broker with an order to buy Intel at 85. This order can either be put in the "book" of business and displayed on the NASDAQ system as an available bid, or else the broker can take the other side of the customer trade. The firm would sell the Intel shares at 85 and hope to buy them in the market at a lower price. Typically, NASDAQ dealers would not take the other side of customers' price orders unless they believed the market was turning, or they have a large block of sells at 85⅛. Firms take virtually all the market orders, which give them the opportunity to buy shares at the bid and sell them at the offer.

I've never traded stocks. But, when business associates or social acquaintances meet me for the first time and they find out I'm an S&P trader, I'm always asked two questions: They want to know what I think about a particular stock. (They look at me like I'm nuts when I explain that I don't trade stocks, I trade stock index futures.) The second question is always, "Why do I get such lousy fills on stocks? I always have to buy on the ask and sell on the bid. . . ." Now they know why.

For stock traders, order flow is the lifeblood of their profession. A case in point: Small brokerage firms that do not have market makers take their orders and place them with a NAS-DAQ member firm. Originally, these thousands of small firms around the country would have to pay a commission to have their orders filled. Say, for example, Joe and John's Brokerage in Omaha, Nebraska, was a small stock brokerage, but did not clear its own trades. Joe and John's Brokerage collected commissions for their customers and had to pay for those orders to be executed by Big NASDAQ Broker Dealer. As capitalism would have it, some NASDAQ broker realized that the greater the order flow, the greater the opportunity to buy on the bid and sell on the ask. This enterprising broker dealer then approached the Joe and John's Brokerages across the country, offering to *pay* for their order flow. I ask all you day traders of stocks to consider how easy would it be to turn a profit if you had first access to thousands of buys and sells, and could pick the ones you want!

When I was the lead order filler in the S&P pit in 1986, routinely accounting for 10 percent of the volume in the S&P pit, I received a strange call from a New York firm that claimed to account for 1 percent of the NYSE volume, trading about 150,000 shares a day. When I met with the firm in New York, I was given my first inside look at the way stocks were traded. The firm had a network of retail and institutional brokers that provided buy and sell orders. When a buy or sell order was received, the firm had a minute or two to decide if it wanted to be part of that trade. I know the SEC has tight rules regarding firms trading in front of a customer order, but customer order flow still presented an opportunity for brokerages. If they bought shares from Broker A in Omaha, they would try to sell to Broker B in Nashville, and put themselves in the middle for an eighth. On 150,000 shares a day, that was a big profit potential.

If this worked in stocks, the firm told me, why not stock index futures? But, that is just the point. It would have been illegal for me to disclose orders to another party. In futures, customer orders are sacrosanct. They must be offered and traded in an open forum where every eligible player has an equal shot at them.

Although the trading systems used in stocks and futures are vastly different, a new similarity is emerging. To me, it is the most disturbing of all—the potential on-line player. I'm not talking about the professional screen trader who, whether in stocks or commodities, studies the markets and trades daily. I'm talking about the amateur or the hobbyist who thinks they can log on to the Internet and trade with the big players. If I had no concern for the long-term viability of the futures markets, I would welcome these new on-line players. As an experienced trader, I could easily make money off these naive investors. One of my rituals over the years has been to joke with new traders who showed up in the pit with "new member" badges emblazoned with bright red stickers to alert us veterans that a novice was among us. I would walk up to them and take them by the hand. "You stand right near me. I'll take care of you. . . . I'll turn your money into my money."

On-line trading and the inexperienced customers it attracts are no laughing matter. It has been a bonanza for discount stock brokers for whom on-line trading is nothing more than an opportunity to draw more participants into the game and to collect more commissions. Industry figures show that assets managed by on-line investors are predicted to grow from over $100 billion to $524 billion in 2001, accounting for more than 8 percent of the total assets held by investors. But, on-line trading by individuals truly amounts to nothing more than a faster way to contact your broker through glorified e-mail. These investors are not entering orders directly to the floor of the NYSE; more important, on-line investors contribute to the order flow that brokerage houses can sell to clearing firms.

On-line stock trading appeals to the masses for two reasons: greed and freedom. They want to make money; we all do. Now, they figure they can. The chance to trade on your own appeals to the ego. I've seen it more times than I can count in a social situation. I've met professionals with MBAs and PhDs and jobs that carry both a big salary and a lot of prestige. But, when they hear that I'm a trader, they want to hear all about the way I make a living. The appeal is even stronger for someone farther down the career ladder, who fantasizes about a sexy, big-money lifestyle. They can picture themselves at their home PC, making money hand-over-fist by trading stocks. Then, they can tell their bosses to take this job and. . . .

When it comes to the legions of on-line stock traders, brokers are happy because there are no concerns over churning, an unscrupulous practice to encourage customers to buy and sell stocks frequently to generate commissions. With on-line trading, the customers decide when to trade, without the advice of their brokers. As more day traders and short-term speculators emerge in the stock market, they are, in effect, churning their own port-folios with the hopes of making a profit. The only way that stock brokerages can make up for the reduced commissions is to increase the volume of trades they handle. (And, remember, bro-kerages are only paying a fraction of one cent to clear a trade.) There is no better net to lure in the public than the Internet.

Just take a look at the advertisements. They invariably show smiling people at their computer screen trading their favorite stocks. At a second glance, however, it's not such a promising proposition. Admittedly, it's not a bad idea if an investor does research on a company and decides to buy shares via an on-line broker to take advantage of lower commissions. The danger is in the temptation to use on-line trading to make quick profits in stocks, which are more than likely to be prompt losses—partic-ularly when commissions and other expenses are factored into the mix.

I fully concur with Merrill Lynch Vice Chairman John Stef-fens, who has publicly called on-line trading "a serious threat to Americans' financial lives." On-line stock trading has given rise to the at-home hobbyists who believe they can day-trade stocks and make a killing. This is a dangerous supposition. Just con-sider the fate of Houston-based Block Trading, which failed in 1998. According to an article entitled "Day-trading Firms Under More Scrutiny" by Pamela Yip, published in the *Houston Chron-icle* (October 22, 1998), securities regulators in Massachusetts filed a complaint against Block Trading, alleging that the com-pany "lured customers with illusory profits and didn't warn them of the risks." The newspaper also reported that Block's failure prompted regulators to investigate whether day trading firms were taking advantage of unsophisticated investors by promising big profits while failing to warn them of the risks, and illegally lending investors money to encourage more trading.

The SEC has a long list of rules aimed at protecting investors from unethical money managers and brokers, who must be licensed and scrutinized. But, there are no requirements to protect unwary investors from losing their own money.

The true electronic day traders in stocks play a difficult game among the eighths and quarters. These professional day traders, however, do not pay retail commissions; their commission costs are only a few cents per trade. These professionals move in and out of the market, scalping profits on small moves, and with the benefit of seeing the order flow. Gone are the days when anomalies in stock quotes on NASDAQ created an opportunity for the astute scalper. For example, one quote system may have shown a bid at 7⅛, while another quoted 7¼. All traders had to do, in theory, was scan the computer screens for the discrepancies between the quotes. This gave rise to the proliferation of SOES trading rooms.

The SOES phenomenon grew in popularity in the early 1990s with a steady influx of would-be stock day traders, looking for an opportunity to make money. But, a tighter quote system on NASDAQ eliminated those discrepancies in stock quotes. Instead, traders tried to buy and sell stocks, hoping to make profits on short-term moves. All the while, they were paying some hefty commissions on the stock trades. I am critical of SOES because, for a short while, I was an investor in a Chicago-based operation. I cannot give the details of that operation because of a legal dispute that arose when the partnership was dissolved, but I saw firsthand just what a controversial business venture the SOES room was. I was approached to become a partner in the SOES operation because of my ability to devise "quality controls" in trading, such as computer controls to keep undercapitalized traders from buying or selling. The appeal of SOES for me was the prospect of branching out into another area of trading.

However, SOES, with the high commissions it charged traders, profited the house far more than it did the traders. When one trader went bust because of bad trades and commission costs, there was always another eager candidate to take his or her place. By bringing traders together, the SOES room used mass psychology. When one trader was winning, his enthusiasm would spread to the others who increased their trading. When somebody had an idea that an opportunity existed in a stock, others were eager to listen, especially if they had losses they needed to recoup. In theory, if a large SOES room generated enough enthusiasm, it could hype a stock.

Disciples of SOES spread their gospel of riches to the masses with courses and seminars. All they needed was one "success story" to tout: "I was laid off from my job, and then I learned to trade stocks. Now, I make $10,000 a week. . . ." Although there were some successful day traders in stocks, they were few and far between. There were far too many stories of people who went through $50,000 in a matter of months, most of it going to commissions. When I saw the SOES operation for what it was, I tried to pressure my partners into cutting commissions that we charged by as much as 90 percent. When they balked, it was the beginning of the end of a partnership that later dissolved. The SOES trader has given way to a new breed of speculator, a virtual cult of computer geeks with money to burn. They buy into the notion that because it is possible, it must therefore be profitable. It's like Mount Everest, which can be climbed by virtually anyone who has the money, if he or she uses oxygen. But, just because they can climb Everest, does that mean they should? Because on-line trading is possible, does that mean it is okay for the average person with no knowledge or study of the markets? Is it ethical?

On-line speculators can quickly become trading junkies. I thoroughly understand the appeal. After 18 years as a trader, I know the addiction to the adrenaline rush. Once you experience it as a trader, you can't get it out of your blood. At the risk of sounding egotistical, I wish I had a dollar for every time someone comes up to me in a restaurant, a car dealership, a store, or some other place and says, "Aren't you Lewis Borsellino? You probably don't remember me, but I used to trade in the S&P pit. I ran out of money, but one of these days, I'm going back. . . ." Even when you've depleted your nest egg on bad trades, nobody can convince you that you're not very good at trading.

Of all the issues in electronic trading, the potential abuse by—and of—individual investors is often overlooked. Trading is not a game for hobbyists. All too often, professionals who have made money in one occupation—doctors, for example—believe that they can apply their considerable intelligence to trading. They ask themselves, "How hard can buying low and selling high be compared with open-heart surgery?" They say to themselves, "I know I must be smarter than the average broker." A high IQ, however, doesn't guarantee success in the market. All it does is give a false sense of ability. Trading requires its own brand of expertise that comes from full-time study. Yes, opportunities exist for computerized day traders, professionals who trade for a living by using all the tools at their disposal. Certain skills to trade the market can be acquired and honed over time, but there is no shortcut to hard work and discipline. I remember standing in that pit—bell to bell—day after day until trading became second-nature. Even at the computer screen, there is no such thing as the occasional trader. This is especially true of day trading.

Day trading refers to entering and exiting trades within the same day. But, I believe it also connotes another meaning: To be a day trader, you have to be in the market virtually every day. Unless you are in the market all the time, you cannot possibly learn market flow, timing, and the price patterns that develop over days. That's why I don't believe the general public should be encouraged to trade futures just because of easy, electronic access to our markets. Despite all the warnings and disclosure statements, this would be a huge disservice to consumers at large.

Perhaps I shouldn't worry about the fate of these amateur on-line traders. Their presence in the market would certainly only help liquidity and enable professionals like me to make money more easily. But, I go back to my feelings after the Crash of 1987 when, in spite of the euphoria of big money, I had the dread that the market had been compromised. In the end, we must defend our market and ensure that trading is conducted for the ultimate good of all participants.

I don't want to go back to chalk and blackboards, nor do I

want to see an exchange dominated by an old boys' network. The pit, like the members themselves, is constantly changing, growing, and adapting. It would be a mistake to write off the trading pit. But at the same time, there is no denying where this industry is headed. Whether broker in the pit or professional techno-speculator, we must all get on board with electronic trading. That is the future of this industry, and the future is now.

That will require far more than the installation of computers and the introduction of electronic trading. Commodity brokers and traders must adopt a new mentality to stay in business and compete. To make that next leap to become markets that are traded worldwide, an electronic exchange is the network with which it can be done. More importantly, the traditional futures exchanges themselves must undergo a dramatic and fundamental change to survive and, in time, thrive in the electronic arena.

CHAPTER 9

Politics, Trading, and the Futures Exchange

The futures exchange is facing the biggest challenge in its history. After enduring everything from an FBI probe, regulatory scrutiny, and foreign competition, futures exchanges are up against a formidable competitor—the computer screen. Electronic exchanges, which offer futures contracts that can be traded virtually anywhere there is a computer and an on-line connection, threaten to make the traditional brick-and-mortar exchanges obsolete. Nowhere is this battle for survival more intense than in Chicago, where futures trading began some 150 years ago.

To combat this competitive threat, the world's two leading futures exchanges—the Chicago Mercantile Exchange and the Chicago Board of Trade—must end their battle and join forces. Their only hope to retain their prominence in the industry is to form a unified front, combining not only their trading operations but adopting the latest in technology as well. Rivalries between the two exchanges, which go back as far as any of us can remember, have to be overcome and forgotten. It's time for the egos to be put aside, because what's at stake is nothing less than their survival. For the two exchanges, this may prove to be the most difficult challenge of all.

Electronic trading, as I outlined in the previous chapter, is here to stay. Inroads will continue to be made as contracts are offered side by side in the pit and in an electronic venue. Contracts that are dominated by institutional players, such as bonds, eurodollars, and currencies, may do well in an electronic format, given the current backdrop of low volatility and high liquidity. Others, such as the volatile S&Ps or the illiquid agricultural contracts, will favor the pit. But, in some form, electronic trading will expand.

This presents both a wake-up call and a reality check for all of us in the industry. Commodity brokers and traders must wean themselves from the idea that the pit, as it now exists, will be the only game in town. Traditional exchanges can no longer rely on the dominance of their contracts to remain competitive. In the electronic arena, virtually any contract can be traded anywhere. The exceptions, of course, are contracts like S&Ps and the Board of Trade's Dow futures, which are licensed products. But, the détente that existed among exchanges that one would not tromp on the other's trading turf is over. We only need to consider the Cantor Financial Futures Exchange, which began trading Treasury bond contracts electronically in competition with the Board of Trade. Although initial volumes on the Cantor Exchange have been small, the existence of such an alternative marketplace is startling. It may only be a matter of time before other electronic venues are introduced or existing electronic exchanges find new partners to expand their technology and contract offerings.

There is no denying that the issue of electronic trading is a controversial and emotional one. Consider the shake-up at the Board of Trade in late 1998 over the issue of the Board of Trade's pending alliance with Eurex. Urging the Board of Trade to proceed cautiously toward a link with Eurex and the adoption of its trading platform, third-generation grain trader David Brennan won the election by a mere 19 votes. He replaces Patrick Arbor, a long-term chairman who had overseen the Eurex project. As of this writing, the alliance with Eurex is over. Board of Trade members rejected the Eurex alliance in a vote taken in early February.

Although I cannot argue the merits of an alliance with Eurex here, I do know that neither the Board of Trade nor any other traditional exchange can simply ignore the advent of electronic trading. For this reason, although electronic trading is perceived to be the threat, the real enemy of futures exchanges is their own attitude. The Merc and the Board of Trade can no longer afford to thumb their noses at each other in a contest to prove which is the bigger and better exchange. Rather, they must join forces, as they are proposing with common clearing, and merge. However, that is not the end of the transformation. The exchanges must revamp their organizations into a for-profit business run in the best interest of all its shareholders.

To do that, however, the Merc and the Board of Trade will have to give up a rivalry that is as long and as storied as the history of the exchanges. The Merc and the Board of Trade have vied over the years to be known as the world's largest futures exchange. The Merc can claim that title on the basis of the dollar value of the contracts it trades, bolstered by eurodollars and S&Ps. The Board of Trade, which is indisputably the world's oldest exchange, can claim to be the largest on the basis of contract volume alone. As this rivalry continued over the years, everyone has looked for the next new contract to be launched, which will carry one exchange or the other to prominence. Consider the competition for the futures contract based on the Dow Jones Industrial Average.

For the Merc, with its roster of stock indexes, including the S&P, Russell 2000, Nikkei, and NASDAQ 100, the Dow contract would have solidified its position as _the_ stock index exchange. The Merc, after all, had pulled off quite a coup in 1982 when it won the right to offer S&P futures. The S&P 500 is the backbone of world financial markets, the litmus test to gauge how well every other stock index and stock portfolio performs. So, why was the S&P contract launched in Chicago and not New York? I believe the answer is simply that Chicago exchanges do futures better than any place else.

When it came to the Dow contract, the Board of Trade, with its long history in trading and the success of its U.S. Treasury contracts, beat the Merc and the former New York Commodity Exchange, or Comex. Between the Chicago exchanges, the competition for the Dow contract was only one skirmish in a long-running battle. (This competition between the exchanges is even put to good use, occasionally, with a charity boxing match between members of the Merc and the Board of Trade!)

The success of the Chicago futures exchanges made them the prototype for every exchange that was launched over the years with an open-outcry system. The first time I walked into the London International Financial Futures Exchange (LIFFE), I thought for a moment that I was back in Chicago at the Merc. Everything was the same, from the arrangement of the pits to the quote boards on the wall. I understand the same is true for exchanges in Singapore and Hong Kong, which also followed the Chicago model. The Merc and the Board of Trade were the prototype; we were the gold standard that everyone else tried to emulate.

When these foreign-based exchanges were first established, the Chicago institutions had no reason to fear them. After all, these were primarily regional exchanges with their own niche markets. The Chicago exchanges would have no more interest in trading rubber or red beans than a Far Eastern exchange would want to trade pork bellies or soybeans. Even though the Nikkei stock index trades in Chicago, it is only a supplement to the primary market in Japan. These offshore institutions brought together local participants from their markets, just as the Chicago exchanges had done.

Futures trading, as we know it today, was born in Chicago some 150 years ago when a group of merchants formed a marketplace to buy and sell grain that would be delivered in the future. But, historians believe the concept of futures trading dates back to the Japanese rice market in the 1650s. A story I've heard puts the founding of futures at an even earlier date. Galileo, it seems, had his sights on more than just the heavens when he invented the telescope. The Italian astronomer used his invention to scan the horizon for ships that were bringing goods to replenish the local merchants' supplies. As soon as he saw the ships, Galileo would rush into town, where shortages had pushed prices sky-high. He would agree to sell goods at the going rate with delivery in a few days. When the ships landed, Galileo would buy his supplies and resell them in town, where the arrival of fresh wares had depressed prices. By agreeing to sell what he didn't yet own, Galileo was the first futures trader and the first short seller.

Despite that heritage, the first future exchange was not founded at the crossroads of trade in Europe. Rather, the first market was established where the Midwest grain crops were brought to market: Chicago. In 1848, a group of grain merchants founded what became the Board of Trade, which remains preeminent in grain contracts. In 1874, the Chicago Produce Exchange was formed to market butter, eggs, and poultry. A division of that exchange, the Chicago Butter and Egg Board, was formed in 1898, and renamed the Chicago Mercantile Exchange in 1919. The Merc expanded by adding frozen pork belly futures and live cattle, but these contracts had a very narrow and predetermined client base.

That changed in 1972 when the Merc launched financial futures with the creation of the International Monetary Market (IMM) to trade seven foreign currencies. At the Board of Trade, a contract was launched to trade U.S. Treasuries in 1977. With these new financial contracts, the exchanges became powerful—financially and politically—commanding the respect of Wall Street, LaSalle Street, and the world's financial institutions. These financial futures bridged the gap to make the exchanges truly worldwide institutions and not just niche markets. Now, banks, institutions, corporations, and any business that had interest rate or foreign exchange exposure could hedge their risks by accessing these markets.

Later, the Chicago exchanges added eurodollars, 10-year Treasury notes, S&Ps, and a gamut of other financial futures. In these markets, the Merc and the Board of Trade were the only games in town. At the exchanges, there were three basic groups of participants: individual traders, clearing firms, banks, or futures commissions merchants (FCMs), and retail customers who trade through FCMs. As members, individual traders, FCMs, and clearing firms paid very low commissions, whereas retail customers paid higher fees. Thus, the value of being a member was clear: It cost less to trade. This economic reality made exchange memberships more valuable, as reflected in the rise in seat prices to a high of $1 million in 1996.

Today, things have changed. The Board of Trade and the Merc are no longer the only games in town. The success of Eurex abroad makes it the prototype for the electronic exchange of the future. Now that alliance with the Board of Trade was rejected, it's possible Eurex may join forces with another exchange. Perhaps that would be a traditional exchange like the Merc, or even NASDAQ or the NYSE, which would allow them to list both stocks and commodities. Or, maybe it will be an upstart partner that rattles the foundation of futures trading as we now know it.

The solution for the Merc and the Board of Trade is as simple as the cliché: If you can't beat 'em, join 'em. The Merc and the Board of Trade must join forces in a merger that will combine both their expertise in trading and their financial resources. If they choose not to pursue an alliance with an existing electronic exchange, such as Eurex, then they must construct a platform of their own. But that would be a lofty and daunting investment; estimates I've heard from those involved with Eurex range between $60 million and $70 million. The Merc and the Board of Trade can also glean another lesson from Eurex when it comes to its management and operational structure.

Eurex was organized as a private, for-profit organization, meaning every policy and procedure had to benefit the bottom line. In addition, Eurex created a level playing field for all participants, with no distinction made in terms of commissions for members, nonmembers, and clearing firms. The Eurex system, itself, became unparalleled for split-second execution of orders through point-and-click technology, which makes trading on a computer as easy as participating in an on-line chat room. The Eurex software interfaces easily with outside systems, meaning participants can trade Eurex from their own terminals. Eurex has become so efficient that it can handle 1,000 transactions per second. With this kind of speed and efficiency, Eurex became the ideal forum for European institutions wanting to trade electronically.

As I have stated previously, despite the overwhelming success of Eurex, I do not advocate going all electronic and shutting down the pits. At the same time, traditional futures exchanges must adapt to this new era. To address electronic trading, some exchanges will adopt alliances. The New York Mercantile Exchange and the International Petroleum Exchange, for example, are merging, a move that is expected to speed the adoption of electronic energy futures trading. For others, it will mean hefty investments in the tens of millions of dollars to develop their own electronic platforms. But futures exchanges cannot sit back and do nothing. Otherwise, the futures industry will join the VCR and the camcorder as a good idea that got its start in the United States, but became more efficient offshore.

As a pit trader, I have always been an advocate of open outcry. To back electronic trading in a side-by-side venue with the pit may strike some as pure heresy. I'm sure that there are brokers and locals who, when they read this, will believe I'm telling them to cut their own throats. Futures trading, however, faces the same question that confronts every business and institution at some time or other: Adapt or die. As traders and brokers, our chance for survival is to embrace electronic trading. For our exchanges, there is no other alternative but to expand into the electronic venue, but not as competing institutions going it alone. Rather, the Merc and the Board of Trade must join forces and give up the isolationist attitude that will otherwise be our downfall. In the new era, the exchanges must implement a trading platform that embraces the best of both worlds—the electronic exchange and open-outcry pit trading.

To be competitive in the new era of electronic trading, the Merc and the Board of Trade cannot rely on GLOBEX and Project A, respectively. These electronic order-matching systems are not truly electronic exchanges. They have not demonstrated the ability to handle the volume and the volatility of the pit. Right now, Eurex has at least a two-and-a-half-year lead time on the Chicago exchanges when it comes to offering electronic trading. To compete, the two Chicago exchanges must swallow their pride and work together.

This will require some fundamental changes at both institutions. As a first step, the Merc and the Board of Trade must convert from member-owned, nonprofit organizations to for-profit companies. This, I believe, will improve management and increase accountability for all members, not just for certain factions represented on the board of governors. Under this conversion, those of us who own exchange memberships will be given shares in the company. I can envision FCMs combining their assets to have a large enough capital base to guarantee the financial integrity of the clearing firms and the exchange. As a result, the caste system when it comes to clearing fees will be abolished, and all participants will pay the same to trade. As a for-profit company, the first priority of exchange management must be to reduce costs and increase volume. This will automatically spark the study of open outcry and side-by-side trading.

The Merc and the Board of Trade must then merge. There is no other way, as I see it, for the two exchanges to compete. There is some glimmer of hope that some kind of unity between the exchanges is possible. In December 1998, the Merc and the Board of Trade agreed to pursue cross-margining and common banking for the benefit of their member firms. Although this is a far cry from a complete merger, it is a step toward cooperation that may, in time, lead to closer ties.

The exchanges need to update and improve their order delivery systems. The expanded use of computerized order entry and handheld devices for brokers in the pit will not only speed the delivery of orders, but provide more anonymity for customers. With a handheld computer that connects customers with the brokers on the floor, a broker doesn't have to worry that his customer's order has been intercepted as it is flashed by hand signal into the pit. With side-by-side trading in most, if not all, of the futures contracts, the decision will then be left to the customer. On each and every trade, the customer at a computer will decide whether to execute trades electronically or via open out-cry. In time, where the liquidity goes the market will follow.

To effect this change at traditional exchanges, such as the Merc and the Board of Trade, individual members will have to take up the cause. As we address the issue of electronic trading, we cannot look to our leadership alone. For one thing, we are each responsible for our own livelihoods. The cynics among us would also note that the leadership in the past has sometimes adopted policies and rules that we vehemently disagreed with. It's no surprise, therefore, that we have not heard from the long-term leaders of the exchanges on the subject of electronic trad-ing. Could it be that the message they know is inevitable, but do not want to deliver is that, for the traditional futures exchange, the writing is on the wall? Or, perhaps the rank and file at the exchange—the brokers and traders—do not want to listen because it is too engrossed in protecting its own turf.

The futures exchange is an independent marketplace. At the grassroots level are a few thousand brokers and local traders who function as individual business units. As a member of the exchange, you set up shop each day on the floor of the ex-change, standing next to your competitors. Traders and brokers do business with each other, but let there be no mistake: Each party is looking out for their own trading account and best interest. This independence is what attracts many people to trading. At the end of the day, you have only yourself to thank— or to blame. But, this kind of independence also engenders a territorial attitude. Most brokers and traders are only concerned about policies that affect the markets in which they trade, or an exchange rule that makes trading more cumbersome, such as the time-stamp requirements for trading cards.

There are, of course, individuals who choose to become in-volved in the governance structure at the exchange. The traders and brokers support the candidates who best represent their interests. The result is a board of governors composed of indi-viduals from the different factions of the exchange—the order fillers, the local traders, the agricultural pits, the financial mar-kets, and so forth.

For individual brokers and traders, rallying around the cause of electronic trading will require a change in attitude and perspective. In my experience, futures traders and brokers do not easily become involved in broader issues. In the past it was difficult, if not impossible, to elicit sympathy in one pit for another. Many futures traders and brokers are narrow-minded in that respect. They only care about what they trade. That's a sorry lesson I saw in the S&P pit.

Even before the Crash of 1987, there were those who sought to limit trading in the S&P pit, particularly when it came to the brokerage groups that had grown in prominence and influence. A blue-ribbon panel of S&P traders and brokers in 1986 was given the task of looking at certain trading practices. At the end of its study, the panel recommended rules that stipulated a broker could only trade a certain percentage for his own account and a certain percentage with members of the same brokerage group. The minute I saw the panel's recommendations, which were set out in a letter that was circulated on the trading floor, I knew where the Merc leadership was headed: a ban on dual trading.

I took the letter over to Howard Dubnow, Leo Melamed's son-in-law and chairman of that blue-ribbon panel. "I'm going to stop you on this one," I told him.

Howard sneered at me. "Forget it. It's a done deal."

I took a copy of the letter upstairs to Maury Kravitz, my partner and former mentor. The only way to stop these rules from taking effect, we decided, was to draft a petition to block it. "Lewis, how are we going to get the other traders to back this?" Maury asked me. "You know how they are. They're not going to take a stand on this for someone else."

"Maury, you can write this petition!" I told him. "I'll get the signatures." I knew if there was anyone who could put the fear of God into the trading floor it would be Maury. He was not only an eloquent attorney, but a man who could communicate beautifully through the written word. Besides, Maury could invoke just the right tone in drafting this petition, the kind that would communicate just how serious these recommendations were when it came to the future of the trading floor. In jest, I had always called Maury "Dr. Doom." From the beginning of my career as a clerk, he has been predicting the demise of the futures exchange.

Maury wrote that petition and we began circulating it on the floor. We only needed 300 signatures to bring the issue to a referendum. That, we knew, was the last thing Leo wanted. A referendum would show dissension in the ranks. The only way to rally that kind of support was to show the Merc membership that this issue went far beyond just the brokers in the S&P pit. With the help of two other traders, we began circulating the petition on the trading floor. We started with the brokers in the S&P pit, who felt the same way I did when it came to preserving dual trading. Several locals and dual traders like myself also saw these rules as potentially dangerous because they could limit trading and, therefore, dampen liquidity. We brought the petition to other pits, where we explained to brokers that this wasn't just an S&P issue; it raised the question of dual trading across the floor of the exchange.

Within a few hours, we had gathered 400 signatures—well beyond the 300 we needed for a referendum. Then I called Leo and arranged to meet with him that afternoon.

"Leo, you cannot jam this down our throats," I told him, handing him the petition. "If you do, I've got enough signatures to take this issue to a referendum. I'll do that if I have to." (At least, that's what I remember saying, although perhaps not quite as tactfully.)

Leo's tone softened as soon as he saw the petition. "Let's sit down and discuss this," he told me.

The meeting consisted of Leo, Howard Dubnow, and about 10 of their people on one side and, on the other side, about a dozen locals and brokers with me. I didn't mince words at the meeting. "You have to change what you're instituting, or I'm putting this to a referendum," I told Leo again.

The next day, Leo called a membership meeting. He praised Howard Dubnow and the panel not only for their hard work but, in his words, their realization that this issue was not going to be accepted by the Merc membership. The panel's decision, Leo told us, was to study the issue further. In the end, we had won our battle over the panel's recommendation, but we eventually lost the war for dual trading.

After the Crash of 1987, the S&P pit came under some tough scrutiny. There were allegations that the S&P contract and the portfolio insurance that it provided had somehow contributed to the Crash. The thinking was that the sell-off in futures, triggered by computerized programs, had weakened stocks—the proverbial tail-wagging-the-dog scenario. To curb S&P futures, some people in Congress who were trying to make a name for themselves suggested that the contract come under the purview of the Securities and Exchange Commission (SEC), which oversees stocks. In addition, there were some who urged the SEC to take over the Commodity Futures Trading Commission (CFTC), which regulates all U.S. futures trading.

Many S&P traders were concerned that if the SEC took over our pit, we would face the same 50 percent margins that are required in stocks. Can you imagine how ludicrous that would have been for a trader to post a $250,000 margin to trade one S&P contract? There would be no one in the pit and no institutional issuers for such a contract.

All the while that the S&P pit was under attack, I saw very little empathy from fellow Merc members outside our pit. To their credit, Jack Sandner, who was chairman at the time, and the rest of the Merc leadership stood behind the S&P pit. But that's where it ended. Traders and brokers in the other pits had heard stories about the fortunes that had been made in S&Ps during the Crash. That kind of fast money sparked jealousy—and suspicion. If traders in the S&P pit had violated any rules, some Merc members believed, then they deserved to be in regulatory hot water. As a result, much of the Merc membership turned its back on the S&P pit, divorcing themselves from our dilemma. At the time, I could not believe that the other traders and brokers were so naive, not realizing that as one pit was scrutinized, the others were going to come under close examination.

This fractious attitude on the trading floor and the rivalry between the Chicago exchanges made unity difficult, if not nearly impossible. In fact, the only time I ever saw the Merc and the Board of Trade come together was when self-regulation was threatened and the exchanges rallied against a common enemy—Congress. Self-regulation has been a tenet of futures trading since the beginning. The exchanges have always argued that no outside party understood the issues of futures trading as well as the insiders, and therefore no one could regulate us better than we could ourselves. The Commodity Futures Political Funds have raised hundreds of thousands of dollars over the years with what seemed like constant warnings that our self-regulation was under attack. We'd hear one day that stricter regulations were going to be imposed, and on the next we were warned that our trades were about to be taxed. Transaction taxes would only increase the cost of futures trading and force the institutional users to go to other exchanges outside the United States.

To appease certain factions in Washington, D.C., and to send a signal that an exchange could regulate itself, the Merc voluntarily tightened its rules. Consider the top-step rule, which was enacted first in S&Ps after the Crash. In the pit, the higher up you are, the better your vantage point for seeing and being seen. The Merc decided that, starting in S&Ps, only brokers filling orders for customers could stand on that top step. Locals were relegated to lower levels. The reasoning behind the top-step rule was that it would keep broker orders confidential until they are offered in an open forum.

By standing on the top step, brokers would have a clear view of the desk managers and clerks, who used hand signals to flash customer orders to the pit. By banning locals from the top step, they could not see the orders as they were flashed into the pit. The Merc decided that a local trader would have an unfair advantage if he saw the broker orders a second or two before the bids and offers were made in the pit. What angered me about the top-step rule was that it gave preference to the brokers and their customers. The institutions and the other customers who traded through brokers were not members. Yet they took precedence over the locals who were members. The result of the top-step rule has been a debate over when an order actually becomes part of the public knowledge: Is it when a bid or offer is made in the pit or when the desk manager notifies the broker?

When the top-step rule went into effect in S&Ps, the other pits did not join our cause to fight it. The prevalent attitude among other Merc members was the top-step rule affected only S&Ps. It did not impact eurodollars, currencies, or other financial futures. But, what the brokers and traders in the other Merc pits failed to realize was the top-step rule in S&Ps made the banning of dual trading across the exchange inevitable. The top-step rule exhibited clearly that there were plenty of brokers at the exchange who were willing to make their living exclusively by filling customer orders. From that premise, it was not too far to ban brokers from trading for their own accounts altogether.

As I've said before, I am a proponent of dual trading, which is a controversial practice and a much maligned one. Critics have complained that dual trading gave brokers in the pit an unfair advantage because they could conceivably trade with the knowledge of their customers' orders. This practice of trading in front of the customer is strictly in violation of the exchange's rules, and anyone who did so was eventually caught by the exchange. To defend the practice of dual trading, all the Merc had to do was show it could effectively police the handling of customer orders through its computer reconstruction tracking (CRT) system. These sophisticated computer programs allow the exchanges to reconstruct down to the tick any trade on the floor.

When it comes to regulating the pit, you cannot underestimate the role of the customer. Any broker who continually put his or her self-interest ahead of the customer's violated the exchange rules—and the poor quality of its fills would be noticed by the customer, who would quickly find another broker to handle the business.

Brokers are successful only when they earn the loyalty of their customers. When I was a dual trader, there were more

times than I wanted to admit that I lost money on my own position because my first obligation was to my customer. That was
precisely the reason I eventually gave up the customer deck. I
had become such a big trader that I had outgrown dual trading;
my personal trading was hurt as I serviced the customers. But it
was my decision to stop filling customer orders. There were
other dual traders who, when the market was busy, focused on
filling customer orders. When things slowed down, they traded
for their own accounts. There was no reason these brokers
should have been precluded from dual trading.

Dual trading, in my opinion, best serves the interests of both
the brokers and their customers. For one thing, dual trading
increased liquidity, which is the lifeblood of our existence. Every
trade in the pit sparks four more. So a ban on dual trading,
which made brokers unable to trade for themselves, had a four-
fold impact on every trade it eliminated.

Moreover, dual trading offered anonymity for clients.
Because I traded large lots for my own account, other locals
couldn't be sure when I was trading for myself and when I was
executing trades for my customers. With dual trading, brokers
always had their minds on the market. They were not sitting on
the sidelines reading a newspaper and waiting for a customer
order. You didn't see, as you do today, a broker suddenly look
around him and ask where the market was because he suddenly
had an order to fill.

Also, as a dual trader, I could effectively stop locals who were
trying to race me on a customer order. Say I had 200 contracts
to buy for a customer and locals were racing me, meaning they
answered my bids with higher ones. If I bid 50, someone else
would bid 55 and then 60. As a dual trader, I could turn to that
local and say, "Sell 'em!" on 10 or 20 contracts for my own
account, and stop that local cold.

The battle over dual trading became a political one, particularly in the wake of the Crash of 1987 and the FBI sting. In the
book *Escape to the Futures* (John Wiley & Sons, Inc., New York,
1996), Leo Melamed, with Bob Tamarkin, admits that there was
"nothing inherently evil" about dual trading, and that "it has

been argued that dual trading benefits market liquidity." His concern was that "dual trading has always given our markets a bad image, and it has been a source of interminable accusations that the practice leads to customer abuses." But, in his opinion, ". . . there was more to be gained from a ban on dual trading than would be lost in market liquidity."

By banning dual trading, the Merc leadership managed to shed that so-called bad image. But the result, I believe, hurt liquidity and caused an irreparable rift between local traders and brokers. In return for risking their own capital, local traders could potentially make far more money than the brokers, who lived by commissions of $2 per contract. With nothing but commissions to make a living, some brokers developed a "fill 'em and bill 'em" attitude. As long as customers got their fills, there was little incentive to go the extra mile on a price. A broker's only concern was to make sure the order was filled without an error for which he or she would be liable.

The ban on dual trading also made for yet another contrast between the Merc and the Board of Trade. The Board of Trade never banned dual trading, and allows its brokers and locals to stand next to each other on the top step—or any other place for that matter. This reflects the Board of Trade's reputation for putting its membership first. Brokers and local traders wield a heavy influence at the Board of Trade, although that exchange has certainly seen its share of dynamic chairmen, including Les Rosenthal, Karsten "Cash" Mahlman, and, until recently, Pat Arbor.

The Merc, in my opinion, has catered more to the institutions since the introduction of financial futures, even at the expense of individual members. A case in point is the Merc's eurodollar contract, which is based on U.S. dollars on deposit overseas. When the eurodollar contract was proposed, many local traders lobbied for the same $100,000 face value as the Board of Trade's Treasury contract. But the Merc leadership caved in to institutional pressure for a larger $1 million contract. Why? Because at $1 million, fewer contracts would have to be traded to hedge short-term interest rate positions. Fewer contracts meant less commissions that would have to be paid.

Another contrast between the Merc and the Board of Trade surfaced after the FBI sting in 1989. Both exchanges automatically barred any members who pleaded guilty to federal charges or actions brought against them by the CFTC. Indicted traders who pleaded innocent were allowed to trade, but both exchanges asked that they do so only for their own accounts and to refrain from executing orders for customers. The difference was seen in the two exchanges' attitudes toward brokers who, accused but not convicted of any wrongdoing, declined to obey the voluntary ban on filling customer orders.

In an article entitled "No Long-Term Damage, Merc Exec Says; Next Counts May Come as Early as Next Fall," by Christopher Drew and Sallie Gaines (_Chicago Tribune_ (August 4, 1989); Terry Atlas, William B. Crawford, Jr., and Gary Marx, contributors), Leo Melamed, who was then chairman of the Merc's executive committee, was quoted as saying the exchange would clamp down on any indicted trader who refused to abide by the request not to fill customer orders. The Board of Trade, however, said it would not take any action against indicted traders who still filled orders. The Board of Trade's attitude of someone being innocent until proven guilty certainly wasn't all that revolutionary. But for some reason, however, the concept was too much of a stretch for the Merc leadership.

At the Merc and Board of Trade, the quality of the futures contract price quotes that are disseminated to the public is held in high regard. Under open outcry, the price at any given time is determined by the last trade. Prices move up and down based on the level at which trades are executed. In a bearish market, sellers have to lower their offers; in a bullish one, buyers have to raise their bids. Every time a trade is made on the floor, the price is reported immediately. Say, for example, I trade 50 contracts at a half. When the trade is made, I turn to one of the Merc's pit recorders and yell, "Trade at a half." The pit recorder then reports the price by walkie-talkie to another Merc employee, who punches the information into a computer, contrib-uting to the continuous time and price record, which is what the public sees.

But there are times when the bids and offers in the pit are out of sync when the market turns volatile. The Board of Trade, in my opinion, has a more realistic attitude when it comes to the way trades are actually transacted on the floor. The Board of Trade acknowledges that there are times in a fast-moving, un-predictable market when a broker who is offering contracts at 50 may not even be aware of bids at 70, or even 90, in other quadrants of the pit. As long as brokers were not negligent in their efforts to fill the contracts, the practice at the Board of Trade is usually to stand behind the trades. Adjustments are not handed out on a regular basis to customers out of fear of losing the business. In fact, as stated in Chapter 6, Archer Daniels Midland's complaints about its orders being filled on the floor of the Board of Trade prompted this agribusiness company to cooperate with the U.S. government in the FBI sting operation.

This is a contrast with the Merc's view that all transactions happen within the proper time-price sequence. At the Merc, brokers have allowed institutions to hold them captive. With dual trading banned, brokers' sole livelihood is filling contracts for commissions. It's rare then that a broker at the Merc will stand up to a customer over a trade when the market is fast and volatile, and prices are out of sync. Their best defense, therefore, is the time-and-price record. Striking out the prices that appear to be anomalies can help a Merc broker keep the customers at bay. To do that, however, requires an adjustment be made to the Merc's office-time-and-price record, the integrity of which can-not ever be compromised.

Here's a typical scenario of a disputed price on the floor of the Merc. Say a broker is offering to sell at 50, but before the broker can execute that trade, bids across the pit are raised to 60. A trade is reported at 60, which becomes part of the time-and-price record reported to the public. Then the market breaks and falls 200 or 300 points. Seeing the trade reported at 60, the broker's customer calls the trading desk and demands to be filled at that price. The problem is, with the market far below that level, there is no way of executing a fill at 60. The broker then has three choices. The broker can explain to the customer that this was not a case of negligence, but rather the trade could not be executed at 60; however, that could cost the broker the customer's business in the future. The broker could give the customer the fill at 60, making up the difference with the current market out of his or her own pocket. Or, the broker could dispute the 60 price, even though trades were made and reported at that level.

When a price is called into question, the bells and whistles sound and a red warning light flashes. Then the pit committee is called upon to make a decision whether the price at 60 should be kept in or stricken from the record. The pit committee consists of about 30 members from various quadrants in the pit, which gives the committee a perspective on what happens across the trading arena. The pit members don't sit in a room somewhere, poring over time-and-price runs. They're in the pit, trading. When a price is disputed, a Merc employee finds the committee members in the pit and asks for a decision on whether a price should be retained or taken out. Based on the majority, a ruling is made. This all happens in a matter of minutes, and trading is not interrupted by the process.

But even on the price committee, the factionalism at the Merc was evident. The pit committee is composed mostly of brokers, who tend to favor price requests from other order fillers. As a major player in the S&P pit, I decided I needed to be part of the pit committee. The price adjustments were having a major impact on my bottom line, and I wanted a say in what prices were left in or taken out. I lobbied Maury to take his place on the pit committee, because he was rarely in the pit anymore. When Maury approached Jack Sandner with my request, he later told me, it was the hardest sell of his Merc career. After all, I was not the most popular guy on the floor. But, eventually, I was named to the S&P pit committee.

The job of the pit committee was to preserve the integrity of the time-and-price run. Even so, the pit committee wasn't immune from vested interests of brokers or locals and personality clashes. When I served on the pit committee from 1984 to 1986, during the time I was dual trading and then became strictly a local, I saw that other members were quick to vote against whatever I asked for or recommended. If I asked for a price to be taken out, the committee left it in. If I wanted the price left in, the committee took it out. The only exception on the pit committee was Marty Potter, a friend and fellow trader with whom I had worked briefly back in 1982 when the S&P contract was first launched.

So I decided to try a little reverse psychology on the pit committee. "Listen," I said to Marty one day, "don't vote for anything that I ask for from now on."

"What?" Marty looked at me like I had finally cracked.

"Don't you get what they're doing? They go against whatever I ask for. So I'm going to ask for the opposite from now on. Then when they vote against me, I'll get exactly what I want."

It's a sad commentary on human nature, but it worked just as I had planned. If I wanted a price to be kept in, I asked for it to be taken out. The committee ruled against me and it would be kept in. I reversed my strategy when I wanted a price struck from the record. I hate to admit it, but I wasn't beyond a few petty games of my own. If somebody I didn't like petitioned for a particular price, I'd add my own recommendation. I'd make sure that everybody saw my "LBJ"—the initials on my trading badge—on that request. It was the kiss of death to any petition brought before the committee.

After two years, I was off the pit committee when I became strictly a local trader. But even though I no longer served on the pit committee, I did not take a back seat at the Merc. My own self-interest demanded that I stay involved. Price adjustments were sometimes costing me and other large locals about $2,000 a day. I figured that, on an annual basis, price adjustments cut my profit by some $200,000. I was concerned about what I saw as an overwhelming bias toward the brokers who filled orders for the institutions versus the local traders. To prove my point, I pulled the price change requests brought before the pit committee. Roughly 90 percent of those requests were granted by the pit committee, and about 90 percent of the requests came from order fillers.

We can no longer afford such division in our ranks, as we've seen in our recent history. The brokers and the locals may be rivals on the floor, but if we don't join forces, we cannot hope to defend our livelihoods. Whether we trade for our own accounts or we fill orders for customers, we are part of a greater whole known as the market.

For the futures exchanges to change, the brokers and traders must first shift their perspective. Fundamental change is always from the bottom up, not from the top down. A merger of the Chicago Mercantile Exchange and the Chicago Board of Trade would be more than just the coming together of two institutions. It would be nothing less than a merger involving some 6,000 independent businesses represented by each broker and trader in the pits of the two exchanges. This grassroots support must be amassed and then spread through the ranks so that the leadership hears a clear message that allows us to embrace the future instead of fear it.

For that to happen, brokers and traders alike must look up from their spots in the pit and the screens in front of their faces to contemplate a broader picture. All of our livelihoods depend upon the decisions that are made today. The competition from electronic trading is a reality. I reiterate that although I do not believe the pits will be closed and open outcry silenced forever, I believe that the trading floor will not be the only venue. Increasingly, electronic trading will make inroads, and new exchanges will not be brick-and-mortar institutions, but computerized ones.

For the Chicago Mercantile Exchange and the Chicago Board of Trade, the challenge is really an opportunity to once again take the lead in the futures industry. Chicago, after all, is where futures trading was born, some 150 years ago. It is only right and fitting that these two exchanges take an active role in determining not only their own futures, but the direction this industry will take in the next century.

CHAPTER 10

From Grassroots to the Global Economy

Everybody is a trader these days, or at least they act like one. They watch every tick of the Dow Jones Industrial Average and every blip of the S&P 500. They tune into CNBC more than they watch their favorite sitcom. The financial pages and the stock columns in the newspapers aren't just for the wealthy or the nerdy. Some might argue that we've become a nation of investors, but I believe that description is too passive. Investors salt their money away for the future, buying and holding blue chips and bonds for their retirement or a rainy day. I say the majority of investors have become speculators—short-term players who, like traders, are acutely aware of whether the market is up or down on any given day.

The emergence of this new speculator is part of the grassroots change in the market. Retail investors have flocked to the stock market through mutual funds and retirement investments, with combined clout that has underpinned the market and bolstered its resilience through the downturns. Fundamental economic changes have also strengthened the market—including corporate reengineering to cut costs and reduce debt and, more recently, a global economic restructuring in emerging markets, post-Communism economies, and even a new pan-European monetary bloc.

Through these grassroots-to-global changes, the impact on the market is likely to be instantaneous and profound. Put another way, this means volatility. Investors who have been used to a smooth upward ride had better buckle their seatbelts. That point was brought home to me on the golf course one day in August, 1998. The Dow was down 200-plus points, as the market expressed its worries over everything from the Asian crisis to a lack of aggressive action by the Federal Reserve.

I had done well in the market that morning, trading from the short side for myself and my customers, and was glad for a break when I headed to the course in the early afternoon. But, when I saw my golf buddies, I felt like I was back in the pit. One guy was checking his pager, just in case his stockbroker had beeped. Another was glued to CNBC in the clubhouse. The third guy's expression was an artist's study in worry.

"What's the matter with you?" I cajoled them.

"Lewis, the market," they groaned in unison. "We're getting killed."

"Good!" I teased them. "Now you know how I feel every day I'm faced with a loss. At last you get a taste of what it's like to be a trader."

I am empathetic to my friends' concerns. I know, firsthand, the agony of feeling a financial loss, even if it is just on paper. But, for a lot of investors, this increased volatility is unsettling. Intellectually, they grasp the fact that the market has become hypersensitive to changes in the global economy. But, emotionally, it's a roller-coaster ride that most would rather forego.

As we've seen over the past year, 100- and 200-point moves are not uncommon in the market today. Just consider that, in the first 11 months of 1998, the Dow ranged between about 7400 and 9400 in the cash market, and 7415 and 9500 in futures. S&P futures, meanwhile, ranged between 929 and 1212 for the first 11 months of the year. To handle this kind of

market volatility, investors can opt to pay no attention whatso-
ever to the market's daily activity and focus only on the long-
term time horizon. That's a fine strategy for investors who have
diversified their portfolios and entrusted their money with good
managers, two steps that help ensure their investments are likely
to perform well over the long haul.

Many investors have done well over the past few years, admittedly not because of any particular savvy in picking stocks, but
because of a strong bull market. Now, armed with a portion of
their profits and a confidence—perhaps falsely—in their ability
to play the market, these investors have evolved into speculators.
They take higher risks with short-term, speculative investments
in hopes of reaping an even higher reward. People who even a
few years ago weren't sure about the role of the Federal Reserve
are acutely aware of every word that Alan Greenspan utters.

Investors have no choice but to adopt a trader's mental discipline. They must stay focused and disciplined about their investment strategy, even when their portfolios are down 15 or 20
percent because of a stock market correction. But, when it comes
to speculators, they must worry about controlling their losses
instead of focusing on the potential gains. It's an adaptation of
one of the cardinal rules of trading: Worry about the losses; the
profits take care of themselves. Speculators should never put too
much of their portfolio in high-risk investments, just as a trader
can never take on too large a position. Don't bet the whole nest
egg on a "can't lose" investment; there is no such thing as can't
lose, unless maybe you're talking about a certificate of deposit.
Control your greed.

Individual investors continue to underpin the strength of the
stock market, although mostly through mutual funds, 401(k)
plans, and other investment plans. This money combines the
collective clout of individuals under an institutional manager.
Prior to the Crash of 1987, retail investors bought and sold
stocks on their own, often on the advice of brokers who collected commissions on every trade. The go-go 1980s led to a lot
of largesse in expenditures, credit card debt, and investment.

Then came the Crash. Some investors had become so highly leveraged in their stock investments that they could not meet their margin calls and were forced to liquidate their positions. Others panicked over their paper losses.

By May 1988, the stock market stabilized. Even a decline that lasted from mid-1990, prompted by the Persian Gulf War, through early 1991, didn't dissuade most investors from the market. Rather, money continued to flow into the market. After the Crash, many individuals shifted away from investing on their own to using mutual funds and other institutionalized investments, following the advice of financial planners and other professionals. This flood of individual money managed by institutions—household names such as Vanguard, Fidelity, and Putnam—has helped fuel the bull market through the early 1990s. It has also made the market more resilient on the downside. Bolstered by the financial planners and advice from the mutual fund companies, investors have stayed the course with a "buy and hold" strategy.

There is another reason for the up-to-the-minute market mentality among people who, not so long ago, didn't know a mutual fund from an insurance policy. Now, people are increasingly becoming fiscally responsible for themselves and their futures. Gone are the days of the defined-contribution company pension. Few of us are counting on Social Security to see us through our "golden years."

In a previous generation, Social Security was the safety net for old age. Whether a retiree received a company pension, there was always Social Security. It was as secure as a promise from FDR himself. Then the demographics began to work against Social Security. Budget deficits, a shrinking birth rate, and a graying of the median population have put a strain on Social Security. The sobering news out of the Clinton White House in November 1998 was that, by 2013, money put into Social Security will no longer be enough to fund what it pays out, forcing the government to dip into the Social Security Trust fund. By 2032, the trust fund will be empty, and the money Social Security takes in will only pay 72 percent of benefits.

While the security of Social Security is debated on Capitol Hill, many Americans are taking their futures into their own hands. There is even some speculation that a portion of Social Security funds may some day be placed with professional money managers. In addition, companies have shifted from defined-benefit pension plans to 401(k) plans, which allow employees to shelter a portion of their salaries. Pay money in now before taxes and save for the future. That has hit home with a lot of workers, particularly Baby Boomers, who have their kids' educations and their own retirement to worry about.

As a result the stock market, which was once the bailiwick of the wealthy, has become very Middle America.

Now, enter what I call the CNBC syndrome. Although I am a fan of CNBC (and I've been honored to be a guest market commentator from time to time), I believe the popularity of this financial network reflects a near obsession that we all have with the market and our money. Everywhere we turn, we're being bombarded with the latest in market information. Pundits give their opinions on what they believe will happen tomorrow, the next day, next week, next year. Mutual fund companies, advertising in print, on the TV screen, and on the Internet, assure us that an investment today means a secure tomorrow. My favorite is the slogan reminding us that the only thing worse than growing old is outliving our money.

With interest rates low and unlikely to be raised in the foreseeable future, there is simply no other place for Americans to put their money than the stock market. A more sophisticated individual knows no passbook savings account or CD bearing 5 percent will generate enough money to provide a livable future, let alone a comfortable one. Just take a look at a few statistics:

According to the New York Stock Exchange, 51 million Americans, or roughly one-fifth of the population, own stock directly. More than 100 million, or about 40 percent of the population, participate in the stock market indirectly through investments by their pension funds, insurance companies, universities, and banks.

Statistics from the Investment Company Institute (ICI) show that 37.4 percent of all U.S. households invest in mutual funds. That's up from 23.4 million in 1990 and from 4.6 million in 1980. Household ownership, in fact, accounts for 75 percent of all fund share assets, either through individual investments or through retirement plans, the institute adds. Not surprisingly, ICI found that 84 percent of those investings in stock mutual funds were investing for their retirement.

Together, household investors and mutual funds account for 61 percent of stock holdings, ICI reports. That's up from 56 percent combined in October 1987. Although shares held by mutual funds alone have risen to 15 percent of the market in 1997 from 7 percent in 1987, it's clear that the individual investor—alone or with the combined clout of a fund—is underpinning this market.

I was reminded of this lesson when I was stopped for speeding one Saturday evening. The speed limit was 30 miles per hour and, well, I was traveling just a little faster than was prudent. A suburban police cruiser flashed its lights and pulled me over.

"They're going to take me to the station," I explained to my wife. "I missed a traffic court date last month."

One hazard of being a trader is that, when the market is very busy, you miss all sorts of things—vacations, business trips, luncheons, doctors' appointments, book deadlines. . . . Throughout much of September 1998 the market was very volatile, with the Dow moving by 200 points or more on a given day. I stayed in the S&P pit longer than I intended one day, managing my trading position and overseeing trading for our clients. As a result, my traffic court date slipped passed me.

"Hello, officers," I said, taking my driver's license out of my wallet and handing it to them. "You're going to find out that I missed a traffic court date last month. And, I missed a date a few months ago, too. . . ."

The police officers escorted me to the back of the squad car for a ride to the station. On the way, one of the officers heard my raspy voice. "Do you have a bad cold?" he asked.

"No, my voice is like this because of what I do for a living."
The police looked at me curiously.

"I'm a trader in the pit at the Chicago Mercantile Exchange.
I trade S&P stock index futures."

"Really?" The cop spun around in the seat while his partner
drove. "What do you think about this market? Is the bull market over?"

Here was yet another example of everyone's preoccupation
with the market.

"I don't think the bull market is over," I told him. "But who
knows if this correction is over yet. A lot will depend on what we
hear next about the Asia crisis."

"So, can I ask you a little friendly advice?" he continued as
we pulled into the police station.

"Sure, if you'll tear up the ticket . . . ," I laughed.

"Can't do that. But we'll give you a cup of coffee."

We sat together in the police station and waited for my wife
to bring me money so I could post bond. "I'm invested in mutual
funds, so this market has me worried," the officer told me. "My
wife watches CNBC all the time, and she tells me we're long-
term investors. We shouldn't even think about taking our money
out of the market."

"What's your investment time line?" I asked him.

"What do you mean?" he replied.

I asked him a series of questions: How old was he? What
percentage of income do he and his wife invest? Was the money
invested with a reputable mutual fund company? What was their
investment objective? The police officer told me he and his wife
were investing to pay for their children's college education,
starting in 10 years.

"I'd keep it in mutual funds right now. If you look at any 10-
year period in history, stocks have outperformed bonds two-to-
one. You're a long-term investor, so your wife is right: Keep
your money in the market."

"Thanks. I was getting worried."

"You'll be fine." I took a sip from my styrofoam cup of coffee and decided it was undrinkable. "So about that ticket. . . ."

Just like that police officer and his wife, we've become by and large a nation of long-term investors. We'll ride out the market highs and lows, knowing that we're in it for the long term. We have to be. There isn't any other option.

Just as investors discovered after the Crash of 1987 that their money was better off in the hands of professionals, companies, too, learned they had to make some fundamental changes. Across Corporate America, companies that had become over-leveraged and overexpanded put themselves on a fiscal diet, particularly when the economy slowed in the late 1980s and slipped into recession in the early 1990s. Corporate downsizing and reengineering mergers, acquisitions and divestitures—the more pink slips that were handed out by companies that believed they could do more with less people, the happier Wall Street became with these lean, mean, money-making machines.

Companies discovered what I call the "UPS effect." Pare down the ranks of the full-time employees, and make up the difference with part-time and temporary workers. United Parcel Service, or UPS, relies on part-time workers, despite both complaints from labor and its own expansion. For UPS, demand for part-time workers was due to the nature of its business: Shipping packages requires everything from warehouses to trucks to be staffed around the clock. Because many people don't like to work the night shift, UPS found itself with a lot of turnover. Their solution was to rely on part-time workers and even temporary help when seasonal demand rose. The Teamsters waged a strike against UPS in mid-1997 seeking to reduce the company's reliance on part-time help. Still, according to news reports, UPS remains heavily staffed by part-time workers who get less pay and reduced vacation time and pension terms compared with full-timers.

At the same time, downsizing has become a widely used word, a euphemism for layoffs and terminations. Over the past decade, layoffs have meant a good business is getting better.

Consider IBM. When I was in college, IBM was the paradigm of Corporate America—the most respected and socially responsible of companies with maternity leave and college funding for dependents. But, even Big Blue was forced to cut its costs. IBM laid off 60,000 workers in 1993 and offered voluntary buyouts to many of its 241,000 employees.

Layoffs and corporate downsizing dampened consumer confidence, slowing the economy in the 1980s. By 1990, the United States was officially in a recession that lasted into 1991. The economy has grown steadily since then, propelling the stock market higher. The strength of the economy is visible in the low unemployment rate (below 5 percent).

Many of those who were laid off were hired back on a part-time or temporary basis. In this new corporate environment, the temporary help services industry has thrived. My first view of the temporary help phenomenon was when I worked summers with the Teamsters at McCormick Place. Whenever the Teamsters needed extra help setting up or tearing down displays, they turned to the "ready men." These itinerant workers were paid only a few dollars a day, and many cashed their checks at the local bar where they drank much of their pay.

Today's temporary help industry—one of the fastest growing sectors of the economy—is far different from the "ready men." Temporary help relies on skilled workers with college degrees, who fill the gaps at companies, but without the costs of a permanent workforce. This practice has become so widespread that the National Association of Temporary and Staffing Services says 9 out of 10 companies now use temporary help. In addition, demand for temporary help has helped spark a whole cottage industry of self-employed consultants and upstart companies that handle outsourced services for major corporations. These new jobs—part of the 50 million new positions created in the 1990s—were offering skills to companies, born from these fundamental changes in the workforce. These self-employed people are also investing to fund their own pensions through IRA, SEP, or other plans.

Now, the widespread changes that swept Corporate America are sweeping across the global economy. The new Capitalist players—including countries like Russia, Poland, and even Vietnam—are undergoing monumental change. For many former Socialist countries, the change is not just economic, it is also political and social. People who were once guaranteed jobs from the state, face rising unemployment. Governments are finding it difficult to fund social programs because of economic turmoil and their own budget crises. Just as we saw a Darwinian survival of the fittest in corporations, we are seeing the same scenario among government regimes, state banks, and financial institutions.

I am old enough to remember the Bay of Pigs standoff between the United States and a Soviet-backed Cuba. When I was growing up, the Soviet Union and the United States were locked in the Cold War. But the world changed in 1989 when the Berlin Wall fell, and Communism was toppled throughout the Eastern Block. I had a glimpse of some of that change as it was happening, although I could only contemplate the enormity of it in retrospect. In 1990, my market technician named Otto, who was of Hungarian descent, approached me with a novel business idea. Otto told me in his brusque Hungarian accent that his future father-in-law had made a very important introduction for certain Russian trading companies.

I agreed to go to New York with Otto to meet with representatives of several Russian trading firms, who had wanted to meet me. I had thought this could be an opportunity for ABS Partners, the brokerage group I was a partner in at the time, to arrange brokerage for them. The Soviet Union—which has the largest gold reserves in the world and is also the largest purchaser of grain—is active in virtually all the commodity futures markets. After our meeting in New York, I agreed to go to Moscow to discuss the project further. Otto and Jim, another technician who worked for me at the time, went to Moscow a few days ahead of me.

I flew from Chicago to New York, where I was going to catch a plane to Zurich and then an Aeroflot flight to Moscow. It was January 1991, and the United States was in the throes of the Persian Gulf War. As I got on the plane bound for Zurich, the pilot told me the United States had just dropped its first bombs on Baghdad.

I took my suitcase out of the overhead bin and picked up my briefcase.

"Where are you going?" the pilot asked me.

"I can't take this flight," I explained.

"Don't worry," he tried to console me. "You don't have anything to worry about. We have very good security. Nothing will happen to this plane because of the war. You'll be safe."

"I'm sure you're right," I told the pilot, who shot me a puzzled look. "I'm a trader and I've got to get back to the market. If we just bombed Baghdad, I've got to get back to the market." The market was likely to be frantic, I knew, which was usually a great opportunity for me to make money.

I boarded the last plane bound for Chicago that night, and the next day I was in the S&P pit, where the market staged a strong rally, and I had a six-figure day. I never made it to Moscow to join Jim and Otto. Because I had not entered Russia on the specified date, my visa expired. When I couldn't get another visa, we agreed to meet a month later in Budapest.

When I landed in that centuries-old city, I was not sure what to expect. To my surprise, I found a beautiful city that was both Old World in charm and Western in convenience, such as the modern hotel I stayed in on the banks of the Danube. Just as I was beginning to doubt all I had read and heard about the inefficiency of the East Bloc, where capitalism was scorned for the good of the state, another image brought me back to reality.

It snowed that evening, blanketing the streets and sidewalks with about two inches of flakes. As I walked down the street, a truck pulled up to the curb. The driver got out of the cab and opened the back of the truck. A crew of men jumped out and began to shovel the snow in the street.

"Why don't they just put a plow on the front of the truck?" I asked one of the men at the table.

"Then the men would have no work," I was told. Even in the aftermath of Communism, everyone had a job, no matter how inefficient or impractical.

The next day, I was taken to the Hungarian commodity and stock exchange in Budapest. There, in a room about the size of my office, three men sat at folding tables. They alternated between talking on the phone and writing down the price of whatever they were trading on a chalkboard. This was as far from the S&P pit of the Merc as anything I could imagine. After 20 minutes, two Russian-speaking men arrived, accompanied by a translator. They were ready to discuss the particulars of the proposed business arrangement: They wanted me to trade on behalf of certain interests in Russia.

I was not trading for clients in those days, but I did not want to turn down the possibility of lucrative commodity futures business with the former Soviet Union.

I was never certain who these men were. All I know was they were very emphatic about having me trade for them. They had set up several accounts in countries outside of Russia, which would be used for trading. The money, I was led to believe, was coming from the Russian government. When I asked why these accounts were being set up in foreign countries outside of Russia, I was not given a straight answer. I was, they told me, on a need-to-know basis only.

"Well, I need to know this before I agree to anything," I explained. "I need to know who I'm trading for."

The men conferred with each other in Russian, then gave me a bare-bones explanation, which they said was highly confidential. Within six months, they told me, the Russian government would fall and Gorbachev, whom I had thought was a very popular leader in his country, would be out of power. Then there would be no more Communism in Russia, they told me. It would happen in about six months' time. In August 1991, just as these men had predicted, Mikhail Gorbachev was ousted as president of the former Soviet Union in a failed coup attempt. It was incredulous as I heard the news accounts. It happened just as I had been told, but the timing was off by a month or so. As for the Russian trading representatives, I never saw them again.

In the past decade, there has been significant change in the global landscape, resulting in far more opportunities for Western companies to invest, sell their goods, and build factories overseas. It's as if these companies operated a convenience store on a busy corner, and a new housing development doubled the population base. Pepsi-Cola is bottled in Poland. American blue jeans are as hot as black market dollars in Russia. The demand has been for everything Western, from Nike to technology. As U.S. companies joined this new gold rush, the stock market has been a beneficiary. As a result, we've seen a rise in everything from stock prices to the proliferation of initial public offerings (IPOs).

But the foundation-rattling change in places like the Soviet Union has not gone smoothly. Inflation, unemployment, and unrest among the people have darkened the outlook in Russia, Poland, and other countries of the region. Then, in a backlash that we should have seen but did not, Russia faced serious economic and political troubles in 1998, including the free fall in the value of the ruble and bond. Russia has suffered a budget shortfall, a problem that is compounded by its large black market economy and the fact that it's difficult for the government to collect taxes even from legitimate businesses. (Perhaps the Russians should send the KGB to the United States to be trained by the Internal Revenue Service. That could be a very effective strategy for increasing tax revenue.)

Russia's economic woes stole the headlines momentarily from the other world economic crisis, the so-called Asian flu. An economic crisis of catastrophic proportions has gripped Asia since July 1997. Investors steeled themselves as the bad news out of Asia was revealed slowly, until we had learned the region was gripped by recession and several Japanese banks were facing failure. The Asian financial crisis began with the collapse of the Thai currency in July 1997, then spread to Indonesia, where President Suharto was forced to resign in May 1998. All of Asia was infected with the crisis, the effects of which were felt in late 1998 in the United States. Companies reporting earnings for the third and fourth quarters of the year complain of declines in Asian demand and overseas sales.

Foreign governments have not been the only casualties in the world economic crises. U.S. investors were burned when foreign markets turned sour. One of the most spectacular failures was that of Long-Term Capital Management LP, a hedge fund that reportedly was down more than 90 percent for 1998 before a rescue was staged.

Hedge funds, in my opinion, are misnamed. They should be called leverage funds. They can turn $5 million in equity into 10 or more times that in borrowing power through leverage. Lofty and often entangled lines of credit may be invested in any number of things, from stocks to foreign bonds. Hedge funds, which often attract wealthy investors, are unregulated, although they are attracting more scrutiny in Washington.

The Long-Term Capital debacle, which caused nervous investors to yank money out of other hedge funds, and which was compounded by a downturn in the market, resulted in some hefty losses and a drain in assets. Although no one should ever gloat over another person's misfortune (it's unlucky, as well as impolite), it's interesting to note that managed futures—often viewed as the ugly duckling of the investment world—have been standing in a better light. As the managed futures industry has been preaching for years, a prudent use of leverage in the regulated futures markets can turn profits for investors. Indeed, managed futures funds with double- or even single-digit returns have attracted attention from institutional and individual investors alike.

The unprecedented volatility that spanned from April 1997 through 1998 reflected the grave uncertainty in the world from Asia to Russia to Brazil, in hedge funds and even the American presidency, as a sex scandal and impeachment hearings put the White House in crisis. Throughout this period, volatility in the market was driven by news and economic fundamentals. In my opinion, what prevented the Crash of 1998, as news headlines had predicted, was the resiliency of the American investor who held steadfast in the conviction that they are long-term players and this was a temporary downswing in the market.

Historically, international crises such as these have been a launching pad for rallies. Consider the Latin American debt crisis of the 1980s and the Mexican peso devaluations in 1990 and in late 1994. Once a solution is found and funded, the market heaves a sigh of relief and rallies higher. I expect nothing less of the current Asian and Russian crises.

One of the most promising steps was to hear Alan Greenspan's testimony before Congress in late 1998, calling for foreign banks to adopt stricter, Western standards to receive IMF economic assistance. This will lead to a Westernization of banking structures and political standards, which I believe will provide a firm foundation to launch the next rally.

After a year and a half of economic bad news, from Asia to Wall Street, there have been glimmers of hope. I came across one missive of optimism while surfing the Internet the other day. An editorial in *AsiaWeek* (November 13, 1998), entitled "Asian Rebound," caught my eye. ". . . Don't look now, but the 16-month-old Asian Crisis may be bottoming out. . . . Government, private analysts and the International Monetary Fund are speaking of recovery taking root as soon as mid-1999. . . ."

The positive evidence cited in the editorial included interest rate cuts in the United States and several European countries, which may ensure that these economies will not slow dramatically and, therefore, will continue to demand goods from Asia. Potential perils include a Brazilian crash that "would sorely test confidence in the U.S. and Europe," an unhealthy Russian economy, and nervousness about other potential losses in hedge funds à la Long-Term Capital Management, *AsiaWeek* stated.

Whether that editorial is premature or on target remains to be seen. But, once these optimistic signs begin to emerge, they become part of the market psychology. Once the market believes a recovery is underway, the patient is as good as cured.

In investing, as in human health, part of the healing is attitude. Doctors will tell you a patient betters his or her chance of recovery with a positive attitude. So it goes with the markets. If the collective market psychology believes the worst is over, the flight of capital will cease or at least slow, investors will come out of the woodwork, and the markets will begin rising again.

On the global economic horizon is the launch of the "euro," the new currency that will be adopted by about a dozen European nations. In time, this may lead to a pan-European market-place where everything from tariffs to prices are unified. The next challenge is the Year 2000 (Y2K) problem. Pessimists have forecasted that computers around the world will crash because they will not be able to handle a "00" date in their systems. That could cripple everything from banks to electrical power grids to air traffic control. But, the optimists believe the Y2K problem will not be widespread. Problems will be isolated and business will be unaffected. If the Y2K problem turns out to be only a hiccup and not a hurricane, that will be more good news to fuel a continued bull market.

I expect this market will continue to be strong into the next century. The Dow, which is now hovering around 9,000, could easily be at 15,000 by 2005, thanks to a global economic recovery. I expect the bull market to continue—although some interim corrections are probable—until 2006, when growth likely will slow as the first Baby Boomers begin to draw down their retirement investments.

If this scenario unfolds as we hope and expect, it will be good news, indeed, for investors who weathered the correction of 1998 with the hope that the long bull market was not over, but merely catching its breath. Whether investors buy and hold for the long term or speculate on short-term opportunities, it's time to adopt a trader's attitude toward risk and reward. As the investment disclaimers state, past performance is no guarantee of future returns. But, if we can extrapolate anything from the past, it is that the market will undoubtedly be volatile and, at times, uncertain.

CHAPTER 11

From the Pit to the PC

Over the years, friends, acquaintances, and sometimes even family members have asked me if I could trade money for them the way I trade for myself. I always hated this question because my answer had to be no, I could not. It wasn't that I was being selfish, trying to keep my skills to myself, or that I didn't want others to reap the same good fortune in the market that I have. I simply could not trade for them the way I trade for myself.

As a pit trader, I make hundreds of trades a day because, as a member of an exchange, my commissions are a few cents. So I can scratch on some trades (buying and selling at the same price for no profit), lose on a few, and make money on the rest. At the end of the day, I've made a tidy profit, and sometimes a considerable one. But, this kind of scalping only works when you're on the floor and paying a member's commissions. There is no way that an investor, paying full commissions, could ever hope to make money through scalping. Even if investors had winning trades 70 percent of the time, commissions and other costs would erode the profit.

My transition from the pit to the PC was the start of being able to trade for others. But, I'm still scalping at the screen. Say, for example, the market fundamentals and technical analysis indicate that S&Ps will move from 1050 to 1065. I may sell when S&Ps test the 1050 support level, and buy when the market holds. Once the price breaks through 1050 and finds support, I'll buy and hold the position while the market ticks up and down on its way to 1065. If I had been on the floor, I would have bought and sold on dozens of those intermediate points between 1050 and 1065. But you can't scalp from a PC the way you can from the floor. You simply don't have the same feel for market flow when you're off the floor. Still, when I'm at the screen, I have the advantage of a member's commissions, which enables me to make several trades a day. Although the frequency of trading at the screen is less than when I am in the pit, the style is still too dynamic to manage client money.

To make the evolution from being a trader to a fund manager required a leap of faith and the tapping of all my skill and experience. Luckily, I had laid the foundation for this move years ago when I became interested in computerized trading systems. Today, my firm, Borsellino Capital Management, trades money for clients using a state-of-the-art computerized trading system. We have developed systems that generate 15 to 20 trades a month that carry a high probability of being successful. We take a conservative approach in our modeling, programming in specific numbers to assume a certain slippage on order fills and making sure the trade is likely to be profitable, even at full-commission costs.

My evolution to becoming a fund manager was not just a way to extend my life as a trader when I no longer have the desire or the stamina to endure the pit. If that were the case, I could just as easily trade for myself from a PC the rest of my life. But, I am the kind of man who loves a challenge—not to compete with others, but merely to test and better myself.

At the pinnacle of my floor trading career there were times when I moved the market, buying or selling with enough conviction to change the market direction. I traded, on average, 250,000 S&P contracts a year. At current face value of $250,000, that means, on a theoretical basis, the equivalent of $62.5 billion worth of stock passed through my hands each year. But it was not enough. For me there has to be more than just the trading floor or the jagged line of the market's tracings on the PC screen. Part of it is the intellectual challenge. As I said previously, to be a successful trader, especially on the floor, you have to become robotic. The less you think and the more you act instinctually, the more profitable you are.

Based on the success I have enjoyed, some people look at me with confusion when I say I believe I have underachieved. What they are looking at is only the material side of my accomplishments. I judge myself by far more than the money I have made. I have challenged myself to evolve as a trader, adopting cutting-edge technology to meet the changes in the marketplace. For me, I am aiming for a reward that is more than just monetary.

To paraphrase Pogo, I have met the challenge, and it is me.

The past year has been a journey, literally. I have gone to Paris, London, Madrid, Monaco, Zurich, and Bermuda to spread the word about the new fund manager—Borsellino Capital Management. It began in December 1997, when my partner, Edward R. Velazquez, II, and I went to Spain and then to London. The purpose of the trip was to meet with potential administrators for an offshore fund we planned to offer, as well as to begin making introductions for ourselves.

From London, we traveled to Paris where, at a cafe on the Champs Élysées, Borsellino Capital became a reality when we received our first $1 million commitment to trade. It was an important milestone, but clearly only the beginning. We returned to Europe in February 1998 for our first bona fide road show at an investment conference in Zurich. We did not take the Zurich conference by storm, as we had hoped. For one thing, the gathering was geared toward hedge funds, and not commodity-trading advisors (CTAs). But, the conference allowed me to evaluate the competition. I also learned a valuable lesson. No matter how good your computerized trading system, no matter how strong you are as a trader, the first year or so for a CTA is the tire-kicking stage. This was a frustration for me because I have spent so many years successfully trading my own account.

Because of the volatility of the market, it is not uncommon for a CTA to have one or two down months in a row, followed by a very profitable month that more than offsets prior losses. It's important that investors not only understand that potential swing in returns, but that they have confidence overall in the fund manager's ability. This confidence can only be engendered by knowing both the fund manager's trading methodology and his personal integrity. This is especially true for European and Asian investors I have met, who prefer to do business with someone they know. They are equally interested in getting to know me as they are in my performance statistics. Many American investors, I have found, are more bottom-line oriented, concerned mostly with returns and not in building a personal relationship.

We also learned at Zurich, courtesy of a few newfound friends in the business, who were the movers and shakers of the financial futures game. We would get a chance to meet them, thanks to a little serendipity, when we returned to Europe in April for an investment conference in Cannes. On the plane from Paris to Nice, I switched my seat to allow a husband and wife to sit together. My new seatmate was none other than a Pacific Stock Exchange trader who was at the top of my list of "people to meet." By the time we got to Nice, I had not only made a friend and a valuable contact, but was invited to a party hosted by another man on my list. The occasion was the "33rd anniversary of his 21st birthday." Virtually every person we met at that party was on the list.

While we were in Cannes, Eddie and I were given another invitation—to meet with our first client, a Greek investor whose considerable fortune was made in shipping and industry. He invited us to his home (one of three, I might add) in southern France for a little socializing and to learn more about us. The old stone house, perched on a hillside overlooking the Mediterranean, was not at all ostentatious by American standards, but had an Old World elegance. A cobblestone walkway led from the gated driveway up a steep incline to a stone patio where I sat, sipping a glass of wine as golden as the late afternoon sunlight.

All around me were olive gardens, terraced into the hillside. The only thing about the place that had changed in the past hundred years or so was the in-ground pool, a discreet distance from the house. I watched sailboats skim over the water, which looked more green than blue that day. It was so perfect—nearly too perfect—as if it were a scene out of a movie.

I looked around and thought to myself, "What the hell am I doing here?"

That's a question that I've asked myself countless times, from the campus at DePauw University to the trading pits at the Merc and now in the international world of money management. In each instance, the answer is the same. I have always welcomed a challenge in my life, and each time I have stepped up to meet that challenge.

People have described me as one of the biggest and the best traders. That's all fine and good, but there is a danger in believing everything the people say about you. If you begin to believe it, without questioning yourself or examining the inevitable mistakes, you make yourself vulnerable. Trading is one profession in which you can never coast along on someone else's efforts. You rise or fall on your own. Each day, you have to evaluate where you are and where you are going. You have to know that, no matter how well you did yesterday, you have to perform again today. And, no matter how well you do, there will always be someone who is a little smarter and performs a little better.

I remember when my brother and I were kids, Dad used to take us to the gym to develop and discipline our bodies. But, he warned us that, no matter how tough and disciplined we perceived ourselves to be, we could never assume we were invincible. "Never go looking for trouble," he'd tell us. "First of all, you're likely to find it. Secondly, you may find trouble from someone who is a little tougher than you are."

Sitting on that patio in southern France, I was presented with a twist on that same theme. Although I have enjoyed success— professional and financial—it could not compare with the wealth around me. It's like you're stopped at a traffic light in a Mercedes sedan when someone pulls up next to you in a Rolls

Royce. Then another car pulls up and it's a stretch limo Rolls Royce. And finally, a fourth car stops and it's a $500,000 Ferrari. When you think you're on top of the world, you look up and realize that you're sitting just a few miles from the equator.

Even when I was starting out, I never was one to count anybody else's money. Someone else's accomplishments or the rewards of their success never made me jealous. It only showed me what was possible if I set my mind to it.

Anything I have accomplished in my life has been through hard work and perseverance. Nobody ever gift-wrapped and handed me anything. But, this is not a chip on my shoulder. Rather, it is a badge of honor that I wear proudly. Too often, people perceive that someone's success is the result of luck or a fortunate fluke. What they don't realize is how hard successful people have had to work. I've seen this firsthand in the lives of successful people I've met, and in the case of many more I've read about. The more effortless their endeavors appear, the more effort they expended behind the scenes or in the early years. They invested time, capital, energy, resources—whatever it took—to reach their goals. For most people, it is a commitment that they cannot make.

But, I would be remiss if I did not take an opportunity again to recognize the important people who have helped me over the years. My father, my mother, my brother, and I were an inseparable, tightly knit family unit that embraced my aunts, uncles, and cousins. Today, I have my wife, Julie, and our children who are my strength and my hope for the future. Nothing would please me more than to look down the corridor of Borsellino Capital Management some day and find my children, stepchildren, nephews, and nieces working with me. Professionally, I was blessed to have friends and mentors like Maury Kravitz and Jack Sandner. I also want to thank my fellow traders, the men and women in the S&P pit who over the years made it, in my opinion, a premiere competitive arena. Above all, I thank God for the abilities He gave me and the people He put in my life.

My life has been and continues to be a study of contrasts. I've driven a truck and I've moved the markets with my own trades.

I shot craps with the Teamsters in a trailer, and I had lunch with President Clinton at an exclusive fund-raiser. I am comfortable in any environment, not because I put on a different identity to please someone else. Rather, it comes from being secure in who I am. I can't and won't pretend to be something that I'm not. I didn't grow up with the silver spoon, the pedigree, and the old family money. Nor did I hang out on the street corner.

I am a man from Chicago, the self-made variety, who knew hard knocks and overcame them. I learned lessons, like the cost of risk and the value of loyalty, from my father. One of the most important things he taught me is to keep everything— both obstacles and success—in perspective. When things turn against you, he used to say, you can never look at it like it's a catastrophe. It's only an obstacle or a temporary setback. And, when things are good, you can never assume that they always will be. In life, there will be periods of good times and bad, victories and failures. I also learned self-reliance, knowing that no matter what, I will survive. This has meant I've never worried about making money. If I lost it all, I would somehow make it up again.

Through my intelligence, discipline, and God-given abilities, I have done very well in the futures markets. Now, I am applying those same skills and expertise in the market on behalf of investment clients. When investors evaluate me as a fund manager, they cannot look at performance alone. Even my 18 years as a successful trader, although I am proud of that track record, is not the full story. Rather, I believe that investors should consider all of my character, my integrity, and my survival. The key questions to be weighed are not just whether I can manage money, a skill I have demonstrated throughout my career, but whether I am disciplined as a person and as a trader. Am I a fighter? Can I handle success? Can I handle failure?

That is what I told the director of research for a midsized U.S. investment firm one day. He told me proudly that he had devised a method of evaluating traders on the basis of certain mathematical performance standards. He then began to recite a long litany of statistics.

"Excuse me, but may I ask how many S&P contracts have you traded?" I asked him politely, but with an obvious point in mind.

"None," the man replied.

"Then how many stocks have you traded?" I asked him again.

"None. I'm not a trader."

"Then how can you evaluate a trader? Performance statistics only tell half the story."

You see, traders and fund managers are more than just numbers. There is a human side to fund management, just as there is an undeniable human element to trading. You can quantify monthly returns, standard deviation, and the peak-to-trough drawdown, but how do you evaluate the intangible? How do you count for the psychological discipline of a trader?

"What about tenacity and dedication?" I asked the director of research. "What about discipline? How can you quantify these things?"

He sputtered a little bit, searching for an answer. "Hopefully, we will get to know the trader in time," he told me.

In trading, we refer to commodities as being fungible, meaning one of something is exactly the same as another. One bushel of wheat is the same as the next bushel, as long as it meets the specifications of the futures contract. By the same token, one barrel of West Texas Intermediate crude oil is the same as another, and one S&P 500 futures contract has the same value as another. This fungibility is what allows futures to be traded.

Traders, however, are not fungible. We have some common characteristics, but we are not the same. Some brokers in the pit are experts when it comes to filling customer orders, but they can't trade their way out of a paper bag. There are locals who are good at scalping, but have never put on a position trade based on an opinion. Among traders there are vast differences not only in ability, but in style and temperament.

But, there is one commonality among traders who are very good at their profession: Once they have mastered the techniques of reading the market, sensing floor-order flow, and understanding technical analysis, they can trade anything. It doesn't matter if it's bonds, stock index futures, currencies, or even agricultural contracts, as long as there is sufficient liquidity and volatility, an expert trader can buy and sell it. I've often said that I'd trade horseshit futures if there were enough liquidity and volatility. It doesn't matter what the underlying cash market is, as long as there is an opportunity to trade. . . .

I've stayed in S&Ps for most of my career because this was my specialty. It was where I first made a name for myself as an order filler and later as a local. It was, from the beginning, "the" contract to trade. That's why, when I look around the S&P pit today, I can't help feeling like the old bull in the pen. I see so many new faces, many of whom want to lock horns with me. I know the attraction to trading. I know the appeal. And, I know what these new players are up against. Some will stay, some will leave, and some will just disappear.

I remember years ago when I began to feel a little paranoid in the pit. I'd be trading when, all of a sudden, I'd spot two or three young traders standing at the edge of the pit, watching me. When I looked up, they would look away. A few minutes later, they'd be staring at me again.

"What?" I'd bark at them.

"Nothing," they'd reply with a shrug, and then leave.

A few days later, there would be another group of traders, all with new member badges, staring at me. It was beginning to drive me nuts.

"Okay, so tell me what's going on? Why are you staring at me?" I asked one of the new members.

"We're taking a class in floor trading," one of the traders explained to me sheepishly. "The instructor said that if we wanted to see the best local on the floor, we should watch LBJ."

I laughed then, and I later related the story to my friend, Mickey Hoffman, who teaches trading courses at the Merc. But, I must admit, I was glad to dispel my fear that these new traders were not part of a new ploy by compliance to drive me crazy. I was merely the homework assignment.

I remember being in their shoes, watching a trader like Maury in the gold pit. I am reminded of that each time I see a new member come into the pit, or when one of the clerks who works for me dons a trading jacket for the first time. When I look out into the S&P pit, I see the faces of so many people whom I brought to the Merc or who were sponsored by someone I knew. When I look out into this pit, which has become increasingly ethnically diverse over the years, I can walk around the floor of the Merc, go into any pit, and see the traders who have come to the exchange—directly or indirectly—because of me. I remember when I first visited the Merc, how I thought this place was off-limits to those of us who had not grown up in the business. I have made it my cause to open the door for anyone who shows promise or talent. It is my way of giving back, remembering men like Lou Matta and Maury Kravitz, who opened the door for me.

When I see the new members in the pit, I remember my early days, when I was trained to handle the deck, keeping the buys and sells in line. I remember yelling out my first bids and offers, for my customers and then for myself. I can tell you that trading provides no better adrenaline rush. But, then there are the down days, which are inevitable. When a trader has lost money, you don't have to look at his trading account, you can hear it in his voice. It's written all over his face.

That's what I read in Julian Robertson's eyes and in his expression when he addressed via satellite an MAR investment conference in October 1998, which was held in Bermuda. It was just days after this legendary hedge fund manager had reportedly suffered a loss of almost $2 billion in one day. The article "Tiger Manager Mauled by Yen, Loses $2 Billion," by Mitchell Pacelle and Linda Sandler (*The Wall Street Journal* (October 9, 1998)), reported at the time that his Tiger Management had lost big when the Japanese yen surged against the U.S. dollar. We later read that Tiger Management had lost 17 percent, or $3.4 billion, by October, wiping out all the gains for the year. This, of course, followed a spectacular year in 1997, when Tiger Management's assets grew from $8 billion to roughly $16 billion.

As I watched Julian Robertson, it was clear the market had humbled him a little. Even though he is a superstar of the investment world, and I was just starting out as a fund manager, I knew what he was going through. It's what I call trader empathy. Nobody can understand the exhilaration of the win or the agony of the loss like another trader.

The Long-Term Capital Management hedge fund crisis left many casualties in its wake. Many hedge funds that generated returns with highly leveraged investments from foreign currency to commodities were left high and dry by unforeseen circumstances. Long-Term Capital was caught when the Russian government defaulted on its bonds, forcing banks that had issued letters of credit to renege on them, citing an "act of God."

Hedge fund horror stories circulated through the MAR conference in Bermuda. We heard about funds with assets from $100 million to $1 billion that had suffered considerable losses in both assets and investor confidence. And, some fund managers who had been expected to participate in the conference were noticeably absent. On the whole, many hedge funds had devised good investment strategies across a diverse universe of financial instruments. But, their downfall was often caused by taking big positions in illiquid markets. When they had to sell out of losing positions, there were simply no buyers—at any price.

At the Bermuda conference, nearly a year after the launch of Borsellino Capital Management, I could sense that our firm was attracting attention. We had a story to tell, and investors were listening. My partner, Eddie Velazquez, is an expert computer programmer, a genius at mathematics, algorithms, and artificial intelligence. Plus, he is an independent trader, who has traded for himself and clients. As for me, I am an 18-year veteran of a profession in which 5 years is a long time. We literally combined two schools of thought in fund management: the systematic and the discretionary. Systematic traders take an objective approach to the market, based on sophisticated computerized models and trading programs. To be a true systematic trader, you must take each and every trade that the computer system generates— regardless of outside variables. Discretionary traders use human judgment and thought processes to trade the market, relying on technical and fundamental analysis.

At my firm, we combine both philosophies in a strategy that we call a responsible approach to discretionary trading. The marriage of the computer and floor trading expertise is a powerful alliance, because we believe that in today's investment climate you cannot rely upon just one. It takes a combination of skills to read and trade the market, to reduce risk and maximize returns.

Here's how it works. At the heart of our trading methodology is an innovative system that combines 18 trading programs, each encompassing a variety of market analysis strategies. Some look for breakout price points at which the market is likely to move higher or lower. Others look for fade-outs, in which a rising market loses steam or a declining one begins to ease its decline. Some programs are based on momentum, and others analyze price patterns over the previous five days. The computer system uses artificial intelligence and neural networks to read the market, and also to learn and adapt itself to certain market variables. Taken together, the trading programs generate trades that have a high probability of being profitable.

But, even the best computer system with the latest in artificial intelligence cannot replace a trader. As sophisticated as this computer system is—with artificial intelligence and a neural network that replicate some functions of the human mind—it is still only an aid to us. There remains a human element to trading, which the computer cannot duplicate. The instincts for reading and trading the market that I have developed over 18 years cannot be put into any computer code. That is where my expertise and market experience come into play. I evaluate each trade that the system generates according to several criteria. Are there variables in the market that cannot be programmed into any computer? Is Alan Greenspan scheduled to speak in the next 15 minutes, an event that always has an impact on the market? Is it Yom Kippur or the day before a major holiday, which reduces the liquidity of the market? Is it options expiration day? Is the contract scheduled to roll over from one month to another? Based on variables such as these, I may decide to cancel or alter the computer-generated trade.

Or, I may decide to enhance the trade. Recently, the computer generated a sell signal with a tight stop just a few ticks above the price at which the trade was to be executed. The market, however, was particularly volatile, and I knew there was a good chance our buy stop would be hit. But, I also believe the market was weakening and that a sell was the correct trade to make. I made the decision to move the buy stop up a few ticks, but to counter the additional risk, we reduced the size of the trade by one-half. The strategy paid off: The market went up a few ticks, then declined as our computer system indicated.

I believe our responsive strategy sets us apart from other CTA firms. We have enough confidence in our computer system and our trading methodology to put our money where our mouths are—literally. The only way I could ethically trade for clients is to trade the same way for myself. Whenever we put on a trade for the clients, we are making the same trade for ourselves.

There is another key difference between my firm and other CTAs. I did not start out with an MBA at a hedge fund or a large institution, trading the house account. I have made my money by my own wits and talents in the front lines of this market. I know what it's like to handle risk, manage money, and reap profits responsibly. Investors who put their money with me know that at the start. I began in this business in the market, not in an upstairs office. I approach the markets as a trader, but as one who has earned his longevity.

It's also important to remember that CTAs do not make money unless the clients are successful. In stocks, a broker reaps a commission no matter if the shares he recommends escalate in value or decline. A CTA, on the other hand, makes an incentive fee only if the fund performs well. Even management fees disappear if returns disappoint investors and they pull their money out.

I expect our first S&P fund will be closed to new investors within a year. After that, other funds will be launched, some offered exclusively overseas and others just in the United States. With our trading expertise and a cutting-edge computer system, we can easily expand beyond S&Ps to trade virtually any high-volatility market, whether financial futures or physical commodity. We are already committing the firm's capital to testing our computer system in international financial futures markets where we hope to someday trade for clients as well. As markets evolve, new opportunities will present themselves, and we will be there to capitalize on them.

I returned to Europe as this book was nearing completion, traveling to Switzerland, Monaco, and Italy to meet with both institutional and individual investors. While I was in Zurich, I could not help but think of my two previous visits to that city. Just a year before, I was in Zurich as a fund manager who was virtually unknown in the money management arena. A year later, people have heard about the company and are eager to learn more.

I can also look back to the trip I made over 11 years ago. I was a trader on a holiday with friends. I can still remember looking at watches at that jewelry store when I spotted the sign on the bank, which delivered the chilling news: The U.S. stock market had crashed. That seems like a lifetime ago, and in many ways it was. I was a 30-year-old floor trader who had just given up the customer deck. I had established myself as the leading local in the S&P pit, trading only for myself.

My life and my world have expanded exponentially since then. I am no longer just a trader, but a fund manager whose reputation is spreading. I know my life and my professional journey are far from over. (In fact, when I was approached to write this book, I hesitated because I consider myself to be at only the midpoint of my life.) But, no matter where I go or what I experience, I know my core remains the same. The nucleus of my life is my family, a precious constant in my life that has seen much upheaval. Some of my family are with me literally, working at my company today; others offer love and emotional support. Together, they are my home.

None of us lives in just a physical dwelling, whether it's a one-room apartment or a mansion on a mountain. We live within ourselves in the company of those we love. That, to me, is home. When I was growing up, my father gave us the proverbial American dream house in the suburbs, but our home was so much more. It was Mom, Dad, Joey, and myself dressed up for Easter Sunday Mass. It was a spaghetti dinner with the relatives in a house that was filled with adult voices and children's laughter. It was hopping over the backyard fence—Dad, Joey, and me—to wake up Uncle Norfe and Aunt Dolly. It was knowing that no matter where we went or what we did, we belonged.

Some people may wonder, as I come to the close of my story, why I have been so candid with my life and my upbringing. Certainly, I came from a family where you did not tell secrets, let alone publicize them. But, there came a time when I had to own my story, to reveal who I am and where I came from. I know the stories that have trailed me all my life, some true, some exaggerated, and some outright lies. The only way to put them to rest was to tell my story myself. If the record was going to be set straight, I had to do it. If I was going to establish a relationship with investment clients, I wanted them to know me personally as well as professionally.

In my new role as a fund manager, asking institutions and individuals to entrust me with millions of dollars, there could be no question about my integrity or my character. The only way to do that was not to hide the past, but to bring it out into the light of truth. I want my investors who read this book to know me as a trader with unique expertise in an increasingly unpredictable market and to know me as a man. I hope they will see that I have the commitment to stay the course and the dedication to stand by them. In investing, as in life, it comes down to a matter of trust.

All of us are the sum total of our own experiences and the lives of those who come before us. Each generation is a link in a chain that connects the past and the future. There may be events we would like to forget or different choices we wish we had made. There, however, we cannot break that generational chain. We must understand the lives of the people who came before us. We appreciate their strengths and forgive their weaknesses. Then, we must do the same thing for ourselves.

This story does not belong only to me. It is part of the history of my family. This is part of the legacy that I will pass onto my children, Lewis, Anthony, Briana, and Joey, who carry the Borsellino name, and my stepchildren, Nicole, Jamie, and Nick, who are like my own flesh and blood. It belongs equally to my brother, Joey, and his children, Anthony, Joey, Johnny, and. Marla. My hope is that this next generation understands Joey and me, and looking beyond us, that they begin to see the grandfather they never knew.

I went to the floor of the Chicago Mercantile Exchange nearly 20 years ago when other doors of opportunity slammed shut for me. I began to trade, and never looked back at what was or what might have been. Some people ask me the key to my success, as if there was a magic pill they might take or a secret formula that explains it all. There is neither magic nor a secret. I became a successful trader because I knew myself. I understand both my strengths and my weaknesses. I mastered myself with a cast-iron discipline that allowed me to stomach risk and handle failure. Although my temper got the better of me at times, especially in my younger days, I never blew up to the point of no return. I reined in my negative thoughts and emotions. By controlling myself, I could master my environment. I learned to act, and not react, particularly in the markets where money, ego, and emotions are a lethal combination. Neither I nor anyone else will ever master the market. That knowledge preserved me in my younger days, keeping me from ever becoming too sure of myself. Furthermore, it helps ensure my longevity as a fund manager, whether I have $20 million under management or $2 billion someday.

I was on the trading floor the other day, a place I go with far less frequency, although I am in the market every day. I stood in my old spot on the second step of the S&P pit, my brother, Joey, beside me. I looked around at all the faces. Some were newcomers who have traded for only a few months; others were relative old-timers who had been in that pit nearly as long as I. Many more were in-between.

We are the market, all of us together. Pit trader and broker. Off-the-floor trader and speculator. Fund manager, investor, and hedger. Together, we are what makes this work. Who knows what the arena will look like in the future, whether there will be a trading floor, a bank of computers, or a virtual reality pit? Who can say what we will trade in the future, or what world economic factors will shake and shape our markets? One thing is for certain: Where there is a market, there will be a trader. Where there is risk, there will be a hedger. Where there is opportunity, there will be a speculator. I may be leaving the pit for the PC, but I am not leaving the arena. The game is far from over, and this competitor has not yet retired.